SHEPPERTON STUDIOS

An Independent View

DEREK THREADGALL

BRITISH FILM INSTITUTE

bfi

BFI PUBLISHING

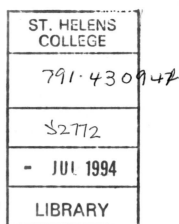
First published in 1994 by the
British Film Institute
21 Stephen Street
London W1P 1PL

The British Film Institute exists to encourage the development of film,
television and video in the United Kingdom, and to promote knowledge,
understanding and enjoyment of the culture of the moving image. Its
activities include the National Film and Television Archive; the National
Film Theatre; the Museum of the Moving Image; the London Film Festival;
the production and distribution of film and video; funding and support for
regional activities; Library and Information Services; Stills, Posters and
Designs; Research; Publishing and Education; and the monthly *Sight and
Sound* magazine.

British Library Cataloguing-in-Publication Data.
A catalogue record for this book is available from the British Library

ISBN 0−85170−421−2
    0−85170−422−0 pbk

Cover by Robert Harland Design
Cover still: *Things to Come* (William Cameron Menzies, 1935)

Set by Fakenham Photosetting Ltd, Fakenham, Norfolk
Printed in Great Britain by St Edmundsbury Press Ltd,
Bury St Edmunds, Suffolk

CONTENTS

Shepperton was the only major UK studio that has been financed by government, was answerable to government and was almost destroyed by government.

Sidney Gilliat

One of the happiest experiences of my professional life was the making of *A Man for All Seasons* at Shepperton Studios, which was then managed by Adrian Worker. The crews and departments were top class and no request was too much trouble. It was a wonderful way to make a movie. There is still a glow twenty-five years later when I think of the lovely time we had.

Fred Zinnemann

Shepperton was my favourite studio. I loved all the nonsense of the (Old) House and the big black and white tiled floor which we had to cross to get to the restaurant and bar. In my day it was a converted conservatory. I remember the story of the dotty lady who threw herself from the gallery into the hall and died, naturally enough. A lot of actors rather wished that they could follow her course having been to 'rushes'.

Sir Dirk Bogarde

ACKNOWLEDGMENTS

Shepperton Studios – An Independent View is dedicated to Sir Stanley Baker, Lew Broom, Len Girdlestone, Guy Green, John Huntley and Andy Worker, each of whom provided a timely morale-boosting opportunity for me to work in the British film industry at different times in my career; to John Bentley, whose purchase of Shepperton Studios in 1972 on behalf of Barclay Securities Limited provided me with a new lease of life when organising the successful public campaign against him; and to 'W' for making this project possible.

Special thanks to Sidney Gilliat, Nigel Hurdle, Kenneth Maidment, Paul Olliver and to producer/director Andy Donally, who sadly died before publication of this book, a major contribution to which was his initial enthusiasm and active support. Thanks also to Roy Pembrooke for his invaluable assistance and dogged detective work on my behalf.

I am indebted to the many individuals who took both time and trouble to contact me with reminiscences, many of which provided vital clues to the frustrating number of key pieces that were missing from the Shepperton jigsaw. Helen Hudson succeeded in making sense of my hieroglyphics before committing them to her typewriter.

The following people offered invaluable help and advice: William Altria, Brian Anthony, Ray Austin, Mike Ayling, Julie Bailey, John Bannon, Hazel Banting, Paul Beeson, Ted Belcher, Dick Best, David Blake, Roy Boulting, Lord Brabourne, Sandra Bradley, Beryl Brown, Michael Bucks, Vera Byrnes, Martin Cahill, Denis Carrigan, Cliff Castle, Annette Caulkin, Karen Chatterton, Dawn Cherry, Charlie Chester, Sir John Clark, Michael Clark, Ernie Clarke, Malcolm Craddock, John Dark, Barry Dix, Natasha Fairbairn (British Film Institute), Bryan Forbes, George Fowler, Roy Fowler, Freddie Francis, Peter Frazer-Jones, Henry Geddes, Leslie Gilliat, Godfrey Godar, David Godfrey, Cherie Goode, Lord Goodman, Vernon Goslin, Laurie Greenwood, Charles Gregson, Sir Alec Guinness, Guy Hamilton, Julie Harris, James Hill, Archie Holly, Cyril Howard, Ken Hughes, Renata Hutton-Mills, Arthur Ibbetson, Charles Jarrott, Bob Jones, David Jones, Roger Langley, Morton Lewis, Ronnie Maasz, Kay Mander, Joe Marks, Angela Martelli, Toni Martin, Geoff Mist, Wilfred Moeller, Frank Nesbitt, Peter Newbrook, Peter Noble, Herbert Parkhouse, Roy Parkinson, John Peddie, Sarah Powell, David Samuelson, Sydney Samuelson, Ken Scott, Peter Graham Scott, David Sharpe (British Film Institute), George Sidney, E. M. Smedley-Aston, Ronald Spencer, David Stark, Richard Stephenson,

Roy Stevens, George Stroud, Stanley Taylor, Alex Thompson, Gordon Thompson, Phyllis Townsend, Steve Watts, Alistair Welch, Eva Welch, Tony Willis, Sir John Woolf, Jimmy Wright, Fred Zinnemann.

I am grateful to BFI Stills, Posters and Designs for all of the film stills. The cover still from *Things to Come* is courtesy of CTE Ltd. This film was a portent of things to come for Shepperton Studios. When Korda bought British Lion and Sound City (the original name for Shepperton Studios) in 1946, he also brought with him from Worton Hall Studio this huge stage built specially for *Things to Come*. It was erected at Shepperton in 1948 and became Stage 'H', the largest silent stage in Europe.

A donation from sales of this book will be made to the Cinema and Television Benevolent Fund. The Fund, founded in 1924, incorporated the ITV industries in 1964 to become the present CTBF. It is the only trade charity in the UK specifically designed to offer financial help, care and support for anyone in the two industries who may need it. Currently the Fund helps to support over 1,100 people of all ages. The CTBF is based at 22 Golden Square, London W1R 4AD (tel: 071 437 6567).

PREFACE

Publication of this history of Shepperton Studios is the final piece in the major British studio jigsaw. Both Pinewood and Elstree Studios have had their respective histories covered both in print and visual form. Until now, Shepperton was the only major British studio not to have had a definitive history written. This corporate history follows a convenient anniversary for the studio of sixty years (1932–1992), but perhaps more importantly this project presents an opportunity to place in perspective the complex relationships between Shepperton Studios, British Lion, London Films, Sir Alexander Korda, the National Film Finance Corporation and the British government's £3 million loan to British Lion in 1948.

It also provides an opportunity to assess the impact on the studio and on British Lion of the City-based owners, the first of whom was Barclay Securities run by John Bentley.

I make no apology for digressing throughout the book into the background to major developments within the industry which helped to influence decisions by managements and government organisations. I hope this will provide a better understanding of the circumstances which influenced the development of Shepperton Studios.

Researching and writing a book can take a long time – in this case, three years. Sadly, during this time three key industry figures relevant to the history of the studio have died: Andy Donally, who was an early inspiration for this project; Milton Subotsky (for whom Freddie Francis kindly deputised in checking and clarifying Subotsky's production record at Shepperton); and the courageous blind film-maker Jimmy Wright, who died within days of providing his contribution.

It is clear to me that there was (and still is) a genuine high regard and, for many, a genuine love for this studio and for the people who have worked there. I consider myself fortunate to have been one of those lucky ones who experienced the highs and lows of working in a major film studio when it was operating to capacity with top international stars, producers and directors. (I worked at the studio in management from 1960 to 1965 and ran the public campaign against Barclay Securities and John Bentley in 1972.)

In my opinion, film-making was more fun then, but perhaps comparison with today's film-making is unfair. My hope is that this book, for the first time, will place both good and bad times at Shepperton Studios in the correct perspective.

Derek Threadgall, June 1993

ix

INTRODUCTION

Historically, Pinewood and Elstree Studios have been part of vertically integrated company structures controlling the production, distribution and exhibition of internally produced films. Pinewood is owned by the Rank Organisation, whose films were distributed by Rank Film Distributors – chiefly to Rank-owned cinemas – until 1979, when Rank ceased to make its own films. Until 1969, Elstree was owned by the Associated British Picture Corporation Limited, whose films were distributed by Associated British Pathé Limited to Associated British Cinemas (ABC).

Shepperton has always been a maverick studio. From 1946 to 1972 it was owned by British Lion, and it is still an independent studio for independent producers.

All three studios have experienced the trauma of takeover, in real terms for Elstree and Shepperton and, in the case of Pinewood, the threat of takeover on more than one occasion. To date, the Green Belt restrictions protecting the Pinewood studio core have put up a strong resistance.

Independent producers can be fiercely critical of, or fiercely loyal to, a studio. Shepperton has a reputation among independent producers for being a friendly studio where things get done – somehow!

Pinewood is renowned for its efficient, military-style operation and Elstree was a very professional film factory. Shepperton has an atmosphere of its own, sympathetic to the different types of producers who work there – from the sophisticated professionalism of John Brabourne, to the 'family' producers of Walt Disney and the hard-nosed, hard-boiled Hollywood independents such as the late Hal Wallis, Carl Foreman and director Joe Losey, with all of whom I had the privilege of working at Shepperton. This studio is an amoeba, changing shape, size and staffing to suit multifarious producer demands.

The success of Shepperton can be summarised by the films produced there, or for which it has provided production facilities. Epics such as Sir Alexander Korda's *Sanders of the River* and Sir David Lean's *Lawrence of Arabia*; classics such as Sir Carol Reed's *The Third Man*, Anthony Asquith's *The Winslow Boy*, Sir David Lean's *The Sound Barrier* and *Hobson's Choice*, John Huston's *The African Queen* and *Moulin Rouge* and Sir Laurence Olivier's *Richard III*. These and many other films reflect the diverse nature of Shepperton and of those who have worked there.

Shepperton is not a cosy studio – it has a rawness and a vibrancy perfectly reflected in some of the hardest-hitting films to come out of the

British film industry. Jack Clayton's milestone film *Room at the Top* and John Schlesinger's slice of Northern life, *A Kind of Loving*, were two such trailblazers. The Boulting brothers, Roy and John, together with fellow long-term studio residents Frank Launder and Sidney Gilliat, produced a string of successful comedies at Shepperton, the most famous (or infamous) of which was the Boultings' satire, *I'm All Right Jack*. Shepperton also tackled large-scale productions such as Carl Foreman's *The Guns of Navarone* and Stanley Kubrick's *Dr Strangelove*.

The big musicals produced at Shepperton – *Half a Sixpence, Oliver!* and *Scrooge* – contrast with the smaller *It's Trad, Dad*, produced by American Milton Subotsky, better known for his string of Shepperton-based low-budget horror films featuring Peter Cushing and Christopher Lee. American producer/director Roger Corman provided healthy competition on adjoining stages dominated by sibilant-voiced Vincent Price.

At Shepperton, Daleks rubbed shoulders with Triffids, the terrors of St Trinian's ran amok (both on and off the set), and American special effects king, Ray Harryhausen, painstakingly breathed life into his miniature monsters.

Since 1946, when Sir Alexander Korda acquired the studio, Shepperton has provided facilities for the production of some 500 feature films, numerous second features, television series and commercials. Even as a 'four-wall' studio, Shepperton has hosted some remarkable films. David Lean completed *A Passage to India* in the studio, and the classic Peter Sellers character, Inspector Clouzot, bungled his way through Blake Edwards's 'Pink Panther' films.

The creative freedom of the 'four-wall' system encouraged greater flexibility both for labour and facilities, sustaining and developing productions such as Ridley Scott's chilling *Alien*, Dino de Laurentiis's *Flash Gordon*, and *Ragtime*, the swan song of veteran Hollywood star James Cagney.

Since 1984, when John and Benny Lee's Lee Electric (Lighting) company acquired the studio, considerable sums of money have been spent on refurbishing the studio's facilities. New workshops were built in 1987 and, slowly, the studio became a hive of peripheral production activity with many specialist companies, such as special effects experts the Magic Camera Company, permanently based at Shepperton. Some sixty service companies now populate the studio grounds, providing a highly concentrated, vibrant production centre with cost-effective life-support systems for all the main production stages.

Handmade Films, run by ex-Beatle George Harrison, was the first production company to base its production arm in the new-look Shepperton, producing all its UK films in the studio. American director Sydney Pollack was sufficiently impressed to complete *Out of Africa* at Shepperton, as were Michael Apted with *Gorillas in the Mist* and Richard Attenborough with *Cry Freedom*.

Since its birth as Sound City in 1932, Shepperton has been influenced by three sets of brothers – the Kordas (London Films), the Boultings (British Lion), and the Lees, who bought the studio in 1984 but who now no longer own the Lee Group of companies.

Today, the future of Shepperton Studios is again on the political agenda.

It is ironic that the Single European Market and the American desire to be part of that revolution are once more drawing the attention of British politicians to the importance of the British film industry in the international sphere. As a leading independent studio with a production track record second to none, including eight productions selected for Royal Film Performance presentation, Shepperton is ideally placed to take advantage of the production and investment opportunities now arising out of a combination of European market unity and American financial muscle.

Time will tell whether, at long last, this nettle will be grasped.

When Commander Sir Edward Nicholl MP said in 1917, 'What I wish to buy is some place where I can walk straight in and hang up my hat', he was promptly sold the 900-acre estate of Littleton. Not until the Commander's bowler was removed from the hatstand did Littleton become a film studio.

This book is a 'hats-off' tribute to the studio known to many as the 'yo-yo' studio because of its many ups and downs through the years. In some miraculous way, often with the help of dedicated individuals determined to protect and preserve it from business and financial rape, the studio has survived.

1

FIRST STIRRINGS

Shepperton Studios are located a mile outside the village of Shepperton in the county of Middlesex, on land close to the River Thames fifteen miles upriver from London. The studios are arranged around Littleton Park House, for many centuries the centre of the Manor of Littleton.

After the Norman conquest, the overlordship of the Manor was granted to Robert Blunt, whose family retained it until William Blunt died fighting for King Henry III at the Battle of Evesham in 1265. A foretaste of the reasonable studio rents to come was the annual rent of one pound of pepper paid around this time by the tenants of the Manor, which remained unchanged for two centuries. In 1346 cannons and yeoman archers from the estate fought at the Battle of Crécy in France. The following year King Edward III rewarded his standard bearer, Sir Guy de Brian, with overlordship of the Manor. Over the following three centuries the Title of the Manor changed hands many times. In 1619 Edward Wood, an Alderman of the City of London, became tenant of the Manor and in 1689 his son Thomas, a ranger at Hampton Court, built the present house, Littleton Park, which owes its design to Sir Christopher Wren. The family purchased the Title to the Manor in 1749 and was in residence until the end of the nineteenth century.

In 1876 the house was partially burnt down. It was repaired in the early 1900s by Sir Richard Burbridge, then managing director of London's famous store, Harrods.

Naturally, no historic house would be complete without a ghost, and Shepperton's Old House is no exception. Shepperton's ghost is reputed to be that of a young woman who, spurned by her lover, threw herself from the first-floor Minstrels' Gallery. Her ghost appears from time to time flitting through a side window in the house facing 'A' stage.

After Sir Richard's death in 1917, the estate was sold complete, including furniture and fittings, to Sir Edward Nicholl, a successful shipping magnate and Member of Parliament. Sir Edward lived on the 900-acre estate until 1928.

During Sir Edward Nicholl's tenure of Littleton Park House, Norman Loudon (1902–67), a middle-class Scot from Campbeltown, had started in business as an accountant. From 1922 to 1924 he was an independent merchant in Germany before becoming Managing Director of Camera-scopes Limited in 1925. Two years later he moved into rotary printing,

4

producing booklets for children. These booklets contained close-up, frame-by-frame pictures of golfers, cricketers and so on, shot in slow-motion with a 35mm Pathé camera (this camera was later used to shoot Loudon's first films). When flicked by a thumb or forefinger, the booklets produced movement of the subject. Film director Adrian Brunel described them as 'little booklets of sportsmen in action'. Loudon was a keen sportsman, an excellent 'shot' when hunting and, according to Brunel, 'a shrewd and resourceful beginner – tough, jolly and with undoubted charm'.

Brian Anthony, as a 17-year-old, worked for Loudon at 113b Earls Court Road, London, producing the 'Flicker' booklets before Loudon moved into film production in 1932:

> When I started work with Loudon, he had bought Littleton Park House, but still ran his business from Earls Court. He had a business colleague, George Robbins, and a business manager, Major Beauville, with whom I had most contact. He also had a photographer, George Dudgeon-Stretton. The 'Flicker' booklets were printed on fairly heavy paper and were about two-and-a-half inches wide by about four inches long. On each cover were details of the sportsmen featured inside. We would select from the photographic action a three- or four-second section which was put into an enlarger. This produced a blow-up from every second or third frame, depending on the action. We printed up the enlargements on register pins to fit the booklet. The photos were about three inches by two inches and were stapled into the booklet at the bottom. A fifty-page book, when 'flicked' by the finger or thumb, would give about two to three seconds of action. It really was the same principle used in the 'end-of-pier' Mutoscope 'What the Butler Saw' machines, when you turned a handle to revolve the photo-cards inside the machine to give the illusion of movement. After we made up the master books, they were sent to Norwood in south-east London for bulk printing and distribution to stores such as Hamleys in London's West End. These booklets were very popular at the time and very cheap to buy.[1]

Anthony recalls being taken by Loudon to Littleton Park House (and cleaning Loudon's car each Saturday morning). Unfortunately, he realised that after Loudon had closed his Earls Court operation, the journey to his new business base at the house would be too tiring:

> But there was no question of me being fired. Loudon was not like that. He looked after his staff. He was kind enough to give me an introduction and reference for an advertising agency in the Strand, where I continued my career.[2]

The success of Loudon's 'Flickers' had enabled him to buy Littleton Park House from Sir Edward in 1928. Out of such simple fantasies were born Shepperton Studios.

However, Loudon was unaware of the tenuous link between Littleton Park House and the British film industry that had been forged by a young girl a year before his purchase of the house.

The children's 'Flicker' book

Six-year-old Julie Harris was to become one of the film industry's top costume designers, but in 1927 she was just another little girl invited to Littleton Park House to play with Lesley and Dodo Marshall, Sir Edward Nicholl's children:

> We lived close to the estate in Laleham village. My parents knew Sir Edward Nicholl, hence the invitation for me to visit. Dodo Marshall eventually married the film producer Frank Bundy (who had entered the industry in 1925, with Herbert Wilcox Productions). The conservatory in the house (where Loudon later was to make his first films) was an aviary stocked with birds. I was fascinated by the ballroom because it had a stage and I wanted to go on the stage. Sir Edward also had a miniature railway running through the grounds and in the conservatory. I rode many times on that railway.[3]

Later, as a teenager, she watched a night shoot of Korda's *Sanders of the River* and, in 1936, persuaded a producer to let her be part of a crowd in a hotel lobby sequence in a film being shot at Sound City. Her first film role ended up on the cutting room floor.

Richard Stephenson, a close friend of Julie Harris, also remembers the narrow-gauge railway running through the grounds. Sir Edward's model railway layout in the conservatory, Stephenson remembers, was lit up after dark. According to Stephenson, Sir Edward fell out with his bank and, knowing that Stephenson's father was a bank manager in Windsor, transferred his account to that branch, thereby ensuring that regular visits were made to Sir Edward's house by the Stephenson family. During one such visit for a children's Christmas party, Richard Stephenson met Julie Harris, both six-year-olds and apparently oblivious to the Guards Regimental Band playing in the ballroom.[4]

In 1930, Norman Loudon registered Flicker Productions Limited with a capital of £3,500 and on 15 December 1931 the 29-year-old Scot entered the mainstream British film industry by buying the seventy acres of land, including a stretch of the adjoining River Ash plus an expanse of woodland around Littleton Park House. The total purchase price of land and house was £5,000.

Loudon was now set, like many others, to take advantage of the 1927 'Quota Act', which was primarily intended to protect British film produc-

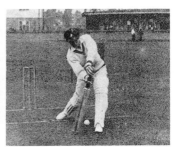

tion against competition from American films. In her book *Continuity Girl* (Robert Hale, 1937), Martha Robinson described her five years' production experience at Sound City Studios (the original name for Shepperton Studios) and observed that:

> The Cinematograph Films Act of 1927 rescued an almost dying industry in England. The subsequent rush of productions demanded more technical assistance than could be found in the country. Even with the absorption of an allowed number of foreign technicians, there was a shortage. The film companies were forced to take on apprentices who were rushed through a rapid training and pushed into positions they were totally unqualified to occupy. Those who showed any special technical or artistic ability found themselves filling two or three positions at once merely because of the incompetence around them.[5]

Under the 1927 Act renters were obliged to offer, and exhibitors to show, a proportion (or quota) of British film footage which rose by annual increases to 20 per cent in 1938. Seventy-five per cent of the salaries of production employees was to go to British subjects and the scenarist (writer) was to be British. Films made anywhere in the British Empire were also eligible as quota. This latter definition led to considerable 'stockpiling' by renters of films, many of them from far-flung corners of the Empire. It would be interesting to know how many exhibitors turned out on 27 December 1929 for the Film Booking Offices' trade show of an 11,000-foot silent Indian film for which they paid less than one shilling (5p) a foot.

Clearly, importers of foreign films, and especially the London renting subsidiaries of the major Hollywood companies, now needed a large number of British films to balance their equally large number of imports. The answer to their problems was the so-called 'quota quickie'. These films were made cheaply and quickly and, if unable to make a profit, were expected to make the smallest loss. Inevitably, this type of film created a new type of producer whose growing ranks Norman Loudon sought to join.

In February 1932 he formed the Sound City Film Producing and Recording Studios with a capital of £20,950, much of it from individuals keen to try their hand at film production.

Later that year Loudon built his first stage (110 by 80 feet). At that time there were some thirty studios in and around London, many of which had

Aerial shot of Sound City Studios, 1932

been built during the silent film period and hastily converted to sound when the new 'fad' had caught on. Loudon had the foresight to make his first stage and subsequent second stage (80 by 45 feet) purpose-built for sound. Both stages were equipped with a Visatone Sound-on-Film system developed by a Captain Round out of ASDIC submarine detection equipment used during the First World War. It was made for the Stoll company under licence from the Marconi Wireless Telegraph Company. Sound City was one of several small studios to use this system, others being Twickenham, Wembley and Rock studios. Electric power was supplied by the latest Ruston and Hornsby eight-cylinder Diesel engines direct-coupled to DC generators. Both original stages were destroyed during the Second World War, but the original first stage, the larger of the two, was rebuilt to become the Scoring Stage (now 'L' stage).

During the summer of 1932 the first tentative film production steps were taken at Sound City, using the conservatory and ballroom in Littleton Park House and a mobile Visatone recording van. By the end of the year Loudon had produced his first seven films: five shorts, *Reward*, *Capture*, *Aerobatics*, *The Safe* and *Pursuit of Priscilla*, and two features, *Watch Beverley* (with Francis X. Bushman, directed by Arthur Maude) and *Reunion* (directed by Ivar Campbell). The production team comprised three directors: Ivar Campbell (a young recruit from the Stock Exchange), John D. Cousins and Arthur Maude; sound recordist J. Kilburn Byers; assistant directors Harold Cox and W. L. Gartin; cameraman George Dudgeon-Stretton and scenario director (writer) N. W. Pemberton (both former members of Flicker Productions); and art director W. L. Daniels. The studio manager was K. H. Bovill; publicity was handled by V. C. H. Creer and construction by carpenter Fred Austin. The chief electrician was Percy Bell, who later rose from the ranks to become a major force in the pre-war development of Sound City. Casting was by John Baxter of Baxter and Barter, based at 91 Regent Street, London. According to film editor Dick Best, the names Baxter and Barter were painted in large letters on the roof of at least one of Loudon's stages. To what effect remains a mystery, considering the paucity of low-flying aircraft at the time.

John Baxter, a Christian socialist and teetotaller, learned the rudiments of directing as assistant to Ivar Campbell on *Reunion* (1932). Subsequently, Baxter created a personal directing style that was to run through all his films made at Sound City, notably *Song of the Plough* and *Doss House* (both 1933). *Doss House* was a remarkable attempt to get away from the phoniness of most productions at that time. Baxter introduced realism and social meaning into this film about the underdogs of British society. All the characters were male down-and-outs. The set was the common room of a doss house. Everyone from Loudon to the clapper-boy prophesied failure, but Baxter produced a masterpiece. When it played at London's Empire cinema in Leicester Square, the usual rowdy Saturday night audience was surprisingly subdued.

Angela Martelli, rated by her peers as one of the best continuity girls in the 1930s, was paid one pound a week (the 1991 freelance minimum rate for a 40-hour week was £386) when she started her first film, *Reunion*. Subsequently, she worked on most of Baxter's films, especially the early ones shot in the ballroom and conservatory of the Old House before the stages were built. She also worked with Ivar 'Midnight' Campbell, so-called because he always worked late, often until the early hours of the morning.

The British class system was much in evidence during the 1930s development of the film industry. The creativity was mostly provided by the educated middle class, whose celluloid dreams and fantasies were given three-dimensional life by craftsmen (carpenters, plasterers, painters) traditionally drawn from the working class. Occasionally, middle-class ignorance of the film industry led to a touch of the 'vapours' when an offspring announced the intention to abandon the real world for that of the 'films'. Angela Martelli recalled that her mother nearly had a nervous breakdown when she told her she was 'going into films'.[6]

Considering the academic and service background of many of the members of Loudon's production team in the studio's early days, it is hardly surprising that, according to Adrian Brunel, who directed *Elstree Calling* (1930), and Baynham Honri, in charge of Twickenham Studios sound department before moving to Sound City as sound consultant in 1939, Sound City was the studio for 'the sons of gentleman'. Using the Old House as a residential hotel for staff and actors, Loudon created a country house atmosphere that was to remain a hallmark of Sound City (and later of Shepperton Studios) throughout the studio's history.

Although 'gifted amateurs' were given an opportunity to buy their way into production, Loudon's business acumen was far from amateurish. In July 1933 he registered Sound City (Films) with a capital of £175,000, and on 2 November that year Sound City bought the main studio lot.

Colonel Blood (1933) was the first 'big' film made at Sound City.

Budgeted at £60,000 (around one million pounds today), it also made a big loss. Written and directed by author and former actor W. P. Lipscomb, *Colonel Blood* featured Peter Cellier, Anne Grey and Allan Jeayes. Also working on the production was John Bryan, a young assistant art director who was later to become one of Britain's most distinguished art directors, winning an American Academy Award for his sets for *Great Expectations* (1946).

Sidney Gilliat knew Lipscomb well as both had worked as writers at Gaumont-British. Lipscomb later went to Hollywood where he wrote the script for the Ronald Colman version of *A Tale of Two Cities* (1935). Unfortunately, the 'jolly camaraderie' enjoyed by Gilliat and his fellow studio writers at that time slowly vanished from studio life.

Norman Loudon was slightly carried away with the exuberance of his first 'epic', sanctioning use of the hall in the Old House for recording the film's music. He thought the hall's acoustics were better for such a prestigious production.

It was no coincidence that the budget for *Colonel Blood* was the same as the reported cash cost of Korda's *The Private Life of Henry VIII* (although the actual cost of Korda's film, including deferments and participating interests, was higher). After 1933, £60,000 became a 'magic figure' and films which were to cost more than this were considered suspect by the financiers, regardless of their content. Certainly the international success of *The Private Life of Henry VIII*, particularly in the USA, made it easier for producers of 'quality' films to raise money, although from 1933 to 1937, when loans for 'quality' productions aimed at a world market were more readily available, this apparent cinematic crock of gold was helped by a slackness in the marine market that persuaded underwriters to turn their attention elsewhere. In this case film production, by way of Korda's film, had proved itself a 'good risk'.

Throughout 1933, Loudon expanded his production team to include two more cameramen, Hone Glendinning and A. A. Austin, an extra sound recordist and two extra assistant directors, Fraser Foulsham and I. N. Watts. Two more 'blue-bloods' joined the ranks. Naval Commander J. L. Freer-Hunt reinforced the directing staff and Naval Commander Anthony Kimmins the scenarist (and later, the acting and directing) pools.

In December 1933, 14-year-old Peter Cull, whose father had been master painter at the studio, became the studio's first apprentice or, to be more precise, tea-boy, cleaner and general dogsbody. He was paid 7s 6d (37½p) a week (1991 Trainee rate for documentary and specialised filming: £150.80 per week for the first year). At that time the studio had carpenters' and plasterers' shops, and later a canteen was built over a well site. Labour was non-unionised, but the first stirrings of unionisation of British studio technical staff had started in 1933. A group of Gaumont-British technicians, and the editor Sidney Cole, had been meeting on a regular basis in cafés around Soho and Gaumont-British studios in London's Shepherd's Bush, to talk film. These informal chats by the 98-member strong Association of Studio Workers led to the Association of Cine Technicians (ACT) becoming a fully-fledged trade union, meeting for the first time as such in February 1935.

10

Assistant property master Ted Belcher introduced Sound City to trade unionism when he used his property room as a recruiting centre. Chief electrician Percy Bell immediately opposed this move, frightening off his electricians for a year before they agreed to sign up. The first official Sound City union meeting was held in Shepperton village hall, although only union officials turned up.

In 1934 Loudon's investment in the huge studio backlot and river location paid off. The big boys came in to shoot a major production at Sound City. At the time they did not come much bigger than Alexander, Zoltan and Vincent Korda. The three Hungarian brothers, Hungarian writer Lajos Biro and American editor Harold Young had registered London Film Productions in February 1932 as a private £100 company. The joint managing directors were Alexander Korda and Conservative MP Captain A. C. N. Dixey. The chairman was George Grossmith, an actor and writer with whom Alexander Korda had worked in America. Zoltan and Vincent worked for the company as, respectively, production supervisor and art director. Financial backing for the company came from, among other influential sources, international banker Leopold Sutro, whose son John represented him on the board. John Sutro worked with Korda until 1940, after which he produced, among other films, *The Way Ahead*, *Men of Two Worlds* and *The Seventh Veil* for Two Cities.

Korda's major production for Sound City had been planned back in August 1933, but was not finished until early 1935. Based in the tiny cramped Worton Hall studios in Isleworth, West London, the film was originally titled *Bosambo*. After its release in 1935, it became better known

Sanders of the River *(Zoltan Korda, 1934)*

11

as *Sanders of the River*. For six months (according to the studio publicity) Sound City played host to some 300 'natives' (black extras) encamped in the African village constructed on the backlot by the river. According to veteran producer E. M. Smedley-Aston, when not encamped by the river, these extras were encamped in their homes in Cardiff's Tiger Bay area. They were bussed to and from the studio when needed. Ever the opportunist, Loudon was not averse to 'borrowing' what was, at that time, a rare commodity in British studios – black extras. *Rolling Home*, starring Scottish comedian Will Fyffe, was one such Loudon production.

Sound City's backlot was not to everyone's liking. Korda's French cameraman, Georges Périnal, constantly complained about the sun 'not being tropical'.

Director Arthur Woods had no such illusions when, in 1933, he brought *Drake of England* to Sound City from Elstree Studios to shoot one sequence by the river. The lot at Elstree was too small for a sequence showing Queen Elizabeth I (Athene Seyler) addressing her troops at Tilbury Docks.

In 1934 Frank Launder, Smedley-Aston's brother-in-law, left British International Pictures (BIP) to become scenario editor at Sound City. Sidney Gilliat recalled Launder's employment as 'rather oddly only part-time and seemed to become more so as the months passed. Our first collaboration at the Bush was, in fact, while he was still attached on this basis to Sound City, but he never seemed to have difficulty in joining me at Shepherd's Bush or Islington.'[7] Launder's department was typical of those in other studios. Unsolicited material continually rolled in from a wide cross-section of the cinema-going public. No amount of rejection letters or silent indifference would dampen their enthusiasm. Norman Loudon's enthusiasm continued unabated. In a double-page advertisement in *Kine Year Book* (1935) he claimed over twenty-five productions made in 1934, including 'five of 1935's biggest films' (referring to the year of release, not production). If nothing else, Loudon was confident of Sound City's future, claiming in the same advertisement: 'They say that three things are necessary in the Film Production Business – money, money and more money.'

Radio Pirates (Ivar Campbell, 1935) convinced Loudon that it was important to keep the trade press happy – with advertising. At a farewell party for South African-born beauty queen and popular actress Molly Lamont, whom Loudon was planning to launch in Hollywood, he engaged a reporter in conversation regarding the imminent review in the trade press. To his amazement, the reporter confirmed what Loudon had suspected for some time. No favourable review would be forthcoming, no matter how good the film, unless the publication had been patronised by the producer's advertising. The knock-on effect was the refusal of exhibitors to book a film with a bad review. Loudon took the hint and immediately ordered some publicity for the film. *Radio Pirates* received an excellent write-up and was heavily booked by exhibitors as a consequence.

By 1935 Loudon had built a formidable team of directors: Ivar Campbell, Anthony Kimmins, Adrian Brunel and Ralph Ince. G. P. Robinson reinforced his writing team and a new general manager, L. Grandfield-Hill, was appointed. The triumvirate of Grandfield-Hill, W. L. Garton (assistant general manager) and Percy Bell (floor manager) formed the managerial foundation of the studio until the outbreak of the Second World War in 1939.

Among the films produced at Shepperton in 1935 was *Father O'Flynn*, directed by Wilfred Noy and Walter Tennyson. Tennyson and his twin brother Alfred were cousins to Pen Tennyson, great-grandson of the poet. Walter Tennyson and Noy had worked in Hollywood before returning to England to set up Film Tests Limited in London's Knightsbridge. Assisted by cameraman (later director) Vernon Sewell and sound recordist Doug Latty, they encouraged people to have a film test for which the client paid, ostensibly to help the client break into films. How many achieved that distinction is not known.

In addition to good personnel, Loudon shrewdly invested in good equipment. In 1935 Sound City boasted four cameras, including the then latest compact model Super Parvo Debrie camera.

On 25 June 1935, at an Extraordinary General Meeting held at Sound City, Sound City (Films) Limited was turned into a Public Company with an authorised capital of £350,000, although no issue took place at the time. The original Articles of Association were replaced by new ones and, in December 1935 Loudon announced that he was to acquire a renting company, this expansion financed by an advance of £100,000 from the Equity and Law Life Assurance Company. He then moved up a gear and closed the studio for redevelopment, allegedly financed from income received from location work on the backlot for *Sanders of the River*. The first phase in the development of Shepperton Studios, alias Sound City – the fun period – was over.

Loudon's pioneering spirit and entrepreneurial flair had pushed him to the brink of becoming a major player in the British prewar volume film production business. He was now poised to expand into the big time, but closing the studio meant also closing down production. His personal production team, many of whom had been with him from his first production efforts in 1932 when he did not have a stage to use, disbanded to find work elsewhere. Many were grateful for the opportunity he had given them to learn their trade under his guidance, and retained a fond memory of Sound City. Others drifted away into obscurity or into other businesses.

Among those hardest hit by a studio closure were the crowd artistes of the day, the 'bread and butter' people who are always taken for granted by audiences yet without whom it would be almost impossible to make films. These people were 'background movement', 'buzz of conversation' or, simply, 'applause'. Prewar Britain was a harsh place in which to live for millions of people. The studios offered a passport to glamour and to a fantasy world much removed from the hard realities of life at the time. Many 'extras' sought only fleeting glory on celluloid for posterity. It was much easier to sit around the studio in evening dress with film make-up on than to work from ten in the morning until eleven at night with a fourth-rate theatrical company. A high proportion of 'extras' were married couples who saw the studios as a means of solving their financial problems, perhaps created by the husband losing his regular job. There was no welfare state to cushion such a blow. Others supplemented a small private income with 'extra' work. The closure of a studio compounded these personal problems.

In June 1936, one month after Denham Studios had been opened by Korda's London Films, Loudon opened the refurbished Sound City. In a two-page advertisement in the *Kine Year Book* (1937), he proudly announced that seven stages covering 80,000 feet of floor space (in fact, taking the quoted individual stage sizes, it was 73,000 feet) were available to independent producers. The new 'A/B' and 'C/D' blocks (the same stages today), each comprised one stage of 150 by 120 feet and another of 120 by 100 feet. Richard Wainright (Wainright Productions) based his company in these new blocks, advertising the fact with his name on the outside stage walls facing the studio main entrance. Another stage (possibly the original first Sound City stage) was 100 by 80 feet and two further stages, each 70 by 40 feet, complemented the new 17,000 square feet concrete pool (for exteriors and special effects) situated beside the Old House (the name by which Littleton Park House was by then more commonly known). The pool site was later transformed into a sunken garden. The Old House was also refurbished to provide hotel accommodation and restaurant facilities. One fatality was recorded during this massive studio reconstruction – a workman was killed when he fell from a stage roof.

RCA High Fidelity Ultra Violet Ray Recording was available with five mobile Visatone trucks. Twelve new cutting rooms and three viewing theatres completed the expanded post-production facilities.

Loudon claimed the largest sound stage in Europe, measuring 268 by 120 feet, but this referred to stages 'A' and 'B' or 'C' and 'D' being combined. He also claimed that 'over 20% of the total number of pictures produced in the country are today made at Sound City'. Since 222 British features were registered with the Board of Trade for 1936, if Loudon's claim was correct his output was at least forty-four films. Twenty-two films were listed for Sound City in the *Kine Year Book* (1937), but as the entry was qualified by the phrase '1936 films include . . .' it seems probable that Sound City output for 1936 could have been around forty films, especially as they were chiefly 'quota quickies', often shot back-to-back.

Loudon's new production policy for Sound City was simple. He would hire the studio to other producers and withdraw from active production on his own account. Throughout 1936 most of the well-known independent producers used Sound City facilities. Probably the best known was an acknowledged exploitation expert, George King. Formerly an agent, King had good connections with Paramount and MGM, producing a string of 'quota quickies' for them during the 1930s, many at Sound City. Between 1928 and 1945 King produced over 150 films, introducing Laurence Olivier, among others, to the screen.

King directed most of the films himself, but also used John Paddy Carstairs and David MacDonald. The only 'star' he had was ZaSu Pitts before she returned to Hollywood. Other producers made this type of film for 15s (75p) a foot and sold them for one pound a foot. King managed to

Opposite: Some of the films made or partly made at Sound City between 1933/34

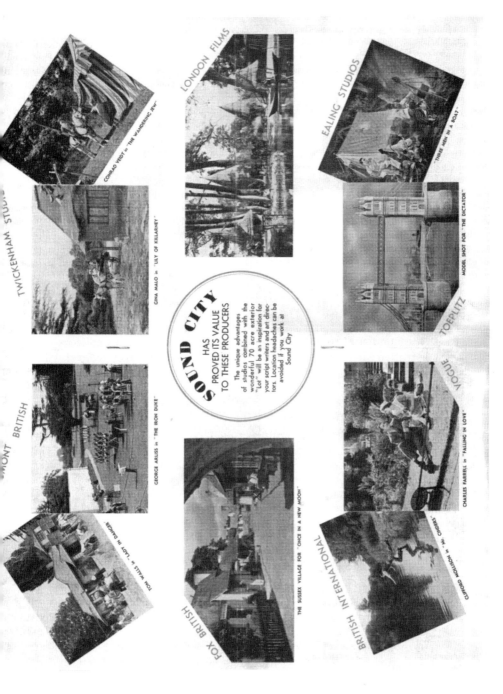

TWICKENHAM STUDIOS

LONDON FILMS

EALING STUDIOS

CONRAD VEIDT in "THE WANDERING JEW"

GINA MALO in "LILY OF KILLARNEY"

THREE MEN IN A BOAT"

MODEL SHOT FOR "THE DICTATOR"

TOEPLITZ

BRITISH

MONT BRITISH

GEORGE ARLISS in "THE IRON DUKE"

TOM WALLS in "LADY IN DANGER"

VOGUE

CHARLES FARRELL in "FALLING IN LOVE"

FOX BRITISH

THE SUSSEX VILLAGE FOR "ONCE IN A NEW MOON"

BRITISH INTERNATIONAL

CLIFFORD MOLLISON in "MR. CINDERS"

SOUND CITY

HAS
PROVED ITS VALUE
TO THESE PRODUCERS

The unique advantages
of studios combined with the
wonderful 70 acre exterior
"Lot" will be an inspiration for
your script writers and art directors. Location headaches can be
avoided if you work at
Sound City

make them for 14s 6d (72½p) a foot, which gave him a Rolls Royce car and a riverside house at Halliford, a short distance from Sound City.

Other studios, including British and Dominion (B & D), British International Pictures (BIP) and Twickenham, also used Sound City, although some films claimed by Loudon for Sound City only used the studio for location work on the backlot. *Sporting Love* (J. Elder Wills, 1936), made at Beaconsfield Studios, and *Thunder in the City* (Marion Gering, 1937), made at Denham Studios, were two such films.

Loudon reshuffled his management pack again and established an office in London's West End at Broadmead House, 21 Panton Street. Inevitably, the office soon moved to Wardour Street (Wardour House) in Soho and on 5 December 1936 Sound City bought the land on which the present North Office block stands.

Production at Sound City peaked in 1937, with productions from all Loudon's main independent supporters and from a few newcomers. Throughout this hectic production period Loudon introduced an export department, although it is not clear what Sound City was exporting or to where. Despite all this activity Loudon sensed that all was not well in the 'quota quickie' world. An attempt had been made in 1933 to inject production finance into the industry through an exhibition-financed production scheme rather grandly called the Empire Co-operative Friendly Society. Member exhibitors contributed to the cost of films made under the scheme in return for priority booking of the films at a favourable rental of 33⅓ per cent. The scheme failed.

In the summer of 1936 another, similar, plan was created by solicitor and Conservative Member of Parliament, Captain A. C. N. Dixey, who in 1932 had been joint managing director with Alexander Korda of London Films. In April 1937 an Agreement was made for studio space and services at Joe Rock's small studio at Elstree. Almost immediately the new British Independent Exhibitors' Distributors Films (BIEDF) began to founder. Dixey resigned at the end of 1937 and Norman Loudon, perhaps sensing that Sound City could benefit more than Joe Rock's studio, took over the company, but with no more success. By October 1938 BIEDF was in the hands of the receiver.

Despite this setback Loudon recruited more staff for his sound and camera departments. Effectively, he was now operating a forerunner of the present 'four-wall' facility studio of which today's Shepperton is one example.

Although he was almost at the end of his cinematic career, Loudon was thrown a brief financial lifeline from a most unlikely source. The talented feet of a champion tap-dancer, 7-year-old Hazel Ascot, had been spotted by director John Baxter when looking for rehearsal rooms for his proposed film *Music Hall*. In his unpublished biographical notes, Baxter commented:

> For those interested in the names of stars who appeared in some of my early films, I will touch briefly on a series of light entertainment pictures. Conditions in the country were not good and comedy and music seemed the best ingredients to offer and, by doing so, I could keep my film unit busy.

Jack Barty joined my regular comedians and a very promising child star, Hazel Ascot, became a firm favourite. She appeared for me in two films, *Talking Feet* (1937) and *Stepping Toes* (1938) ... Both films were made at Sound City studios in conjunction with Norman Loudon and the distributors, Frederick White and Gilbert Church (Ambassador Films).

Hazel Ascot was quite a remarkable dancer – quite unequalled in this country. So popular were these two films with family audiences that they were selected to open several of the new Odeon cinemas, which, during the late 1930s, were being opened by Oscar Deutsch at the rate of about one a week. Hazel was entirely unspoilt and, in contrast to the more sophisticated American screen youngsters of that period, she had natural charm. Her father, who ran a very successful dance academy in Charing Cross Road, had trained her himself and she was thoroughly professional as well as being a most attractive, charming little dancer with twitching feet.

To accommodate Hazel, Baxter rewrote *Music Hall* to become *Talking Feet*. Hazel's second film, *Rhythm of My Heart*, was retitled *Stepping Toes* when Baxter discovered that Bing Crosby was making a film with that title. A third film (in colour) was planned for Hazel, but the outbreak of the Second World War forced its cancellation.

For someone who made only two films, Hazel Ascot, now Hazel Banting, married with three children and working as a primary school teacher not many miles from the studio where she found brief fame, had a short but remarkable career. After the war, she was old enough to apply for a licence to work on the stage and appeared in West End shows and revues. Despite critical acclaim, the war had really ended her film career. 'The last time I danced on stage,' she recalls, 'I was nineteen. It was a big film industry dinner. I danced, got changed and went home and that was that.'[8]

Until 1970 Hazel Ascot believed that her past, kept secret from all but her family, was safe. Unknown to her, and in true 1930s Hollywood tradition, an ardent fan who had first met her in 1937 at the Paramount Theatre, Tottenham Court Road, where she was performing live on the stage during the interval between films (her own film *Stepping Toes* was the main feature), was determined that she should not be forgotten. When he returned from the war to discover her name fading from the limelight, Tony Willis started the Hazel Ascot Appreciation Society and turned his home into a shrine for the child star whose two films had helped Norman Loudon to survive. Willis's objective was 'to remind the British people that they once had a home-grown child star far greater than Shirley Temple', a comparison Ascot was unhappy with.

Shirley Temple was an all-rounder, pretty and cute. I wasn't. I was very ordinary, but had very good feet – better than Shirley Temple's. I hated being compared to Shirley. I was dark and slim; she was short and fair, a very pretty child and she could act. I couldn't act like that. All my talent was in my feet. [According to Willis, Hazel Ascot could dance for an hour non-stop without repeating a step.] John Baxter recognised that.

Like Sonja Henie and Esther Williams, I had become a champion in my field – tap-dancing. I was paid £25 per day for eight weeks' work on my first film.[9]

Having started Ascot's fan club in 1947, Willis was faced with the task of finding the star. Advertised requests for copies of her films led him to Ascot's brother, who arranged for him to meet Ascot in 1970. In 1977 Willis bemused Londoners with a massive poster campaign throughout London's underground system. Alongside sepia-toned pictures of a little girl tap-dancing runs the text:

Film fans!!! Remember America's Shirley Temple? … Of course you do … ! But … did you know that … Britain's own 'Shirley Temple' – Hazel Ascot – is today almost forgotten … ? That she was the most talented dancing and singing star to appear on the screen?

In 1978 Willis's hard work paid off when Ascot's two films were shown again as part of a season of British musicals of the 30s at the Lambeth Film Festival in south London. Ironically, Ascot's father used to live alongside the main subject of the festival – Charles Chaplin. Now in his seventies, Willis admits that the steam has gone out of the Hazel Ascot Appreciation Society, but his tireless work on behalf of his idol has been rewarded. In an interview with Geoffrey Levy in the *Daily Express* (7 December 1977), Hazel Ascot wondered what would have happened had she continued in show business: 'Perhaps I would have ended up like Judy Garland – all showbiz and no life.' When she joined her local Barn Theatre Group, she was asked by the director whether she could do anything (he was unaware of her past). She replied: 'I used to dance.' They made her choreographer!

Eventually the parlous state of the British film industry, and the un-certainty surrounding the imminent Cinematograph Films Act of 1938, persuaded Loudon to close his studio for a second time – not for refurbishment, but for survival.

An attempt by Two Cities Films, under Italian banker and international lawyer Filippo del Giudice, to shoot Anglo-Italian multilingual films at Sound City and in Rome did not really work. The name Two Cities was originally used by Ludoveco Toeplitz in 1937 for a film linked with the Italian company Pisorno. By August 1938 the company had a new board of directors and capital of £40,000. Its only real success was in 1939 with Anthony Asquith's *French Without Tears*, based on the Terence Rattigan play. One of the strengths of this film was its ambitious camerawork (by Bernard Knowles and Jack Hildyard). One scene involved a long take accompanying streams of dancers at carnival time; and another scene with bicycles required some complicated timing as the characters weave in and out of frame, a tracking shot filmed on a road near Shepperton village without the aid of back-projection or post-synchronisation of sound.

Loudon had not entertained such an array of big names in his studio since the Kordas with *Sanders of the River*. *French Without Tears* boasted producer David E. Rose, executive producer Mario Zampi, director Anthony Asquith, writers Anatole de Grunwald and Ian Dalrymple, designers Paul Sheriff and Carmen Dillon, and a young David Lean as editor.

For Loudon it was the last throw of the dice. The new version of the so-called 'Quota Act', which had first created the opportunity for him to produce films, received the Royal Assent on 30 March 1938, its terms effectively killing off the 'quota quickie' and, with it, Loudon's prime source of income. Loudon did not like the term 'quota quickie', preferring 'modest second feature'. The differences of opinion between him and other producers were due to the large volume of cheap films, upon which studios such as Sound City survived – just what the quality producers wanted to stop. The new 'Quota Act' did it for them.

The first signs of this disaster for the British film industry appeared in January 1937, when receivers were appointed to Julius Hagen's companies, Twickenham Film Distributors, Twickenham Film Studios and J. H. Productions Limited. In the same month pay cuts were made at London Films, and Isidore Ostrer announced that 'Unless we can get a bigger return from the American market for British pictures, Gaumont-British will be compelled to abandon production.' Two months later Gainsborough published a loss of £98,000 for the previous year and it was announced that the Gaumont-British studios at Shepherd's Bush were to close, that a limited number of films would continue to be made by Gainsborough at Islington Studios and that these films, together with the Gaumont-British newsreel, would in future be distributed by GFD because it was no longer economic to keep Gaumont-British Distributors in full operation. General Film Distributors (GFD) had by then become the largest British distributor and was handling as many long films annually as the American renters.

Although later in the year London Films restored its pay cuts after announcing a profit of £36,000, the more general story was a succession of losses and receiverships. By the end of the year the boom started by the success of Korda's *The Private Life of Henry VIII* in 1933 was over, although a number of films were finished by additional loans in order to save something from the wreckage.

A legal action in 1939 illustrated the chaotic financing of film production at the time. Before Mr Justice Singleton on 1 May, the Westminster Bank (now the National Westminster Bank) brought thirty-five actions against fifteen insurance companies. Describing the scene in court on the opening day of the case, *The Times* (2 May 1939) reported that 'So many King's Counsel and junior counsel were engaged that there was not room for them in their usual seats ... Such a state of confusion existed when the Judge came in that he adjourned for a few minutes while the lawyers sorted themselves out.'

The state of confusion was not confined to the court. During the six days in which it was heard – before being settled out of court – the case revealed an incredible state of confusion in the financing of British film production. The production companies concerned were the Capitol Group, which also distributed films through United Artists, although neither United Artists nor GFD, with whom Capitol had connections, provided the finance for production. This was largely done by what had now grown to be the normal method of short-term loans. By the end of 1936 the Capitol Film

Corporation had outstanding charges amounting to about £1.5 million with a firm called Aldgate Trustees Limited, set up in July 1935 by Lloyd's member F.C. Ellis and insurance broker L.H. Wilkins, both members of the City broking firm Glanville Enthoven and Company. Aldgate had guaranteed advances to other film producing companies involving at least another £1 million. Of the £1.5 million, averaging £68,000 per film, two-thirds were lost on production – hence the legal action.

Sir Stafford Cripps appeared for the Westminster Bank and in his long opening speech, which was not completed before a settlement was reached after eight days, he explained the method of financing involved. Referring to the foundation of the Capitol Group in 1935, Sir Stafford said:

> About that time there was a good deal of talk about encouraging British film production as against American production. Everybody apparently thought that it was the easiest way in the world to make money and that it did not matter how much was spent on production, or how it was spent, as the inexhaustible resources of the people who went to see the films would be sufficient reimbursement of whatever money was spent. Because of their small capital resources, it became necessary for the Capitol Group to borrow money to finance the production of films and a number of other companies were in the same position at the same time. Some ingenious person in the City of London devised a way by which the necessary money could be raised by these various companies without any difficulty and this method had given rise to the present actions.

> So far as this case was concerned, the protagonists of the method were a firm of well-known brokers in the City [Glanville Enthoven and Company] ... The producing company who desired to raise money would get into contact with the Brokers and tell them what the requirement was. It might be that they desired to raise two loans of £50,000 in order to produce two named films. Thereupon the Brokers would go to a number of underwriters in the marine underwriting market and ask them whether they would be prepared to issue guarantee policies for some share of the total amount of £50,000.

> The Brokers assumed that these policies could persuade some bank to advance the cash against the security of the policies. Relying on the security of the guarantee given by the marine underwriters, the bank would advance the cash. After the first few dealings in that way it appeared that it became nearly automatic for these companies to adopt this procedure and get as much money as they wanted ...

> Out of the sums advanced were taken the premiums which had to be paid to the underwriters and commission which was paid to the Brokers and a further sum was set aside into a reserve account to guarantee the payment of interest to the bank on the loan. A trust company, called Aldgate Trustees Limited, which had been set up by the Brokers, would then take a charge from the producing company over all the receipts for the particular film in respect of which the loan was made ...

> That charge was made effective by giving instructions to the distributing company to pay direct to the bank money which it owed to the

producing company in respect of a particular film. At a later date that charge, which was in the first case a specific one, was converted into an 'umbrella' charge which covered the receipts from all the films of a particular company. The bank had no part of any kind in those arrangements. If, at the end of the period of twelve months, the company had not paid off the loan, or had paid off only part of the loan, the underwriters would have become liable to pay the bank whatever had not been paid by the producing company. But, in many cases, there was a renewal, by the extension of the policies, for a further period. Most of the underwriters apparently reinsured the whole, or part of, their risk.

At that time, no one seemed to think why this very delightful state of affairs should ever come to an end ... The companies got as much money as they wanted and that enabled them to give the distributing companies a very favourable deal.

The actors were able to charge most fabulous fees. The underwriters got a great deal of what appeared to be most lucrative business at a time when the marine market was very dull. The Brokers were doing very well indeed by reason of their commission and the bank were finding a sufficient use for their money at a decent rate of interest with the guarantee of the insurance companies behind them.[10]

The end came in April 1937 when the underwriters, alarmed no doubt by the general uneasiness about the profitability of production as well as by the affairs of this particular group, set up a committee of investigation. Its findings revealed a state of affairs which caused the investors to bring to an end this part of the production boom and, by its repercussions, made a slump inevitable.

Loudon would not be beaten. If he could no longer take his product to the public, then he would bring the public to his product. At the Annual Meeting of Sound City in 1938, he announced plans that were, by his own entrepreneurial standards, daring. He decided to build a zoo and pleasure park in the studio grounds alongside his production facilities. His decision anticipated Walt Disney's theme parks by seventeen years.

Loudon had a huge scale model of his project built on the floor of what today is 'L' stage. Peter Cull, the studio's first apprentice, and his brother helped build this remarkable concept, which covered most of the stage floor. Today, Norman Loudon could be forgiven a wry smile. London Zoo's salvation could be planned around its conversion to a theme and leisure park, yet it was to London Zoo, known in 1938 as Regent's Park Zoo, that Loudon turned in his survival bid for Sound City. He recruited Canadian-born former assistant curator Alan Best to draw up the plans and designs for his new concept. During 1938 Best was in charge of the Children's Zoo and Pet's Corner at Regent's Park and was well qualified for the task Loudon had set him.

A fascinating and ambitious Draft Prospectus (now with the British Film Institute) was produced by Loudon, incorporating humorous but detailed illustrations by artist Alan Gregory. The prospectus showed potential

Overleaf: Loudon's proposed Sound City Zoo and Wonderland

investors how the zoo and pleasure park activities would be developed alongside the day-to-day operation of a major film studio.

To finance this scheme, Loudon devised the Sound City Tontine Plan, to be marketed by Tontine Zoo Limited which was owned by Sound City Zoological Society. According to Loudon's prospectus, the Tontine principle of 'gain for the survivors' first evolved in 1653 with Lorenzo Tonti, a Neapolitan. An example of a British Tontine is the first Richmond Bridge over the Thames, built in 1774. A sum of £20,000 was subscribed by 200 people, who each invested £100 in return for a fixed sum of £800, part of the toll-gate receipts divided each year among the surviving subscribers. Loudon's return to his original investors was to be one-fifth of the annual gate receipts shared equally among surviving investors. A Foundership was to cost £5 and a Fellowship £1, with all investment and associated privileges secured by a bond.

The Sound City Zoo and Wonderland was to be the only zoo of its kind – a place of beauty by day and a floodlit fairyland by night. It was to set a new standard of animal display and show wildlife of the world against vividly realistic backgrounds, a wonderland of mountains, deserts, icebergs, tropical rivers and jungles. A spectacular circus, Noah's Ark and children's paradise were to contain new thrills and amusements as planned by the craftsmen of Sound City.

To achieve his dream, Loudon envisaged fifteen different 'theme' areas populated by over a hundred different species of animal and bird, many in 'natural' surroundings. To ensure visitors were able to find this wonderland, the 'Sign of the Giraffe' was to be placed at advantageous points on the main arterial roads from Land's End to John O'Groats giving the mileage to Sound City Zoo. Quite why anyone should wish to travel to Shepperton all the way from Land's End or John O'Groats apparently did not trouble Loudon.

The Draft Prospectus appears to be an original since it is in 'paste-up' form with many hand-written amendments to the typeset copy. Sound City Zoo and Wonderland was to open in 1940. Sadly for Loudon and for Sound City Studios, the scheme was frustrated by the Second World War.

Notes

1. Author's interview with Brian Anthony.
2. Ibid.
3. Author's interview with Julie Harris, 9 December 1992.
4. Author's interview with Richard Stephenson, 11 June 1993.
5. Martha Robinson, *Continuity Girl* (London: Robert Hale, 1937).
6. Author's interview with Angela Martelli, 26 May 1991.
7. Author's interview with Sidney Gilliat, 27 February 1993.
8. Author's interview with Hazel Banting, 2 February 1993.
9. Ibid.
10. *The British Film Industry*, Political and Economic Planning (London 1952).

2

WAR WORK

Before the outbreak of the Second World War six major American companies (Columbia, Paramount, MGM, Warner Bros., Fox, RKO) distributed
over 50 per cent of all British and foreign features in the UK. The seventh
American major, United Artists, judged by the number of films it distributed, was now only a medium-sized renter, but its influence on the
structure of the industry had been considerably greater than this number
indicated. The eighth American major, Universal, had its films distributed
by the leading British renter, General Film Distributors (GFD), which then
handled over sixty features and was equal to the leading American renters.
Also operating at this level was British Lion, who since 1935 had handled the British release of Republic's films. One other British renter, Associated British Film Distributors (ABFD), part of the group that owned
Ealing Studios, handled over twenty films. Two or three other renters
distributed more than ten films each and the remainder rented only occasional films.

By 1939 the scale of British production had been reduced, with several
production units of the major organisations not making full use of their
studios. These organisations were the General Cinema Finance Corporation (GCFC) group, with Denham, Pinewood and Amalgamated studios and
affiliated to General Film Distributors; the Associated British Picture
Corporation (ABPC) group, with studios at Welwyn and Elstree and linked
to Associated British Film Distributors (ABFD); and the Gaumont-British
group, with studios at Shepherd's Bush and Islington, distributing its films
through General Film Distributors. These major organisations together
owned about half the existing British studio space.

British Lion and Associated British Film Distributors were both renter/
producer concerns. British Lion owned its own studio at Beaconsfield and
ABFD was linked to product both from ABPC studios at Elstree and
Welwyn and from Ealing Studios. However, ABFD did not handle the first
release of Ealing films, whose major releases in 1939 were handled by
United Artists. In addition, there was a decreasing number of independent
British production companies, some owning studios which either distributed their films through affiliated renting companies or through one of the
other British renters, or produced 'quota' films for the Americans. By this
time five American companies had established production subsidiaries in
the UK: Warner Bros. (with studios at Teddington), 20th Century-Fox (who
owned Wembley Studios), MGM, Paramount and Columbia.

Three main circuits (Odeon, ABC and Gaumont-British), each with about 300 or more cinemas, were linked to the three main groups (Rank, ABPC and Eagle-Lion, the forerunner of General Film Distributors). Together, these circuits owned 1,011 cinemas in Great Britain, about 21 per cent of the total. Excluding these main circuits, other circuits with ten or more cinemas controlled 15 per cent of the country's cinemas as opposed to 16 per cent in 1935. Half of this percentage was owned by eleven circuits which had more than twenty cinemas, the largest of which, the A.B. King circuit, had seventy-five cinemas. By 1939 the fourteen circuits with over twenty cinemas controlled nearly 30 per cent of the total, against 25 per cent in 1935.

There was virtually no exclusive American control of any British circuit, but United Artists and 20th Century-Fox and Warner Bros. all had a share interest in the control of a major circuit. The small first-run Paramount circuit was sold shortly after this to Odeon, but several American companies had important pre-release cinemas in London's West End which they used as shop windows for their films.

In September 1939 the British production industry was still suffering from the effects of the 1937 decline. The concentration of studio power in the hands of the major organisations with large financial resources had not raised the level of feature production. Many studios, including Amalgamated and Pinewood, were either dark or working below their capacity.

The Second World War reversed this situation and, temporarily, solved the problems of unemployment among technicians, lack of adequate finance and excess studio space. The government requisitioned many studios for war purposes, including the production of its own propaganda films. Altogether, more than half the studio space available in 1939 was taken over for one war purpose or another.

In 1944 an official committee, the Palache Committee, reported that 'in present war conditions, the decisive factor which limits the amount of British film production is the shortage of studios.' Compounding this problem were other wartime shortages such as materials, staff and film. Despite these difficulties, between 1939 and 1945 the British production industry managed to make an average of sixty features each year. In some quarters there was a feeling that this output could have been higher if there had been a more effective use of studio space. An increasing number of films were expensive productions which occupied scarce studio space for longer periods than less ambitious films would have done.

From September 1939 pressure on that space, including that of Sound City, was intensified when the government made use of requisitioned studio space for purposes other than film-making. This change of emphasis was reflected on 7 September 1939 when a top-level meeting was convened at Royal Air Force Bomber Command Headquarters at High Wycombe. The topic under discussion was the feasibility of establishing dummy and decoy airfields designed to fool the enemy. On 2 October 1939 preliminary plans were drawn up for the construction of sites and submitted to the Deputy Chief of Staff Committee for approval. Ten days later, the Air Ministry sanctioned the building of two dummy airfields, one for daylight, code-named 'K', and one for night, code-named 'Q'. Colonel Sir John F. Turner, given the responsibility of supervising these measures, decided to establish his department at Sound City Studios. By January 1940 one example of each dummy airfield was completed and by the end of that month the organisational structure of the new counter-measure had been drawn up. Sound City, the forerunner of Shepperton Studios, was now at war – for real.

By 1940, twenty-two studios were operating in and around London, offering sixty-five stages covering 647,652 square feet. The British film industry was effectively killed off when the War Department decided to utilise the larger stages for purposes better suited to the conflict. One of the last films to be made at Sound City before the war was *Spy for a Day*, a comedy starring Duggie Wakefield, produced and directed by Mario Zampi for Two Cities Films. During filming, the 'phoney war' mentality was evident in the way some of the crowd artists, dressed in German uniforms, nonchalantly strolled one lunch-time along Shepperton High Street, oblivious to the resulting panic.

Sound City Studios may have been a celluloid fantasy factory but it failed to escape the harsh realities of war. On 21 October 1940, 15-year-old Edward Swindells and 17-year-old Geoffrey Hebdon were killed during a German air raid on the studio. Both boys were sheltering together by a corner of 'C' stage (the same 'C' stage today) when a bomb fell on the stage roof and bounced to the ground before exploding. A simple plaque commemorating this tragedy can be seen in Littleton Church near the present studio entrance.

On 23 February 1944 nine people, including 40-year-old Nurse May Durrell, were killed during another air raid on the studio. Nurse Durrell was on duty at the studio first aid post during the raid, refusing to use a shelter in case she was needed elsewhere. Durrell Way in Shepperton is a memorial to her courage.

The huge Queen Mary reservoir behind the studio was the target for many air raids when landmines and bombs were dropped into the water. Not all reached their target. During one night raid a time-bomb missed the reservoir to lodge itself under 'D' stage. The Royal Engineers were called in to dig it out. It was rumoured that Barnes Wallis's famous bouncing bomb, used by the Royal Air Force in Germany, was tested on the Queen Mary reservoir. But that seems unlikely. A thirty-foot high tower by the reservoir was manned twenty-four hours a day by a team of wardens, as was the observation tower on the roof of the studio's Old House. No one reported any such testing on the reservoir.

After requisitioning Sound City in 1941, the Ministry of Defence used stages 'A', 'B', 'C' and 'D' to store sugar for manufacturers Tate and Lyle. When the Vickers aircraft factory at Weybridge near the studio was bombed and badly damaged, the sugar was removed from 'A' and 'B' stages and replaced by Vickers workers making Wellington bomber parts and spares.

Despite these unfamiliar activities, Sound City's wartime destiny was to be in the hands of its own craftsmen. Art director Peter Proud was one film professional who saw no reason why his work in a studio should not be extended to location work even when, as Captain Proud, his location was

Tobruk in North Africa. Proud was a camouflage expert. He decided to protect his garrison's drinking water supply using his own 'wreckage' to create an illusion of successful German bombing on the water distillery he was responsible for protecting. After a raid he organised numerous small 'bomb craters' to be dug among the buildings, accenting them with shadows made from oil or coal dust. Debris was then widely scattered. On the roof of the main works his squad simulated other damage with canvas, paint and cement. Unused parts of the station, including a large cooling tower, were blown up with pre-set charges.

Major Jasper Maskelyne of the Royal Engineers Camouflage and Experimental Section would have been impressed with Proud's efforts. At the time Maskelyne was the acknowledged expert at visual deception. Sound City Studios supplied him with many of the dummy guns, tanks and men he used in Egypt to support General Wavell's offensive against Rommel. Maskelyne's ingenuity knew no bounds. He hid naval harbours, launched a fleet of dummy submarines, each 258 feet long, and, incredibly, built a dummy battleship 700 feet long to fool the enemy. As he wryly remarked after the incident, 'It goes to sea. It falls to bits, but its job is done!'

When America entered the war in 1941, the guns of an anti-aircraft site at Addlestone near the studio were taken to help defend New York. They were replaced by dummy guns made at Sound City. In 1942, British Film Commissioner Sydney Samuelson had his own brush with an 'explosive' situation.

I was working for Gaumont-British in their newsreel cutting rooms at Lime Grove, Shepherd's Bush. GB News had vaults in the grounds of Sound City. Some of the film stored was very early library footage going back to Gaumont Graphic which was, I think, the silent newsreel which predated the famous GB News whose Editor/Commentator, E. V. H. Emmett, was my boss at the time. This film was all on nitrate stock, much of which was decomposing and, generally, was in a very dangerous state. I remember opening some cans, presumably containing reels of priceless images, instead finding a lump of semi-liquid goo. We (the labourers from GB News sent to deal with the time-bomb-in-waiting) were told that the Sound City stages were being used as government storage for hundreds of thousands of tons of sugar. Apparently, the fear was that the decomposed nitrate could explode at any time, setting off the whole of Sound City, which, in turn, would set off the whole of Shepperton.

We took everything in a hired truck to a place in Southall where a machine boiled off what was left of the emulsion and extracted the silver content. It took two days to remove all of this film, the tedium being relieved by the over-imaginative mind of this particular 16-year-old who elevated the mundane job in hand to the status of a bomb disposal squad saving St Paul's Cathedral in London.[1]

'Operation Starfish' (originally called 'Operation Crashdeck') was another military operation that used Sound City's craftsmen. Started on 2

December 1940, 'Operation Starfish' involved setting decoy fires to mis-direct German bombers.

All this paled before the assignment given to the studio's craftsmen in support of the 'D'-Day invasion of Europe in 1944. Norman Loudon and Percy Bell had remained at the studio co-ordinating its new role as defined and administered by Colonel Turner. It was not that different from what they had been doing since 1932. Now the audience for their fantasy world was to be the German armed forces. Who better to produce dummy weapons, buildings and men than film craftsmen whose trade it was to create that special kind of magic? So began Sound City's remarkable contribution to one of the war's greatest deceptions.

General George S. Patton Jnr was 'in command' of a huge phantom army based under the codename Fortitude North 'Skye' in Scotland and For-titude South 'Operation Quicksand' in England. Its purpose was to keep the Germans guessing as to where and when the invasion of Europe would begin. Sound City's scenic designers and craftsmen faced a task bigger than any previously encountered on a film set. From a design by one of England's leading architects, Professor Basil Spence, they built a giant oil storage facility and docking area near Dover. This installation, stretching along several miles of shoreline, consisted of pumping stations, pipelines, storage tanks, jetties, truck-bays, terminal control points, troop barracks and anti-aircraft defences. Further credence was given to the project when King George VI and General Montgomery both paid inspection visits to 'approve' the project, these visits duly noted in the press. General Eisen-hower, Supreme Commander of the Allied Forces in Europe, attended a special celebration dinner for the project's 'engineers and construction workers'. Guarded by military police, the whole facility was a complete fraud. It was built entirely by the set designers and camouflage crews from painted canvas, wooden scaffolding, fibreboard and sections of old sewer pipe, the only real oil being in the army trucks used to move the staff around.

The Germans believed that the complex was one terminus of an under-water pipeline that would eventually extend to Calais, heralding an imminent invasion in that area. 'Most of us were film and theatre people,' recalled one of the workers, 'so naturally we wanted a proper dress rehearsal.' The Royal Air Force obliged by sending a low-level photo-reconnaissance aircraft over the Dover stage 'set'. The resulting aerial prints were examined and alterations made.

The hoax was successful. German photo-reconnaissance aircraft were forced by British fighters and anti-aircraft fire to take pictures from around 30,000 feet. The resulting pictures 'showed an authentic terminal' which was paid a further compliment of a few long-range artillery shells from German emplacements at Gris-Nez on the French coast. In response the camouflage crews created suitable 'fire damage' using sodium flares and mobile smoke generators.

The Sound City designers also contributed to the war effort by building hundreds of dummy landing barges made of canvas and wood that floated on empty oil drums. The fake vessels, resembling the Allied LCTs, were known as 'big blobs'. Other dummy invasion craft, built of inflatable rubber, were known as 'wet blobs'. Some of these were moored in creeks and inlets between Great Yarmouth and the Thames estuary, but the majority were concentrated in the Ramsgate/Hastings area along the south coast.

The only case on record in which an Operation Fortitude decoy took part in actual combat was when a bull accidentally got loose in a field where a platoon of rubber tanks had been stationed. It charged one of them and was somewhat perplexed as the punctured tank slowly deflated.

Occasionally, the men engaged in this deception were carried away with their work, incensed when German aircraft attacked them, forgetting the purpose for which the sites were designed. RAF Flight Lieutenant Robin A. Brown recalled a conversation over a field telephone between a Flight Sergeant and his Pilot Officer:

Flt. Sgt. (agitated):	Sir! We're being attacked.
Pilot Officer:	Splendid, Sergeant. Good show.
Flt. Sgt.:	They're smashing the place to bits.
Pilot Officer:	Yes. Excellent. Carry on.
Flt. Sgt.:	But, Sir – we need fighter cover. They're wrecking my best decoys!

Surely the best tribute to the work of Sound City's craftsmen during the war.

Note

1. Author's interview with Sydney Samuelson, 2 December 1992.

3

KORDA

During the Second World War the major British studios requisitioned by the government for 'war work' included Sound City (Shepperton), 1941–45; Pinewood, 1940–45; MGM, 1940–46; ABPC (Elstree), 1940–45; Nettlefold, 1942–45; Worton Hall, 1941–44; Islington, 1940–41; and Beaconsfield, 1940–45. More studio space might have been taken over had not producers Edward Black and Michael Balcon agreed to make representations together to the Board of Trade.

After the war ended, the production side of the industry, having been handicapped throughout by lack of personnel, limited studio space and out-of-date equipment, found rehabilitation a slow and difficult process. Government departments were slow to hand back the studios and, even when they were freed, the dollar crisis prevented purchase of American equipment (in particular the Mitchell camera) and Treasury officials were cautious about granting permits for the import of essential equipment from other countries. Even when films were made, the reduction in the amount of raw stock available adversely affected both renter and exhibitor. The laboratories had insufficient stock to print copies and despatch departments had difficulty in arranging 'cross-overs' to supply theatres. The exhibitors were handicapped by the poor quality of the celluloid strip supplied, which often needed major repairs before it could be screened.

Weekly attendances at cinemas had peaked during the war at 31 million, but had fallen back in 1945 to 30 million, providing box office receipts of £117 million. In the year to September 1944 only 20 per cent of the total footage shown in the UK was British – the British Film Producers' Association (BFPA) listed only sixty-four films completed in that period. However, by that time British films had become fully acceptable to the British public, prompting J. Arthur Rank to remark later that, as far as his circuits were concerned, British Quota was not strictly necessary.

Sir Alexander Korda was the catalyst for persuading the government to start releasing studio space back into the production centre. Following London Films' loss in 1936 of £330,000, Korda's main backer, the Prudential Assurance Company, took control of Denham Studios in 1938, depriving him of his production facilities. Korda went to Hollywood, returning to Britain in 1944 to launch a £2 million production programme in collaboration with MGM.

In April 1945 the Board of Trade had confirmed that 200,000 square feet of studio space would be released within the next few months and gave details of stages already released. These included the whole of Nettlefold (Walton-on-Thames), one stage at Denham and one stage at Sound City. It was estimated that 130,000 square feet of studio space would still be in government hands by the end of that year.

Following discussions between the BFPA and the Board of Trade, the Board confirmed in August 1945 that by the end of spring 1946 British studios would be able to increase production by 50 per cent. The Board hinted that the Ministry of Information, Army and Royal Air Force film units were prepared to move from Pinewood if they could find alternative accommodation. According to *Kine Yearbook* (1946) the government announced in November 1945 that film studios were to be given priority second only to the nation's rehousing campaign. Studio release then went ahead steadily and producers anticipated restarting production on their 'borrowed' space at least by the summer or autumn of 1946.

Financially, production in British studios at that time had been divided between producers who had advocated lavish, expensive films and producers who had concentrated on more modest pictures. The £1,300,000 cost of the Rank-financed *Caesar and Cleopatra* (Gabriel Pascal, 1945) contributed to the budgetary arguments of the day. Pascal was the first member of the newly created Independent Producers Limited. Next to join were Michael Powell and Emeric Pressburger, followed by Launder and Gilliat, Cine-Guild and Ian Dalrymple's Wessex Productions.

Caesar and Cleopatra's budget was originally £550,000 but the chairman of Independent Producers, J. Arthur Rank, claimed to be able to sell six other films on the strength of *Caesar and Cleopatra*, the final cost for which would have been around £1,500,000 as the accountants allegedly forgot to include the bank interest in their calculations. Interest was not always allowed for in original budgets, but the responsibility for it was taken over by the production distribution companies.

In April 1945 Maurice Ostrer, Executive Producer for Gainsborough Films, commented on how British studios should allocate money for films. He argued that British films should be budgeted to make a profit in their own market – 'correctly priced commercial pictures'. It was generally accepted in the immediate postwar period that the British market could recoup on its own up to around £200,000 from each film. Ostrer kept to a production cost of around £150,000 for each of his films, the 1945 equivalent of the £75,000 production in 1938. In support of his argument he produced figures showing the proportionate departmental expenditure on a film, citing the lavish *Man in Grey* (Leslie Arliss, 1943), which cost £95,000. That amount was divided approximately into the following percentages: story and scenario (5%), direction (3%), production (5%), acting (17%), art department (1%), camera department (2%), recording and re-recording (5%), sets (16%), lighting (2.5%), film stock (4.5%), wardrobe (4%), make-up department (2%), music (2%), location (0.5%), insurances, etc. (4%), miscellaneous (4%), studio rent (13%), production fee (3%), royalties (recording) (1%).

Clearly, from these figures, the war years had caused certain costs to rise out of proportion. Set costs for *The Man in Grey* were £16,380, including a wage bill for carpenters, plasterers and property men of £6,300 and a props rental of £4,600. An interesting comparison is Launder and Gilliat's first film for Independent Productions, *The Rake's Progress* (1944), which cost around £216,000, and their second, *Green for Danger* (1946), the first film into Pinewood after the Second World War and which cost around £10,000 pounds less. They never succeeded in getting below those figures for any of their next four films for Rank.

Against this background (which included a change of government in Britain when the Labour Party under Clement Attlee won the 1945 General Election on 26 July), Norman Loudon announced that Sound City would open again in September 1945, with two large stages and one small stage.

Unable to find space of their own in Pinewood, the Rank Organisation gave Loudon his first film in postwar Sound City. Costing over £1 million, *London Town*, released by Eagle-Lion on 23 September 1946, starred Britain's Sid Field and was produced and directed by American veteran Wesley Ruggles, who also provided the original story. With photography by Erwin Hillier, lyrics and music by Johnny Burke and Jimmy van Heusen and a popular cast including Greta Gynt, Kay Kendall, Sonnie Hale and Claude Hulbert, *London Town* was to be Britain's answer to the Hollywood musical.

It wasn't. From the beginning the signs were not good. When Ruggles started shooting at Sound City, broken-down wartime aircraft were still being patched up on the adjoining stage. Writing in the *British Film Yearbook* (1947–8), Peter Noble commented:

> *London Town* was the supreme example of a British film made with one eye (or both) on Hollywood; it proved once again that although Britain could make certain types of film superbly, we could not make good film musicals. We could make *The Way Ahead*, but not *Blue Skies*; we could make *San Demetrio, London*, but not *Night and Day*. In the history of British films, it has constantly been clear that when we have attempted to make films in the Hollywood idiom, we have failed. *London Town* proved yet again that an American director, lyric writer and composer could not, did not, breathe an authentic English atmosphere into a pseudo-Hollywood musical and certainly failed to bring out the best in an essentially native comedian.

Sidney Gilliat recalled that Gaumont-British had made the same mistake in the 1930s. '*London Town*,' he ventured, 'did not prove that we could not make musicals, but instead proved that you don't use old hacks to make them.'[1]

Within a year of the *London Town* disappointment, a contribution to which was the demand of an audience which had seen the wartime documentaries for less set-bound, more realistic films, Norman Loudon relinquished control of Sound City and quietly vanished from the British production scene. However, he did not vanish from the British business scene.

When Loudon left the studio, he reputedly did not own anything he stood up in, but he was a man of courage, a big man in every sense – and an entrepreneur. Sir John Clark and his brother Michael, respectively Chair-

London Town *(Wesley Ruggles, 1946)*

man and Deputy Chairman of the giant UK Plessey Group, were well ac-
quainted with Loudon. He was a personal friend of their father, Alan Clark.
Sir John first met 'Uncle' Norman in 1942 when he was sixteen years old.

> Physically, he was a big man, bull-like, with a soft, pale skin and a mane
> of hair of which he was very proud. He stood about five feet eight inches
> tall and had a terrific sense of humour and entertained lavishly. He was
> an excellent shot when hunting and a great womaniser, frequenting
> London clubs such as Mirabelles.[2]

Loudon had married for the first time in 1940, to Mabel Wright. The
marriage was short-lived and Mabel remarried in 1946, leaving Loudon to
his 'womanising' and to his long-term secretary and mistress Alice Preston.
Towards the end of his tenure at Sound City, Loudon had installed an
aspiring young actress in Alice's place in his affections. Alice won him
back at a price – marriage – in 1947. Loudon despatched the actress to
Ealing Studios, where she stayed until she moved briefly to Pinewood as a
contract star with Rank.

Loudon was not actually homeless when he left Sound City and Littleton
Park House. He had another house in Beaulieu, Hampshire, and before the
war had bought the seventy-five acre Tite House estate in Runnymede,
which he leased to Canadian servicemen during the war. He never lived in
the house and, after the war, employed a caretaker, John Parsons, to live
there. Parsons was followed by Loudon's chauffeur, Herbert Parkhouse,

who lived in Tite House with his wife for fifteen years. Parkhouse had taken over from Loudon's first chauffeur, Jack Davis, who in 1947 had decided to train as a Catholic priest.

In November 1946, Loudon and Percy Bell (who had decided to accompany his boss out of the studio) were involved with a company called Bellrock Construction, through which they acquired the engineering works of White Bros & Lamden in London Street, Chertsey, Surrey – not too far from the studio. With the help of plasterers and carpenters from the studio (it is not clear whether this was a 'moonlighting' operation by these craftsmen or whether a deal had been struck between Loudon and Korda sanctioning the work), Bellrock manufactured moulds to make plaster building panels for housing, at that time a major priority for the government. A factory at Harefield in Middlesex was later set up to produce the panels and the Chertsey works concentrated on engineering, producing entire processing plants, which were sent under licence to builders both in the UK and abroad. Loudon travelled extensively throughout postwar Europe and the Middle East promoting and marketing his company's products.

However, Loudon's 'pot of gold' was to come from Jamaica. Here he acquired from an American businessman, Bob Connell, literally a mountain of gypsum (a hydrated calcium sulphate used to make plaster of Paris, or as a dressing for crop land). Indeed, so vast was Loudon's source of gypsum that he contacted the British government in 1953, following the disastrous east coast floods in January of that year and offered to transport his product from Jamaica to Britain to help rejuvenate the ground which had been impregnated by salt from the sea-water floods. In anticipation of a government order, a jetty for loading was specially built in a Jamaican port, but to Loudon's frustration the government declined his offer.

His frustration was understandable as, in 1947, he had attempted to revive his Sound City zoo and theme park concept, this time for Runnymede Park. He had tried to launch the scheme through the London Stock Exchange, but the scale of the project and the postwar shortage of materials thwarted him yet again.

In 1961, the Chertsey works were closed and production continued at a quarry site in Staunton, Nottinghamshire, where gypsum plaster was quarried and processed to make Loudon's next product, plasterboard again, widely used in house-building at a time when builders were looking for cheap, mass-produced building materials.

Ultimately, time began to tell on Loudon's health. He had acrimoniously parted company with Percy Bell over a conflict regarding product diversification and money, although it was generally believed by those who knew both men that Bell had the brains but Loudon had the money.

Following the court case which ended their partnership, Bell worked at Kingston, Surrey with Hawkers Aircraft Company. He bought a motorised bicycle and was involved in a serious accident when the front lamp fell off and into the front wheel. He was in hospital for some time before reluctantly selling his house to buy a small general store in Alton, Hampshire. He died in 1957, aged 54.

Although Norman Loudon had leased a property in Scotland, Knock

House, for weekends and shooting parties with enthusiasts such as Sir John and Michael Clark, and often stayed at London's Connaught Hotel, he had a permanent double penthouse flat in the Carlton Tower Hotel. It was here that Norman Greenlees Weir Loudon, founder of Sound City and Shepperton Studios, died on 13 March 1967, from liver disease developed when he contracted jaundice and hepatitis during a shooting trip to Spain.

Loudon's wife Alice died soon after on 20 October 1967. Those who knew her, such as Sir John Clark, were of the opinion that she died more from a broken heart following her husband's death only seven months earlier. Norman Loudon was cremated on 21 March 1967 and Alice on 31 October 1967. Their ashes lie together in Weybridge cemetery, Surrey. After Loudon's death, his company was acquired by British Gypsum, who continued to manufacture his products.

In his own entrepreneurial way, Norman Loudon had been an impressive influence on the British film industry and on the people with whom he had worked, but the ending of the Second World War saw the re-emergence of a different breed of entrepreneur in Alexander Korda.

Korda, who had helped Loudon into mainstream British production in the 30s with *Sanders of the River*, had reconstituted London Film Productions in January 1946 as a private company following his brief period as head of MGM UK. The authorised capital of the company was £825,000. All but 2 per cent of the shares were held by Korda and members of his family (with Korda as the main ordinary shareholder). In 1943 Korda had bought back from the Prudential earlier London Film productions for £42,500 and had subsequently reissued them throughout the world through London Films International, a company with an authorised and issued capital of £100, and which was concerned with the overseas distribution of the Group's films in countries other than the US. (From the end of 1950, US distribution was through Lopert Films Distributing Corporation, jointly formed by British Lion and London Films and the City Investing Corporation of New York. President of Lopert Films was Ilya Lopert, who owned and was associated with both art and popular cinemas in key US cities.)

In 1935 Korda had been given shares in United Artists by Douglas Fairbanks Snr, who had been impressed by *The Private Life of Henry VIII*. Korda had sold these shares for $950,000, making a profit of nearly a million dollars on an investment of zero. Added to which was £141,000 from Rank in March 1945 for Korda's controlling interest in Denham Laboratories.

Under Korda's chairmanship, joint managing directors of the new London Films were Harold Boxall and Henry David St. Leger Brook Selwyn Cunnynghame (Bart.), who was always referred to as 'David' Cunnynghame. Other directors were Hugh Quennell QC (Korda's lawyer), John Jackson of Amalgamated Studios (Elstree) and Vincent and Zoltan Korda. Since 1939, Boxall had worked with Korda's London Films on productions including *The Thief of Baghdad* (Zoltan Korda and Michael Powell, 1940) *Major Barbara* (Gabriel Pascal, 1940), and *Forty-Ninth Parallel* (Michael Powell, 1941).

35

In 1946, London Films acquired control of British Lion Film Corporation. British Lion owned Beaconsfield Studios, 50 per cent of Worton Hall studio, and was a production/distribution company. Because Korda's distribution deal with United Artists had been severed, this latter asset of British Lion was of particular interest to him. The British Lion board now comprised Korda as production adviser and studio general manager, Quennell as chairman, and Sir Arthur Jarratt from Gaumont-British as managing director and deputy chairman. Other directors were Sidney Myers, Boxall and Cunnynghame. The old British Lion board remained represented by A. J. Mitchell, Sir Claude Dansey, stockbroker Charles Flower and secretary L. C. Sennitt.

The British Lion Film Corporation had been founded in 1927 to use the talents of novelist Edgar Wallace. In 1926 Wallace had made overtures to several film companies, hoping to sell the exclusive film rights of his novels. He had been successful in adapting his crime stories for the stage and the next logical step was the cinema. In 1927 he was invited to join the board of the new British Lion Film Corporation as chairman. British Lion had been floated as a public company with capital of £210,000 under the managing directorship of Samuel Woolf Smith, who had been in film distribution since 1910.

It was clear that Wallace's chairmanship was window-dressing. Part of the contract was that the company should have exclusive film rights of everything he wrote. In consideration, he received a down-payment of £10,000 in the form of shares which he immediately sold before they could appreciate. In addition, Wallace was to receive £1,000 for every film made, 10 per cent of the gross receipts and a nominal director's fee of £500 per annum. Wallace made only around £26,000 from his five-year association with British Lion, far less than if he had sold film rights for his novels to other competing film companies.

The company acquired the ramshackle George Clark silent studio at Beaconsfield, and in less than a year had converted, re-equipped and reconditioned the studio with its single 6,235 square feet stage (a second stage was added later).

Silent films of Wallace's *The Ringer, Chick, The Forger, The Man Who Changed His Name, The Clue of the New Pin, The Valley of Ghosts, The Flying Squad* and *Red Aces* were raced out in the first eight months. Wallace directed only one film, *Red Aces*, but he was indifferent as a silent film director, being steeped in stage techniques and unable to adapt at short notice to the different requirements of film. Wallace's assistant on *Red Aces* was the young Carol Reed, who had acted in one of his plays and became his assistant stage manager.

In 1929, having been in production for less than a year, British Lion had to face the expensive problem of complete reconstruction to cater for the 'talkies'. At the 1929 Annual Meeting, Wallace announced a loss for the company of £49,428, but the studio reconstruction continued for the next nine months. Between the arrival of the 'talkies' in 1929 and November 1931, British Lion lost £91,000. At the end of that month Wallace left for Hollywood on a well-paid two-month contract with RKO, with an option for a further two months. He died alone in Hollywood in February 1932, leaving personal debts of £140,000. The principal creditor (for £58,000) was ironically his own limited private company, R. H. E. Wallace Limited, set up in 1927 to reduce his income tax and which had been assigned all his copyrights for the period of his lifetime. At the time of his death his liquid assets were practically nil.

After Wallace's death, the character of British Lion changed. From mid-1930 space had been leased to Basil Dean, who made the first five Associated Talking Pictures (ATP) films at the studio. Michael Balcon had produced a series of joint Gainsborough–British Lion films at Beaconsfield, using experienced directors and technicians from both companies' studios, the films being distributed by Gainsborough.

In 1930 British Lion formed a renting subsidiary and, from early 1931, had imported films from abroad; at first only minor Westerns, but much later, bigger films including Harold Lloyd's *Safety Last* (1923). Now, under new chairman Sir Robert John Lynne MP, Samuel Smith remained in charge. In December 1932, Herbert Smith, Samuel Smith's younger brother, who had been assistant director on *Red Aces*, became production supervisor, taking an increasingly important part in production.

In 1933, *The World Film Encyclopedia* (London: Amalgamated Press) published an interesting description of Beaconsfield and the studio.

Films have brought the hum of modern industry to old, sleepy places. Beaconsfield, in Buckinghamshire, was a typical English country town, with its wide main crossing, its two main streets empty at most times and its cluster of quiet weathered houses dreaming under the mid-day sun.

The British Lion Corporation came and its studio rose to stir the town to activity. Today, Beaconsfield mothers bring their babies to act in child scenes at the studio (there were fifty of them there one day during the summer). Beaconsfield boys go to see what film stars do to earn their salaries.

The studio is, in effect, a single production unit under one high roof ridge, but there is ample floor space for all film requirements. Alongside the main building there is a row of flat-roofed workshops containing plasterers', property carpenters' and scenery rooms. Separated from the main block by a concrete causeway are projection theatre, offices and a row of film vaults.

The whole studio stands in a wide tract of grassland surrounded by a high fence. This space is frequently used when the film necessitates the building of extensive exterior sets.

It is essentially a breezy studio, although these days, a sense of sadness hangs over the place. For the British Lion studios will never be quite the same as they were when Edgar Wallace, the merriest, the most cheerful of all those merry film-makers, was alive and the ruling genius of the studios. He was, of course, Chairman of the British Lion Film Corporation as well as the author of some of its most successful films.

Beaconsfield is not a pretentious studio. It is not built of white marble and chromium and the cafe does not run with champaigne (*sic*). But some of the finest of Britain's films have been made there and there exists in this country no more efficient and cheerful band of film-makers.

However, a new policy was evident in the British Lion films of 1933. Output expanded with small, safe short features, many of them comedies. The company discovered an easy source of material in revue items and for the next few years filmed the acts of singers, comedians, dancers and dance-bands from variety, cabaret and radio. Many single-reelers and a number of long films composed entirely of revue items were released. Herbert Smith, beginning with the direction of single items for the short films and then for the longer collection of turns, finally graduated to features in 1935. In 1942, he joined Two Cities as associate producer, working on *Demi-Paradise* (Anthony Asquith, 1943), *Men of Two Worlds* (Thorold Dickinson, 1945) and *Odd Man Out* (Carol Reed, 1947).

Some of British Lion's short films were taken by MGM and Fox, but the company's imports continued to increase and it needed its own films for its quota. By mid-1934 British Lion was showing a small profit. In 1935 a franchise to distribute all of the American company Republic's films was signed. This enabled British Lion to reconstitute its capital to £750,000 – this capital was introduced by Sam Smith, Major Holt of the Royal Bank of Canada and Paul Nathanson. Holt and Nathanson were made directors and, although the original share capital was lost, shareholders were given an option to acquire extra shares for five years.

In 1937 British Lion made several films with Hammer Productions. Hammer had been founded in November 1934 as a £1,000 company by joint managing directors Henry Fraser Passmore and G. A. Gillings. The chairman was Will Hammer, who for years had been a producer and performer in music hall, revue and summer shows. He re-entered films in 1947, at the age of sixty, starting the later Hammer Films with the Carreras family. Will Hammer was Chairman both of Hammer Film Productions and Exclusive Films. A Liveryman of the City of London and a member of the Clockmakers Company, he also was chairman of a London building society and had interests in jewellery shops and hairdressing salons.

However, by early 1937, British Lion was in difficulties. Nothing was produced for a year after May 1937. Production restarted in May 1938, and in 1939 producer George King occupied the studio to make some melo-dramas as Pennant Pictures for British Lion release.

Beaconsfield was requisitioned by the Ministry of Aircraft Production for use by small motor manufacturer Rotax, a part of the Lucas Group. Overnight the studio was stripped of all its film-making facilities and equipment. Studio manager A.W. Osborne hurriedly located storage prem-ises in an old variety theatre in Paddington, and in a cinema at Harrow-on-the-Hill. Later in 1940 British Lion distributed Noël Coward and David Lean's *In Which We Serve* (a Two Cities Film) for which it put up a staggering £300,000 guarantee. The film was booked by two of the three major theatrical circuits and made British Lion enough money to declare a dividend for the first time.

In 1944 it was decided that the requisitioned Beaconsfield Studio would no longer be large enough for British Lion's production needs. The Crown

Film Unit moved into Beaconsfield from Pinewood on a twenty-one year lease from British Lion, who then acquired Worton Hall Studio for around £60,000. The new studio company, Worton Hall (1944) Limited, was jointly owned by British Lion (50 per cent), Panton Street Nominees (40 per cent) and Irish entrepreneur the Honourable Frederick Fergus MacNaghten (10 per cent). The chairman was W.T. Vint of Panton Street Nominees.

Worton Hall had started life as a studio in 1914. G. B. (Bertie) Samuelson had been so enthusiastic about the cinema that he employed Walter Buckstone as his cameraman before he even had a studio in which to shoot his films. Through Buckstone, Samuelson heard that George Pearson, director for the London branch of the French firm Pathé Frères, was in difficulties. Pearson had been with Pathé for about a year and had been unsuccessful, through technical problems, in persuading them to open a new studio at Alexandra Palace in north London. He had subsequently made educational films. Over lunch at the Waldorf Hotel in London, Samuelson persuaded Pearson to join him in making films.

Samuelson had probably already decided upon the location for his studios before he met George Pearson. He had learned that the house and estate of Worton Hall, Isleworth, until recently occupied by Colonel Cecil Paget, were for sale. This may have been in March 1914. Pearson thought Samuelson first rented the Hall with an option for buying it for what seems the incredible sum of £200. The grounds of the late eighteenth-century mansion had originally comprised some thirteen acres, but by the turn of the century upkeep was becoming expensive and by 1913 the estate had been reduced to about nine acres. The Hall had forty rooms with two wings. The rooms in the left wing were converted into dressing rooms for women and those in the right wing for men. The ground floor of the centre of the mansion was converted into offices, and later contained property and wardrobe rooms, projection theatre, cutting room and a canteen. The first and top floors, which had eleven bedrooms between them, were partly converted into flats to accommodate those who might need to stay over-night. The ballroom and dining hall were left intact and used for filming until they were later converted into property rooms.

Samuelson, Pearson and Buckstone selected a site for a glass studio with a stage 50 by 40 feet (later enlarged to 65 by 40 feet), and within a month the studio was completed at a cost of a little over £1,000. The trade press announced Samuelson's acquisition of Worton Hall on 23 April 1914 and reported that three films were already planned: *A Study in Scarlet*, *Christmas Day in the Workhouse* and *A Cinema Girl's Romance*.

On 30 May 1914 the Samuelson Film Manufacturing Company Ltd was incorporated with a nominal capital of £2,000 in £1 shares. The original subscribers were Samuelson and Harry William Engholm, a journalist who was also secretary of the company. Engholm wrote the scenarios for most of Samuelson's films up to the end of 1917, and in collaboration with George Pearson while the latter was at Worton Hall.

Worton Hall was officially opened on 1 July 1914. The invited guests from the trade and press were met in the morning at the Queen's Hotel, Leicester Square, by a retinue of cars. The drive to the Hall was photo-graphed along the way and the film shown on the screen in the Hall later that afternoon together with other scenes shot during the day. The famous music-hall star of the day, Vesta Tilley, performed the opening ceremony.

An important part of the day's itinerary was the guests' visit to the set of *A Study in Scarlet* to watch George Pearson direct a scene. It was a dummy run, no film being in the camera, but the report in the *Middlesex Chronicle* is interesting in relation to Pearson's methods:

> Contrary to general opinion, no dialogue was used. The focus having been adjusted, lighting arranged and the stage limit chalked out, the producer simply explained by precept and example what he wanted the actors to do and kept up a running fire of instruction while they did it. The performance – that of a murder by strangling – was gone through three times, the first being explanatory; the second rehearsal and the third the finished article. In actual film-making, the producer explained, an act had often to be gone through six or seven times before he was satisfied, but no dialogue was ever used and there were no parts to learn. The actor was simply told what to do and kept on doing it until he did it right.

Clearly there was still confusion over the respective roles of producer and director. The parlous state of the British film industry in 1921 persuaded Samuelson to try his hand elsewhere, while retaining Worton Hall as a valuable asset. In the spring of 1921 he went into the coach business; but one year later, with much of his capital outlay in this business lost, he returned to film production at Worton Hall. Samuelson needed financial backing for production and was able to interest Sir William Jury in the formation of a production company which would release its films through Jury's Imperial Pictures. Sir William was at this time probably the best-known man in the British film industry. Born in 1870, he was well-established in the trade as a renter before the First World War. For his impressive war service, including connection with the War Loan and various war charities, he was knighted in 1918. By 1922 he was also a director of Provincial Cinematograph Theatres and of another recently formed renting concern, Associated First National Pictures.

The new company, British Super Films, was registered as a private company on 1 February 1922 with a capital of £50,000 in £1 shares 'to acquire and carry on the business of film manufacturers and producers heretofore carried on by the Samuelson Film Manufacturing Company'. The directors were 'Bertie' Samuelson, Sir William Jury and William Firth, a director of Jury's Imperial Pictures who also had interests in cinemas and theatres in various parts of the country. The price paid by the new company for the freehold mansion, Worton Hall, grounds of 6.5 acres, studios etc. was £21,500, of which £8,000 was paid in cash and £13,500 by the allocation to Samuelson of shares in British Super Films. Although no longer the sole owner of a production company, Samuelson retained the controlling interest in British Super Films with 13,500 shares as against Jury's 10,000. However, the main advantage of the arrangement to Samuelson was the guarantee of distribution.

The first film scheduled by the new company was *Stable Companions*, an original story probably by Samuelson himself, with a script by Walter Summers, who had joined Samuelson at Worton Hall following war service and a spell with Hepworth as an assistant director to Henry Edwards. *Stable Companions*, a conventional horse-racing melodrama, was directed by Albert Ward and photographed by Jimmy Rogers, who made a name for himself by continuing to photograph the hero's racing stables burning down despite knowing that they were burning down for real.

> I think I must have been mad, but I kept my head down and went on turning. I think the spectacular scene hypnotised me. I certainly obtained some fine shots before the more sane members of the crew dragged me and my camera clear. The entire building collapsed before our eyes.[3]

According to Walter Summers, in the race scenes, the jockeys' coats and caps were coloured by a stencil-colour process done by hand by three elderly ladies in a garret in Paris, using a magnifying glass and tiny brushes. With this process, when the film was projected and therefore magnified there was a tendency for the colour to spill over from the coloured objects – here the jockeys' coats and caps – onto the rest of the screen. Clive Brook appeared as the 'heavy', one of his earliest film parts before he had established his later image as the thoroughbred English gentleman.

By the end of 1923 Samuelson, in common with other British producers, was finding the going heavy. Trade improvement in the first nine months of the year had not been maintained. Confidence suffered because of an uncertain political situation and a General Election. A high cost of living and high taxation led to a decline in spending power and therefore in cinema attendances. At the end of January 1924, *Kine Weekly* reported that 75 per cent of British studio workers were idle.

Some of those workers were from Worton Hall. The demise of British Super Films led to the liquidator ordering that Worton Hall be put up for auction on 16 January 1924. Included as one lot were the mansion, the stabling which had been used as carpenters' shops and stores, various out-buildings including two scene docks, property rooms and dressing rooms, a daylight studio 100 by 35 feet, a dark studio 93 by 45 feet, film printing laboratories with equipment, and the grounds with cedars, acacias and elms interspersed with herbaceous borders. Also included was a large quantity of sets and wardrobe equipment.

A special feature, not included in the property for auction, was the electric storage battery plant, housed in a brick, coke-breeze and rough-cast building about $16\frac{1}{2}$ by 45 feet. This was divided into two compartments, one containing a motor generator set, the other a large storage battery with a capacity of 2,028 ampere hours. The plant, which had been installed in the autumn of 1920, was designed to deal with any load up to 2,000 amps, 120–130 volts. The power was distributed to the stages by means of paper-insulated, lead-covered underground cables. There were special features for dealing with the widely fluctuating demands of film production. The installation had been made by the General Electric Company, with whom it was arranged that the plant could, if desired by the purchaser, be included in the sale price of £3,820. This plant was believed to be unique at the time, as film studios normally obtained their power supply from the mains and were sometimes in trouble through overloading the circuits.

Perhaps because of the uncertainty of the time, Worton Hall did not find an immediate purchaser and was put up for sale again in October 1924, still without success. Eventually, in December 1924, it was sold to Worton Hall Estates Limited, for an undisclosed sum. The company then hired out studio space to production companies.

In October 1925 *The Cinema* reported that Rex Wilson would shortly commence production at Worton Hall, and in early March 1926 Geoffrey Malins started work there on a boxing series for H. B. Parkinson, one of which, entitled *The Game Chicken*, featured the British boxer 'Bombardier' Billy Wells.

It was not until 1928 that a new production company, British Screen Productions, bought Worton Hall studios and grounds for £19,000, with George A. Cooper as producer and supervisor and Frank Miller as director. The managing director was George W. Pearson (not to be confused with Samuelson's old colleague), who had been general manager of British Screen Classics, distributors of the *Empire News Bulletin*. The arrival of sound created problems for Pearson, so in 1929 he launched an £850,000 scheme to raise finance. The public applied for only 3 per cent of the shares and the underwriters acquired the rest. An attempt to save both his own company and that of his competitor, George Banfield, was thwarted by shareholders in Banfield's company, British Filmcraft Productions, which led to that company being dissolved. An amalgamation of various companies controlled by Banfield and Pearson under the name of Audible Filmcraft, with a capital of £350,000, also failed. In August 1932 all went into voluntary liquidation.

In 1932 Fidelity Films, financed mainly by Duncan Stuart MacDonald, whose sound technicians came from British Talking Pictures at Wembley, had developed a non-royalty sound system called 'Fidelytone'. The 'inventor', Captain Ryan, worked the system's camera with recordist John Rea. MacDonald took a lease on Worton Hall Studio and started business as a service studio and manufacturer of sound recording equipment. The company sold a number of fully equipped vans to India and at least one to Spain.

At the time Worton Hall had two stages, each 100 by 40 feet. One stage, called the 'light' studio, was built with glass roof and sides. The floor lighting was from storage batteries charged by a generator with current from the local supply. Retired production accountant Archie Holly remembers having to feed half-crown coins (12½p) into the meter since that was the only way the local authority would supply the studio following some problems in payment of their bills. Eventually, Fidelity moved on to the Blattner Studio at Borehamwood in a tie-up with the Ludwig Blattner Picture Corporation.

In the summer of 1931 Worton Hall enjoyed a brief respite when Captain the Honourable Richard Norton (later Lord Grantley), a former officer in the Brigade of Guards, set up a programme of production at Worton Hall and

Walton Studios involving six films for United Artists. They cost between £3,000 and £7,000 each, but according to Norton, 'They had some box-office value.' As 'quota quickies', their value was limited. Norton's influence with United Artists had helped Alexander Korda to finish *The Private Life of Henry VIII* (1933) when he was running out of money. Subsequently, all prewar Korda films were distributed by United Artists.

Around 1933 Worton Hall was used by 'Bertie' Samuelson to shoot a series of short films for New Era National Pictures. The series idea was conceived by New Era's Sir Gordon Craig as a means of supplying capital for New Era to compete with larger concerns. Entitled *Spotting*, the series was the basis of a competition for cinema patrons. Twelve short feature films, each produced on a lavish scale, included a number of deliberate minor mistakes which were claimed to be readily observable by the audience. The films were booked en bloc by cinemas and were shown on twelve consecutive weeks, during which audiences were invited to spot the errors, paying 6d (2½p) per entry. It was estimated that if only 5 per cent of the regular patrons took part, £300,000 in entry money would result, of which one third would go to the Cinematograph Trade Benevolent Fund, one third to the British Charities Association (who would handle entries) and one third to New Era as the organisers.

A total of £100,000 prize money was offered with four first prizes of £10,000, four second prizes of £4,000, four third prizes of £1,000 and forty consolation prizes of £100 over the whole series. For each film there were to be forty-eight prizes of £500, forty-eight second prizes of £150, forty-eight third prizes of £50 and 480 consolation prizes of £5. Lord Askwith, Field Marshal Lord Milne and the Marchioness Townshend of Raynham were appointed as adjudicators.

Each of these *Spotting* films ran between twelve and eighteen minutes. An example of the deliberate mistakes occurred in *A Touching Story*, when in a supposed crinoline age, a petrol lighter, a current banknote and a picture of the then Prince of Wales were seen. Unfortunately, Sir Gordon's enthusiasm for the *Spotting* series and optimism as to the future of New Era proved to be misplaced. At the end of 1935 the company went into liquidation.

Perhaps it was appropriate that Samuelson, as the founder of Worton Hall Studio, should direct his last film there: *The Crucifix*, a 1934 sound remake of the silent feature *In Bondage*, for New Era.

Also around 1933, Edward Gourdeau, a film importer, with his company Interworld Films, bought Worton Hall through his father-in-law, J. W. Almond, whose sons George and Arthur worked at the studio. The studio was extended and modernised, new stages were built and the old glass studio was converted into dressing-rooms and a sound department, where a Western Electric system was installed.

In 1934 City Film Corporation, founded by Harry Hughes and Basil Humphreys at Worton Hall, started producing indifferent light entertainment films used as quota by various renters. The company had a paid-up capital of only £100 and was wound up after May 1936.

From 1 January 1935 London Films had taken a lease on Worton Hall at £35,000 per annum, although Korda had been based at the studio in 1934 when shooting *Sanders of the River*.

Probably the most famous prewar owner/occupier of Worton Hall was Douglas Fairbanks Jnr, who, with his father, had come to Britain in 1933. The Hollywood career of Fairbanks Snr had come to an end and Fairbanks Jnr had been consistently unable to repeat his father's success. Both were impressed by Korda's *The Private Life of Henry VIII*, and Fairbanks Jnr agreed to appear in Korda's next film, *Catherine the Great* (1934), directed by Paul Czinner. Eventually, through both social and industry connections, Fairbanks Jnr secured backing and worldwide distribution from United Artists. He registered Criterion Film Productions, a £10,000 company, in June 1935. Other directors were Marcel Hellman, Paul Czinner and the Independent Member of Parliament for Marylebone, Captain A. Cunningham-Reid, who was married to Lady Mountbatten's sister.

In January 1936 they acquired Worton Hall from Almond. Four £100,000 films were planned, including *Jump for Glory*, *Accused* and *Crime Over London*. By the end of 1936 the company was in disarray. Czinner, who had played no part in the company, had resigned. Fairbanks wrote to Cunningham-Reid: 'Our pictures, for what they are, have been disastrously expensive.' No more were made and Fairbanks returned to America. In 1939 Grand National, under Maurice Wilson, leased the studio.

Sporadic productions at Worton Hall included *Things to Come* (William Cameron Menzies, 1935), for which Korda built a huge silent stage 250 by 120 feet, the largest of its type in Europe. This stage was moved to Shepperton Studios in 1948 and is still in use today, even though one end wall with LONDON FILMS painted in large letters was erected incorrectly so that LONDON FILMS became an anagram, DONLON LMSFI or something similar. Some of *Things to Come* was shot in the Consolidated Studio, Elstree (formerly the Whitehall Studio), with exteriors shot at Denham Studio.

Other films produced at Worton Hall include *The Man Who Could Work Miracles* (Lothar Mendes, 1936), with exteriors shot at Denham; *Moscow Nights* (Anthony Asquith, 1935; the only film he made while under contract to Korda); and *Mademoiselle Docteur* (Edmond T. Greville, 1937) for Grafton Films. Perhaps the saddest film made at this studio was the multilingual *The Invader* (Adrian Brunel, 1935) for British and Continental Film Productions. Produced by the flamboyant Sam Spiegel, this slow comedy starred the unfortunate Buster Keaton, then arguably at the lowest point of his long career.

In 1944 the first task for the new Worton Hall company was to get the studio derequisitioned from the government. Company secretary Ken Maidment worked hard and within a year this was achieved and the studio refurbished. The equipment that had been astutely stored when Beaconsfield Studio had been requisitioned was moved into Worton Hall. It included two standard Mitchell 35mm cameras, one of which was subsequently sold to American producer Charles Schneer for use with his 'Dynamation' process in the late 1950s and early 1960s.

In 1946 Worton Hall was back in production with its first major feature, *The Shop at Sly Corner*, produced and directed by George King for British Lion and photographed by Norman Loudon's stalwart cameraman, Hone Glendinning. This was followed by *White Cradle Inn*, directed by Harold

French, which London Films had been discussing when Korda took over the British Lion Film Corporation in 1946 in a deal agreed with Samuel Smith's brother-in-law following Smith's death. The film was shot on location and fitted into Worton Hall because there was no space at Sound City.

On 3 April 1946 three new directors joined the board of Sound City: Sir Arthur Jarratt, David Cunnynghame and Harold Boxall (Vincent Korda joined them on 11 July that year). Also in April 1946 British Lion bought a 74 per cent interest in Sound City (Films) Limited, which owned Sound City Studios, for £380,000. Sound City was then the largest British studio after Denham, although Rank owned well over 50 per cent of all British studios at the time.

At the British Lion Film Corporation's ordinary general meeting in May 1946, chairman Hugh Quennell was reported in the *Financial Times* (23 May 1946) as claiming that British Lion's record

> showed that the company can continue to make a steady and satisfactory profit from distribution. But we want to go further. We want to be able to offer full facilities to independent British producers. We are confident that British pictures will continue their upward trend of success and we believe that this company can play a big part in assisting the British film industry if it puts itself in the position to offer the full facilities which are required by the independent producer.

These facilities were listed as studio space, production finance and distribution. Adequate studio space was provided by the acquisition of Sound City, but the cost of this acquisition and the need for adequate production finance made the British Lion directors decide to raise an additional £1 million by issuing four million ordinary shares of one shilling (5p) each at five shillings (25p) per share. London Film Productions subscribed for 1,600,000 of the new shares on underwriting terms, thus retaining effective control of British Lion. There was no lack of subscribers for the remaining 2,400,000 shares. British Lion had paid an ordinary dividend of 50 per cent for the previous six years and, according to the *Financial Times* (19 June 1946), there were over 24 million applications for the issue.

On 11 November 1946 Korda, through London Films, completed the purchase of Sound City Studios, allegedly through a deal struck within twenty minutes of meeting Norman Loudon in the studio canteen. Korda renamed the studio the British Lion Studio Company Limited, under Chairman Hugh Quennell. Vincent Korda was Managing Director and his fellow directors, Cunnynghame and Boxall, were joined by P. C. Stapleton and Sir Arthur Jarratt (who was also Chairman and Managing Director of Humphries Laboratories, Chairman of Mole-Richardson [England] and Deputy Chairman of the Royal Navy Film Corporation).

The British Lion Group now comprised the British Lion Film Corporation (which was itself controlled by London Film Productions) and four subsidiaries: the British Lion Studio Company, which owned the Group's studios at Sound City and Worton Hall; British Lion Film Productions

Limited; Shepperton Productions, which held certain assets such as film rights; and British Lion Production Assets, which provided the means of making films at Sound City other than those made by producers with their own companies, such as Launder and Gilliat and the Boulting brothers. In addition, Korda still had his own production company, Alexander Korda Film Productions. To complete his relaunch into film production in August 1946, Korda had bought the Rialto Cinema in London's Leicester Square to showcase his films.

Sound City, as the British Lion Studio Company, was now primed for its quantum leap into British 'A'-stream film production.

In his book *Charmed Lives*, Michael Korda, Alexander Korda's nephew, describes a drive through the studio grounds in his uncle's Rolls Royce.

The studio policeman swung up the barrier and saluted, and we drove around the perimeter road of my father's [Vincent Korda] private domain, for it was instantly apparent to me that here was the one place where he was at ease. We passed the huge sound stages, the prop warehouses, the long low red-brick row of cutting rooms and screening rooms (with their distinctive smell of film cement and emulsion), the carpentry department (run by old 'Pop' Day, who was then in his eighties), the plasterers' sheds, the special-effects stages, the huge generating plant, the covered walkways to the performers' dressing rooms and then, crossing over a beautiful little stream, we swept into the courtyard of an old English mansion, surrounded by carefully designed

Vincent (left) and Alexander Korda, c. 1951

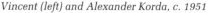

grounds, with a view over a small lake on which were a Gothic arched bridge, several ducks and a mass of lily pads.

As always, my father had managed to preserve what was there and build the studio around it. He liked traditional surroundings, as did Alex, and he was not about to sacrifice a good solid Victorian building, however inconvenient it might be to work in, simply to replace it with a modern office. Shepperton Manor [the Old House] was his home away from home and he liked its mosaic tiles, the mullioned windows, its Ruskinian eccentricities of design, the baronial staircase, the minstrel's gallery and the conservatory, a kind of glassed-in miniature replica of the Crystal Palace, in which a gardener now raised flowers and ferns for Vincent's sets and Alex's home and office.

The Korda influence on Sound City was a prelude to heavy production involvement by London Films which was to be supported by money loaned to the British Lion Film Corporation by the government as a result of a promise made to Korda by Winston Churchill during the Second World War. Churchill did not envisage this loan for Korda's 'services rendered' coming from the then opposition Labour Party (as it did in 1948 following Labour's General Election victory in 1945), not unreasonably believing that he would still be Prime Minister after the war. Korda's 'services rendered' had started well before the outbreak of war in 1939. Churchill had operated his own group of secret agents, mostly business-men, who provided him with information about the German military build-up. He then used that information to try to persuade the British government to prepare the country for the war he believed was inevitable. Korda's many contacts were able to provide that service.

During the war Britain's Secret Service used the film industry to move people around from one country to another to see what was going on. In 1940 one of Churchill's personal agents, William Stephenson (a Canadian businessman who, before the war, had invested in Sound City [Films], the company operating Sound City Studios), was chosen to set up the British secret intelligence centre in America. Until 1941 this operated clandes-tinely from the Rockefeller Centre, New York, and was known as BSC (British Security Co-ordination). Churchill code-named Stephenson 'Intrepid', for operations had to be kept secret from the US State Depart-ment, which was at that time determined to stay out of the war.

BSC grew into a major intelligence force, helped by some of Hollywood's biggest names. Stephenson hired director John Ford to make propaganda films in Canada, and top Hollywood make-up artists were among those who helped agents with disguises. Other back-room staff were taken to Canada to give acting lessons. Among the pilots who flew from Canada for Stephenson was Captain Hughie Green, who had shared star billing in prewar films with Freddie Bartholomew. Green later became a popular host on British television with shows such as the talent show *Opportunity Knocks*.

One of the most tragic incidents was the killing of British actor Leslie Howard. According to William Stevenson in his book *A Man Called Intrepid* (1976), Howard was on a secret mission for Stephenson. The unarmed plane in which he was travelling was shot down by the Germans over the Bay of Biscay in 1941. Howard's death could have been avoided. Thanks to British boffins' success in countering the German military code machine 'Enigma' with their own automatic decoder 'Ultra', the allies were aware that German fighters would attack Howard's plane, having intercepted the Luftwaffe's orders, but were forced to ignore this information to keep their code-breaking success secret from Hitler.

Noël Coward was another of 'Intrepid's' travelling spies, reporting all he heard and saw during his travels throughout the war. 'My celebrity value was wonderful cover,' he recalled on the eve of his death in 1973. 'So many career intelligence officers went around looking terribly mysterious – long black boots and sinister smiles. Nobody ever issued me with a false beard. And invisible ink? I can't read my own writing when it's supposed to be visible. My disguise was my own reputation as a bit of an idiot. . . .'

Greta Garbo was used as one of Stephenson's agents through her contacts in her native Sweden. Stephenson was able to check on German spies in Stockholm, set up escape routes for allied escapees from occupied Europe and order vital war supplies from this (officially) neutral country.

Korda was one of Stephenson's 'willing helpers' outside the BSC, helping Stephenson build Camp 'X', a training centre thirty miles west of Toronto where espionage agents were given coaching for missions in occupied Europe. Korda re-created German locations for exercises and scoured film vaults for clips that would familiarise spies with their European destinations. He knew Europe well and would study plans and photographs before duplicating the key points of exit and entry. On these scale models BSC agents practised their burglary skills.

When Korda was not making films such as *Lady Hamilton* (which apparently made Churchill weep each of the eight times he saw it), he would hop back and forth across the Atlantic in unheated Liberator bombers, 'cooking things up with Bill Stephenson', said Korda's wife Merle Oberon years later. Between 1935 and 1945 Korda made twenty-four Atlantic crossings, many of them arranged by Stephenson. Korda's willingness to help may have been influenced by the appointment of Sir Connop Guthrie as Head of Security Division at BSC. Guthrie had been instrumental in persuading the Prudential Assurance Company to back Korda in the prewar London Films boom and had represented Korda on the Board of United Artists following Korda's acceptance of an owner-membership of United Artists in 1935. (Korda had joined the British board of United Artists in 1937.)

Zoltan Korda was more at home in Hollywood. He did not take kindly to his patient and painstaking work at Camp 'X' being destroyed on an order from some unseen authority. Worse, there were no movie producers at Camp 'X' for him to bully. According to Sir Michael Hordern, Zoltan's bullying was almost second nature.

There were only two famous directors with whom I did not get on and who were hopeless at any sort of tactful direction. They were John Huston and Zoltan Korda. Korda, for whom I made *Storm Over the Nile*, was absolutely hateful. He just loved having a whipping boy who was inexperienced, and I was ideal for his purpose.[4]

Alexander Korda's undercover activities took two forms: acting as a secret courier between British and American intelligence centres, and allowing his New York office in the Empire State Building to be used as a clearing house for intelligence information.

When the American counterpart to BSC, the OSS (Office of Strategic Services), was formed in June 1941, playwright Robert Sherwood, who had previously worked with Korda, became Head of the Foreign Information Service of the OSS, and Korda became friends with General William Donovan, who directed all the OSS's activities.

Korda's activities had not gone unnoticed by the Germans. His name was on the Gestapo arrest list issued around July 1940. It contained the names of those British people whom the Gestapo planned to interrogate once Britain was invaded. This information had been collected by German agents between 1937 and 1940. Each entry concluded with a series of code letters representing the particular department of the Nazi Central Security Agency which would undertake that person's interrogation (the area in which a person was a potential threat). Korda's code letters in his entry on page 109 were RSHA 11 D 5. The 11 D 5 signified 'Investigation of the Opposition', 'External Problems', 'The English Imperium', and presumably referred to Korda's film work in, or regarding, the British Empire.

The only other film producer on the Gestapo arrest list was Isidore Ostrer, whose code letters 11 B 2 designated 'The Jews' and 'Ideological Opposition'. It seems strange that Korda was not considered in this category, but rather under one which related to the possible ramifications of the films he had produced. Others on this list included Winston Churchill, J. B. Priestley, Aldous Huxley, Virginia Woolf and Noël Coward. Understandably, Korda was proud to be included in such illustrious company, but many personalities of the day became 'celebrity agents' during the war. Underwater scientist and explorer Jacques Cousteau, authors Malcolm Muggeridge, Roald Dahl, Graham Greene and John Le Carré, novelist Dennis Wheatley, historian Arnold Toynbee, playwright Benn Levy (husband of actress Constance Cummings) and David Niven, a star of *Bonnie Prince Charlie*, Korda's first postwar film at Sound City Studios, were all involved in espionage in some way. In recognition of his services, Alexander Korda was knighted in 1942.

To help cope with the anticipated increase in production, a resolution supported by chairman Hugh Quennell was passed on 5 December 1946 at an Extraordinary General Meeting of the British Lion Studio Company. This authorised the purchase of the remaining 50 per cent of Worton Hall Studios (1944) Limited for £80,000 cash and a balance of 818,182 fully paid ordinary shares at two shillings (10p) each. (Launder and Gilliat's *State Secret* was one of the last films to be made at Worton Hall before the studio was sold in 1950 to the National Coal Board Research Establishment.)

Industry personnel had grounds for thinking that 1947 was to be the beginning of an exciting new British film industry. Sixteen studios offered fifty-three sound stages covering 524,697 square feet, although the derequisitioned ABPC Studios at Elstree remained closed for reconstruction until 1948. Box-office receipts in 1946 had peaked at £121 million (the average seat price was one shilling and sixpence [7½p]), providing the Exchequer with £41 million in entertainment tax. Unfortunately, there was also an open dispute between American distributors and the British government.

In the last three prewar years, the annual remittance to the US from film earnings in Britain was officially given as some $28 million. For a period during the war (1939 – 1943), the government restricted these remittances, which would otherwise have risen substantially as a result of the increase in box-office takings. This official concern was vindicated when unrestricted remittances were again permitted and American annual earnings more than doubled in 1947 to about $70 million.

In the summer of that year the balance of payments problem had become so acute in Britain that the government was forced to cut imports from hard currency areas. Food imports were to suffer to the extent of £12 million a month, and in the general retrenchment films, although accounting for only 4 per cent of British dollar expenditure in the US, could hardly expect to be exempted. On 6 August the Treasury made an Order under the Import Duties Act 1932, imposing a Customs duty of 75 per cent of the value of all imported films. This duty has sometimes been referred to as '300 per cent *ad valorem*' (in proportion to estimated value of goods).

Despite an attempt by Mr Glenville Hall, Financial Secretary to the Treasury, to defuse the situation by passing the buck to HM Customs and Excise, blaming them for the confusing terminology surrounding the new duty, such reassurance fell on deaf ears in the US. Although legally all imported films were affected, it was the American industry which had most to lose from this 'Dalton Duty', named after the then Chancellor of the Exchequer.

The American reaction was immediate. The duty was imposed on 8 August 1947. On 9 August the Motion Picture Association of America (MPAA) announced that all further shipments of films to Britain would be suspended indefinitely. Perhaps it was more than a coincidence that this announcement was followed immediately by the appearance of posters on London hoardings advertising a new Paramount film. The posters gave no indication of where the film was to be shown nor did they specifically refer to a film at all. They simply showed an eagle and, in bold lettering, the words *The Unconquered*. (Paramount did release a film at that time called *Unconquered*, directed by Cecil B. DeMille, starring Gary Cooper and Paulette Goddard.)

Insinuations that the new duty was either retaliatory for American indifference to British films or that it was introduced purely as an additional means of protection for British producers were repudiated by Glenville Hall:

> I want to make it clear that neither is it intended to obtain additional revenue nor is it an aggressive act against Hollywood in the interests of our own British film industry. The step has been taken simply and solely because the country cannot afford to allocate the dollars necessary to

pay for the exhibition of American films in this country at the present time.

Whether it was intended or not, while it lasted the duty did result in complete protection for British production and was seen by some as the first really big opportunity that the film industry had had. But opinions were divided, even among producers. Certainly, the exhibitors were wholly opposed to the duty. Tom O'Brien MP, then Secretary of the National Association of Theatrical and Kine Employees (NATKE), complained that:

> When this measure was first introduced by the Chancellor of the Exchequer, he promised that there would be consultations with the appropriate interests, but that promise was broken. No consultations were sought, or had. If the government, the Chancellor, or the Board of Trade had convened a meeting of the appropriate interests, American, British and so on, including the trade unions, we would have been able to find a solution for the government which would bring to the government the ends they had in view without the bitterness which has been occasioned.

The film supply situation which resulted from the American embargo was not immediately critical. It was estimated that American distributors had about 125 unreleased feature films in Britain at that time, which would satisfy demand for some months. But with American films occupying about 80 per cent of screen-time in British cinemas, the situation would soon deteriorate. Recourse to extended runs, single-feature programmes and reissues might have a depressing effect on the box office. Not unnaturally, exhibitors campaigned for a more acceptable scheme to be substituted for the duty; and in this they were joined by the American industry, which could afford a temporary embargo but not to lose 25 per cent of its net earnings indefinitely.

British producers were in a dilemma. On the one hand they seemed to have lost their main competitor overnight, which presented an opportunity to dominate their home market, a challenge they could not ignore, yet on the other hand it was a challenge beyond the bounds of economic possibility. The American market was now closed to British films and there were serious doubts whether the home market alone was large enough to cover production costs. This market itself was likely to contract as a result of the American embargo. The shortage of new films would have an adverse effect on attendances and would eventually force cinemas to close, thus further reducing the chances of profitable production. The British industry alone could not hope to produce enough first features to fill the gap left by the Americans and so keep cinemas open. Maximum output, according to the President of the Board of Trade, would be about seventy-five first features a year, less than half the minimum number required annually. Worse, this output would only begin to be possible after studio reconstruction had been completed in the summer of 1948. There were also serious doubts whether, even if film production could be made profitable by severe reduction in costs, adequate labour and materials would be available to producers.

Before the end of 1947 it was announced that discussions were taking place between the Treasury and MPAA representatives aimed at finding a solution that would limit the dollar expenditure on films and persuade the American companies to withdraw their embargo. By early January 1948, no solution was forthcoming, although the government had proposed a scheme that would allow extra earnings for foreign films to be taken out of the country to the extent that British films earned more money overseas. This would allow the American companies to take out more than the one-fourth of their net British revenues remaining untouched by the duty, but, it was hoped, in return for a genuine effort to show British films in the American market.

The outcome of these negotiations was announced on 11 March 1948. An Anglo-American film agreement had been reached which was to cover a four-year period with provision for review after two years.

The main clauses included the 75 per cent duty being removed (it was repealed on 3 May 1948); for the two years beginning 14 June 1948, $17 million (the one-fourth of the net British revenues remaining untouched by the duty) could be remitted each year from the earnings of American companies in the UK; this figure could be increased by a sum equivalent to the earnings of British films in the US (known as the 'B' Pool); American earnings not disposed of in this manner could be used in other ways under the supervision of a joint control committee (investment within the film industry on film rights, prints, acquisition of studios etc., and investment of up to £2.5 million outside the film industry); at the end of two years, one half or £2 million of the sterling not remitted, whichever was the greater, could be carried forward into the second period.

Harold Wilson, the President of the Board of Trade, estimated that a saving of about $33 million would result, since Britain was then still paying out dollars at an annual rate of $50 million on reissues and on the stock of American films. This figure hardly testified to the success of the 'Dalton Duty' as a dollar-saver, but no one could reasonably have expected its effects to have become fully apparent by then. A few more months on would have seen the complete exhaustion of the renters' stocks of new American films. With British production insufficient to fill the gap, con-tinual reissues would have led to steadily diminishing returns at the box office, as audiences drifted away in search of other entertainment. What-ever the shortcomings of the 75 per cent duty, a solution on the lines finally agreed was impossible in August 1947, owing to a clause in the Anglo-American Loan Agreement which precluded Britain from freezing money.

According to Sidney Gilliat, then working with Rank, it was no exaggera-tion to say that he (Rank) was shattered by news of the tax and did his best to get it reversed. He later blamed the financial problems that his organis-ation faced in 1948 on the absence of American films over the previous months and the flood of them which occurred when the tax was just as abruptly lifted. Gilliat did not believe that Rank's 'dismal series of "Inde-pendent Frame" pictures' helped much. They were reputed not only to keep people out of the cinema during the week they were showing, but during the weeks before and after as well. (Independent Frame was a system of film production techniques combining preconstructed sets on movable platforms with still and moving projection backgrounds designed to introduce greater efficiency into studio operations.) John Davis (now Sir John Davis) clearly recalls the background to the 'Dalton Duty' and in particular its effect on the Rank Organisation at that time.

At the end of the Second World War, this country was, for all practical purposes, bankrupt and certainly in so far as the US dollar was concerned. The government was looking for ways to save dollar payments to the American companies. At that time, Arthur Rank and I were in America and were told by the American industry that the British government intended to bring in legislation which would restrict the flow of dollars to America.

At that time the Americans thought incorrectly that Arthur Rank was sponsored by the British government. We were trying to negotiate with the Americans to arrange for British films to be shown in the United States with the support of their industry. They told us that they would support any scheme which conserved dollars, *provided it was voluntary* and not by legislation. They were afraid that, if it was by legislation, other countries, also short of dollars, would follow the same road. Arthur agreed to send me back with a message to the Chancellor of the Exchequer. I spent a whole day sitting outside the Cabinet Office and was not seen by anyone until the end of the day, when I was told that the problem was settled. Consequently, I could not convey to the government that they would get voluntary support from America if they produced a scheme which would control sending dollars to America.

In a nutshell, the government intended to impose legally an *ad valorem* duty on all foreign films imported, basically American. This duty was to be calculated by estimating what a film would earn, and this had to be deposited with the British authorities before the film could be released to the public. This, of course, would involve large sums of money which the Americans either didn't have or were not prepared to put up.

Sir Stafford Cripps and Mr [Harold] Wilson came to see Arthur, at which meeting I was present, saying that the country desperately needed his help to provide British films to replace the American films whose import would be restricted. Needless to say, Arthur agreed to support them. We were told that we 'would be taken care of' when the *ad valorem* arrangement came to an end.

We stepped up film production (in retrospect, beyond the capacity of the creative people), and ultimately incurred a loss of some £20 million. The problem was further complicated by international politics. The Americans at the end of the Second World War were very generous in providing Marshall Aid to help restore Europe's economies and industries. Many Americans thought that we, the British, should only receive Marshall Aid if we were allowing films into this country, with the Americans having the right to remit dollars to pay for them. The outcome was that the Americans sent over one of their top people to negotiate a deal with the British government, which cancelled the *ad valorem* duty, without, as far as I know, consulting any members of the British industry as to the effects of doing so.

The fact was that a large backlog of American films, many of them great box-office attractions, flooded into the British market without any restriction, which explains the disaster with which we at Rank were faced. We had to work our way out of the problem without any help from the government, but fortunately the National Provincial [now National Westminster] Bank gave us a lot of help which enabled Rank over a period of time to pay off the bank with slow recovery.... The real question was that the British government could not afford the dollars that the importation of American films incurred. They produced a lot of money and we (that is, the British film industry) could not afford to pay the dollars back to America because we were desperately short of hard currency, particularly dollars, at the end of the war. As to whether we could fill the gap with British-made films, Arthur Rank was pressed very hard to do his best, which he did. Some films were good, some were not, and that created the problem.[5]

Seemingly undeterred by this mayhem around him, Korda leased a third studio, British National, at Borehamwood. His flagship studio, Sound City, now employed 611 people, including 179 technicians, 265 construction personnel and 167 clerical staff. Both Pinewood and Denham Studios employed larger work forces, respectively 941 and 1,000, but the ratios were different. Denham employed only 100 technicians against 800 construction personnel; Pinewood's ratio was 110/74 and its 90 clerical employees were considerably fewer than for both Sound City and Denham. These figures reflect both management style and production values of the day.

Korda's first film at Shepperton under the London Films banner was *Bonnie Prince Charlie* (1947), directed by Robert Stevenson until he parted company with Korda following a disagreement concerning the production and Anthony Kimmins took over as director. Started in the summer of 1947, the film was completed after thirty shooting weeks, easily one of the longest British shooting schedules at that time, largely because of disagreements between Korda and producer Edward Black. Other long schedules at other studios during that period included *London Belongs to Me* (Sidney Gilliat, 1948: twenty-two weeks – not helped by a drastic change in casting and photography); *The History of Mr Polly* (Anthony Pelissier, 1949: twenty weeks); *Scott of the Antarctic* (Charles Frend, 1948: nineteen weeks); and *Cardboard Cavalier* (Walter Forde, 1948: eighteen weeks). Conversely, *Under Capricorn* (1949) was completed in under ten weeks, being one of Hitchcock's 'ten-minute take' films.

In 1947 the average British feature production schedule was around eight weeks; the American film industry turned out a feature in forty to fifty days. But Sidney Gilliat recalled:

The American film industry did not suffer from the trade unions. There was no nonsense about 'taking the quarter' [when a director asked for an

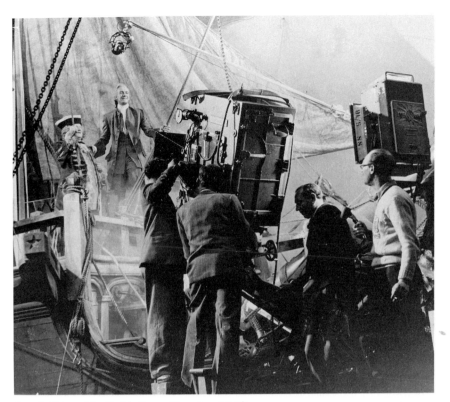

Bonnie Prince Charlie *(Anthony Kimmins, 1947)*

extra quarter of an hour after the normal day's shooting so that a scene could be completed, necessitating approval of the extra overtime by the unions] or works committees having to sit the night before to decide whether they would be gracious enough to allow a little late shooting the following evening.

Because of its long schedule, *Bonnie Prince Charlie* was not the first film to be released by Korda's British Lion. That honour fell to *An Ideal Husband*, the last film that Korda himself directed. Other films from Sound City in 1947 were *A Man About the House*, directed by Leslie Arliss, and *Mine Own Executioner*, directed by Anthony Kimmins (hailed as the first 'adult' film to come out of postwar Britain).

1947 also saw the first in a series of films produced at Sound City by Herbert Wilcox and his Imperadio Pictures. *The Courtneys of Curzon Street* starred Anna Neagle and Michael Wilding. It was typical of the light comedies Wilcox produced at the time. He had entered films as a salesman in 1919, starting a company with his brother. Later he went into film production, promoting such Hollywood names as Dorothy Gish and Lionel Barrymore in Britain. From 1932 his career was almost totally involved with that of the star he created, Anna Neagle, whom he later married. Their first film together was *Goodnight Vienna* (1932), in which Neagle starred with Jack Buchanan. *Nell Gwynne* (1934) was a commercial success for

55

A staff Christmas party in the 'Big Ben' cafeteria, 1948

Wilcox and Neagle which they followed with two films based on the life of Queen Victoria, *Victoria the Great* (1937) and *Sixty Glorious Years* (1938). Other Wilcox films produced at Sound City include *Spring in Park Lane* (1948), *Elizabeth of Ladymead* (1949), *The Lady with the Lamp* (1951), *Derby Day* (1952), *Trent's Last Case* (1952), *The Beggar's Opera* (1952), *Laughing Anne* (1953) and *My Teenage Daughter* (1956).

Until the end of 1947, when the studio working week was reduced from five-and-a-half to five days, it cost around £15,000 a week to keep a production unit working in a major British studio. But the demand for films continued. To cope with the increasing numbers of technicians, stars, producers, directors, crowd artists working at Sound City, the 'Big Ben' cafeteria was opened in 1948. Over a thousand people could be catered for in one sitting and the cafeteria also provided the studio's annual Christmas dinner. The main studio restaurant remained in the Old House, and tea was served in the conservatory.

Britain at this time had twenty-three studios with sixty-eight sound stages available and 4,706 cinemas providing one seat for every ten people in the country. Two thousand of these cinemas were registered as first-run houses. In addition, there were thirty news theatres, each seating between 250 and 500 people. Many of these were situated in major public transport termini such as London's mainline stations, providing a comfortable and (in winter) warm place to pass the time while waiting for public transport.

Total box-office receipts for 1947 were £108 million (rising to £112 million in 1948).

In July 1948 the postwar studio rehabilitation was completed with the opening of the rebuilt ABPC Studios, Elstree. Unfortunately, the Labour government's President of the Board of Trade, Harold Wilson, had announced a 45 per cent exhibitors' quota in June. By November twelve studios were idle.

The British film industry was once again in serious trouble. With the exception of Rank, almost the whole of the industry faced imminent collapse unless more working capital could be made available to the country's independent film producers. Despite these problems, British Lion released four Sound City features in 1948: *Night Beat*, directed by Harold Huth, *Anna Karenina*, directed by Julian Duvivier, and two films destined to become classics of their genre, *The Winslow Boy*, directed by Anthony Asquith, and *The Fallen Idol*, directed by Carol Reed.

In 1947 Harold Wilson had set up and chaired the National Film Production Council to examine ways in which British film-makers could 'achieve maximum output on a sound economic basis'. After six months of preliminary investigations, the Council discovered that this aim was unlikely to be realised because of the parlous state of the industry. Pleas to City investors fell on deaf ears since they were still licking the wounds incurred ten years previously. It was finally left to the government to intervene.

The first government intervention in the affairs of the British film

Anna Karenina *(Julien Duvivier, 1948)*

industry was the 1909 Cinematograph Films Act, which was concerned simply with the physical safety of cinema audiences. The government then moved to a wider concern for the audience – they should have the opportunity to see British films. Given the predominance of the American film industry, British films would only be available for British audiences if the government provided protection for British producers, if only on a temporary basis. The second stage of quasi-temporary protection lasted from 1927 to 1938 (the first 'quota' period), but by then it had become apparent that protection, in some form or another, must be permanent. During the third stage of protection, which lasted until about 1948, doubts began to arise as to whether the extent and incidence of this permanent protection was adequate in the light of the industry's changing structure.

The first doubts were cast by the film technicians' trade union, the Association of Cine-Technicians (ACT), which had developed its full power as a union during the war years. Evidence of its concern is to be found in a number of pamphlets. *Film Business is Big Business – an Investigation into Film Production Finance* [6] was published just after the outbreak of war and argued that 'the move towards the greater concentration on the part of the employers must be met by a corresponding concentration of the labour forces.' In 1941 another pamphlet was published containing more detailed proposals for the reorganisation of the industry. *A State Film Industry?* [7] recommended that the government should supplement the private production of films by setting up a 'State Production Enterprise', together with a nationalised distributing company, state-owned studios and laboratories and a 'Films Credit Corporation to finance approved private production enterprises prepared to submit accounts to public inspection', all to observe trade union conditions and to be subject to public control.

Clearly the government was being called upon to ensure not only that there was a British production industry, but that some part of that industry should be independent of the combines. Direct government sponsorship through the creation of a film finance corporation appeared to be the only logical and sensible option available. A detailed plan for such a corporation had already been submitted to the Board of Trade by the Films Council in February 1940, but no action had been taken. A steady supply of finance at reasonable terms was indispensable to continuous production, and without continuity there could be no successful production. Because of the nature of the product, every film was a unique commodity but of course not every film was commercially successful. Production only stood a chance of being profitable if the losses on the failures could be counterbalanced by the profits on the successes. Such a balance demanded continuity of production – and continuity of finance.

Logically, a film finance corporation should also establish a distributing organisation to which the small producer could entrust his product purely on merit and without fear or favour. Independent producers had long felt that the main distributors' integration with their own production companies was not in the best interests of the independent producers, some of whom had circumvented this concern by setting up their own small but costly distributing companies. A national organisation would have the economic advantages of large-scale distribution and the resources to promote British films overseas through a British organisation specialising in overseas distribution.

Following the Anglo-American Film Agreement, in the summer of 1948 an Organising Committee began to consider how the government should manage an official loan scheme and who should be the beneficiaries. On 1 October 1948 the committee evolved into the National Film Finance Company, 'empowered to borrow up to two and a half million pounds from its bankers on Treasury Guarantee'. [8] Lord Reith was appointed chairman (until his resignation in 1951 when he became chairman of the Colonial Development Corporation) and J. H. Lawrie was managing director. The other directors were S. J. Pears, C. H. Scott and R. J. Stopford (who replaced Lord Reith as chairman in 1951), all of whom had been on the organising committee. Nicholas Davenport had also been a member of the committee and a director of the Company, from which he resigned on 16 January 1949.

Sir Wilfred Eady, Second Secretary of the Treasury, whose son David was to make three documentaries for Korda (*Bridge of Time, 1950*; *Edinburgh*, 1952; *Road to Canterbury*, 1952) and to direct the 'You Killed Elizabeth' sequence from *Three Cases of Murder* (1954), convinced his associates at the Treasury and the Board of Trade to make a special recommendation to the National Film Finance Company for the granting of immediate aid to Korda's British Lion. A major reason for this support was that British Lion owned no cinemas and was a haven for independent producers. Indeed, for most of the National Film Finance Company's working life, Rank and ABC films were not financially assisted.

Although British Lion had shown a profit (£61,154) in 1946/7, heavy production losses totalling £2,187,016 for the 1948 fiscal year had brought the company to the verge of bankruptcy. Eady and others expressed their fear that if British Lion, the second largest production/distribution company in the country, was allowed to collapse, the rest of the industry might well follow.

On 11 November 1948 their recommendation was accepted and Korda's company agreed a £2 million loan from the government through the National Film Finance Company, with fixed 4 per cent interest. Originally, the Organising Committee had informed British Lion that a loan of £1,600,000 (perhaps to be increased later) would be made available when the National Film Finance Company was established. British Lion had estimated that £2 million would be required to finance its production programme. Before any money was lent, an independent investigation by accountants was required; meanwhile a temporary loan of £1 million was made. The investigation showed that the estimate by British Lion was quite inadequate and the government loan was subsequently increased to £3 million secured by a mortgage debenture.

In March 1949 Parliament passed the Cinematograph Film Production (Special Loans) Bill, which sanctioned the loan scheme, established the National Film Finance Corporation (which superseded the National Film Finance Company) and allocated £5 million for the five-year project. The government's objective (and the responsibility of the Organising Committee, the Company and the Corporation) was the maintenance of British film production, then in some jeopardy. This objective was even more desirable owing to the dollar-saving which could be achieved. Moreover, a high British quota had been fixed in the expectation of a certain number of films being produced, an appreciable proportion of them from independent producers. That proportion had become uncertain because of the lack of private finance. The government hoped that temporary assistance from public funds, by way of loan, not subsidy, would carry the independent producers until the confidence of private investors was restored. This would ensure the preservation of the valuable independent production units and contribute materially to the continued projection of British films on the screens of the world.

Concomitant achievements would be maintenance of stable employment in the industry, provision of films to meet the quota, earning (as well as saving) of dollars and training of technicians. It was also felt that it might be possible to establish more economical standards and perhaps a higher code of commercial practice. Something, at any rate, seemed to be necessary if the industry were to regain the confidence of private investors. It was realised by all concerned, including Parliament, that the financial risks were considerable and that losses, though inevitable, would have to be justified by overall achievement.

The new National Film Finance Corporation, set up in April 1949, in its first Annual Report, commented tersely on the union problems which since 1946 had contributed to the difficulties of the industry. The NFFC appealed to the ACT for 'less rigidity', citing the case of a unit 'called out' (on strike) because the producer refused to take overseas four members of the sound crew for whom there was no work. The union had rejected the usual conciliatory machinery but eventually withdrew its claim on condition that the producer contributed £500 to the union's benevolent fund. As this production was NFFC-financed, the NFFC, aware of the alternative, consented to payment being made, though not unreasonably did not consider it a proper use for NFFC funds. [9]

The first film in which the NFFC had a financial interest was registered on 12 May 1949, but the Corporation's much larger financial interest was in the inherited Korda/British Lion loan. Many people, both inside and outside the industry, were unhappy with this arrangement, believing that the money should have gone not to British Lion but to individual film producers. They failed (or refused) to understand that the National Film Finance Company loan was an emergency rescue operation approved before the National Film Finance Corporation guidelines for loans had been established. The Company had decided, rightly or wrongly, that the best way to inject working capital into the independent sector was to give a blanket loan to the British Lion Film Corporation, then home for many independent producers, rather than waste valuable time assessing the merits of individual applications for assistance.

Although the popular belief is that Korda received the loan, it was neither Korda nor London Film Productions who benefited directly, but the British Lion Film Corporation. Many producers not directly affiliated to Korda worked at British Lion's studio (Shepperton) and, if in financial difficulty, they were all to have access to the government money. In practice, London Films, as the largest single unit functioning at the studio, consumed most of the loan (all of it, according to some industry observers) and subsequently was to take the largest share of the blame when things started to fall apart.

To comply with the government instruction that the production and distribution spheres of an organisation receiving state aid should be separated, Harold Boxall, Hugh Quennell and David Cunnynghame, who were prominent in the London Films company, resigned from the British Lion Film Corporation board of directors. A City financier, Harold C. Drayton, was appointed Chairman of British Lion and Korda became 'production adviser'.

Drayton was Chairman of British Electric Traction, which had loaned money for Korda's *Bonnie Prince Charlie* and *Anna Karenina* through Arthur Jarratt. The government hoped that Drayton's appointment would help persuade the City to invest in the film industry. Drayton had agreed to his appointment only if someone else ran the day-to-day operation of the company. Chartered accountant Wilfred Moeller, who had worked for chartered accountants Binder Hamlyn and was then working with the National Coal Board in South Wales, was approached by a friend from Binder Hamlyn, Sir William Lawson. Moeller was anxious to return to London for health reasons and, despite having had little to do with business finance for some time, accepted the position of Drayton's man at the studio. Based in Korda's sumptuous offices at 146 Piccadilly, Moeller visited the studio about twice a week. If he had problems, he would ask Drayton to see him in Korda's offices. Moeller recalled:

> This was completely new ground for me, but it was obvious to me that the £3 million government loan to British Lion was not enough. I had grave doubts whether British Lion could work it out with that amount. Anyway, one of the first things I had to do was to pay out around £1 million to British Lion's creditors, so in fact we only had £2 million to play with. Because film-making is a cyclical business, we did very well for the first two or three years. Then things went badly. If we'd had £5 million and not £3 million, we could have survived. We went into receivership in 1954 because we could not meet our commitments.[10]

After Drayton was appointed Chairman of the British Lion Film Corporation, Korda's responsibilities were restricted to production matters and he had no power to spend money. That dubious privilege was shared between Moeller and Harold Boxall on behalf of the parent company and as directors of the British Lion Studio Company. Vincent Korda was also a director of the studio company but, according to Moeller, 'knew nothing about anything, appearing at Board meetings, but not really getting involved.'

Effectively, the studio was run by Moeller and Boxall, supported by Lou Thornburn, who was in charge of production. According to Moeller, the studio was more like an industrial company because all it did was rent space. For two years (1948–9), 20th Century-Fox rented over half the available studio space. When they left, a large financial hole was left at the studio, which led to the decision in 1950 to sell Worton Hall Studios. Sidney Gilliat had no doubts about Moeller's valuable contribution to British Lion. 'Wilfred Moeller became a great friend of British Lion film-making and of Shepperton Studios,' he recalled. 'I remember meeting him on the steps of 146 Piccadilly just after the Receiver had been appointed. He was extremely upset and I remember him declaring that he would never trust the Treasury again.' [11]

When the National Film Finance Corporation was fully established, it considered applications from producers before production had commenced. Each application would be examined with regard to the experience of the producer, the merits of the film script, the likelihood of finance being easily obtainable elsewhere and the existence of a distribution guarantee (not a guarantee of distribution). The NFFC also demanded certain prerequisites. The producer, in most cases, must already have found some capital of his or her own to spend and must have secured a financial guarantee from a distributor upon which a bank loan for the rest of the 'front money' (approximately 70 per cent of the budget) could be raised. The NFFC would then offer a loan to cover a percentage of the 'end money' without which the production could not be completed.

In 1950 the Anglo-American film pact had been remodelled to make it easier for American companies to use their sterling currency to make films in the UK. Against this, Rank curtailed its own production activities while lending sponsorship to independents; Welwyn studio was closed by ABPC; Teddington and Worton Hall studios were operating a virtually 'care and maintenance' regime and the Gate studio (Elstree), Riverside and Southall studios were in 'suspended animation'. A large country house studio opened at Bletchingley in Surrey, but only one film was made there. Sixty-two first and twelve second features were produced in fifteen studios (five first-features at Shepperton), but the labour force in the industry was, at 3,422, lower than that for June 1945, before men returned to the industry from war service.

1950 also saw the establishment of ACT Films Limited, the only film company owned by a union, the ACT (later the ACTT, now the Broadcasting, Entertainment, Cinematograph and Theatre Union or BECTU). ACT Films arose out of the parlous employment state of the industry in the late 1940s and early 1950s. At the union's annual general meeting in 1949 it was agreed to set up the company with three main objectives: to make 100 per cent British films, to give work to unemployed ACT members, and to prove that films of quality could be made on reasonable budgets while observing all the appropriate union agreements.

In 1950 Derek Twist directed ACT Films' first feature, *Green Grow the Rushes*, financed by the NFFC (two thirds), after some gentle prodding by Harold Wilson at the Board of Trade. The Co-operative Wholesale Society Bank provided the remaining third of the budget. Shot mainly on location at Romney Marsh, Hampshire and at Elstree Studios, the film was completed for £4,000 less than its £100,000 budget, and British Lion agreed to distribute it.

In its first thirty years ACT Films made twenty-four films, one of the most notable being Don Chaffey's *The Man Upstairs* (1958), produced at Shepperton Studios and partly financed by its distributor, British Lion. Also produced at Shepperton was *The Kitchen* (1961), directed by James Hill and based on the Royal Court Theatre play by Arnold Wesker, for which the NFFC provided the total budget of £30,000, – the first time the NFFC had agreed to wholly finance an ACT Films production. However, had British Lion not agreed to distribute these films, it is debatable whether the enterprise would have succeeded. ACT Films was dissolved in January 1993.

Paradoxically, the creative and box-office success enjoyed by Korda during this period failed to hide the deepening financial crisis affecting the government loan to the British Lion Film Corporation. London Films recorded a loss of £127,000 for the financial year 1949–50 (British Lion had already lost £1,388,797 for the preceding financial year). A lifeline for Korda was the setting up of the British Film Production Fund, the 'Eady' levy (named after Sir Wilfred Eady, who had been instrumental in persuading the government to make the original loan to British Lion). The fund was a way of increasing producers' receipts from their own films. Cinema exhibitors, in return for Entertainment Tax relief, paid a levy into the fund from which producers of British films, as redefined in the 1938 Cinematograph Films Act, were entitled to benefit in proportion to their respective billings. When the levy was introduced on a voluntary basis for one year from 9 September 1950, it was clear that anomalies would arise and the contributions of British cinemas would be assisting films made in Commonwealth countries instead of aiding the development of a United Kingdom industry. Subsequent legislation took these and other anomalies into account.

The basis of the levy was relatively simple. Cinema-owners paid one farthing per ticket sold into the Fund; in return, they enjoyed a reduction in the amount of Entertainment Tax for which they were liable, which was a variable sum depending on seat price (for example, a 1s 9d [9p approximately] seat paid $8\frac{1}{2}$d [4p approximately] Entertainment Tax); seat prices were increased, but cinemas with gross box-office takings of less than £125 per week were exempt. It was calculated that these changes would reduce tax receipts by £300,000 and give the film industry an extra £3 million annually, with Korda being a major beneficiary. Unfortunately, the formula by which producers were to be paid from the Fund (after an annual special allocation to the Children's Film Foundation) proved to be totally inadequate.

The year ending 4 August 1951 brought in a total of £1,197,841, leaving £1,180,244 for distribution to producers after expenses had been paid. Payments made to British producers against net receipts from box-office averaged about 15 per cent 'bonus payment' against returns. Maximum payment for a feature was £32,000 and about 4,300 cinemas contributed an average of £6 each week per cinema. 449 features and 554 short films benefited; the maximum benefit for a short film was £3,654. During the first three years of the Eady scheme, up to August 1953, £6,051,820 had been distributed. In that three-year period, the amounts for apportionment to their respective films were: Gaumont Film Distributors, £1,741,683; British

Lion, £933,622; and Associated British-Pathé, £748,122 – a total to the 'big three' of £3,423,427.

A new plan was evolved in 1951, substantially increasing payments to the Fund, which in turn increased payments to producers; but it was soon realised that, partly because of the failure of some exhibitors to make payments into the Fund, it was necessary to put the Fund on a statutory basis from 1957. Customs and Excise collected contributions from the exhibitors and the British Film Fund Agency, which had replaced the British Film Production Fund, paid out appropriate sums to producers. Between 1957 and 1985, a variety of statutory instruments were introduced by government, which affected the collection and distribution of the levy, taking into account the needs of exhibitors and producers.

Despite this, after 1957 cinema attendances continued to decline and both producers and exhibitors suffered increases in costs. Contributions to the Agency gradually diminished, to the point where the value to the producer became marginal. With the increasing rate of cinema closures, a complete reassessment of the industry's economics was undertaken. At the low point in 1984, it was ultimately recommended by the Cinematograph Films Council, comprising representatives of producers, distributors, exhibitors and trades unions, that the 'quota' system for exhibitors should be abolished and the British Film Fund Agency wound up. The deregulation of the British film industry was virtually completed in the Films Act of 1985.

Kenneth Maidment, who has for many years been closely involved with the workings of the 'Eady' levy, believes the scheme has been widely misunderstood:

The 'Eady' levy never was a government subsidy. It was, in effect, a reallocation of box-office receipts which benefited the makers of British films. Foreign companies, particularly the American majors, were happy to accept this as long as they were entitled to make British films themselves. Indeed, it has only been during the periods when American finance has supported the making of British films, both for theatrical and television distribution, that the so-called 'British' film industry has flourished.[12]

According to Bryan Forbes, the Americans helped to wreck the Eady Plan.

What happened was the moment the Eady plan was introduced, there were back-door routes through which Americans could come to Britain and finance films through British companies, because they weren't allowed by law to be American companies. These companies would then get Eady money which would then go back to the American financiers, instead of flowing back into the industry. Most people took the Eady money and ran, but Allied Film Makers and Beaver Films used the money to go back into business. ... No governments are really interested in cinema. Wilson pretended to be, and took credit for it when he was Minister of Trade, but I think it was a political gesture rather than a gesture in favour of the British film industry. Nobody since has been interested at all.[13]

From December 1950, Sir Michael Balcon, in addition to his many other commitments in the film industry, was an unpaid adviser to the NFFC. He was not responsible for the decisions of the Corporation, which were taken by the Board of Directors, but there is no doubt that his judgment was extremely valuable on such matters as the experience of loan applicants and the box-office potential of scripts and subjects. His appointment reinforced the fact that the provision of production finance could not be divorced from the rest of production activities. If the state was to lend money for film production, its financing organisation could not be indifferent to the content of films in which public money was to be invested. However, Balcon's impartiality was questioned by others in the industry when Ealing Films became one of the principal beneficiaries of the scheme.

In February 1951, the NFFC announced improvements in film budgets at British Lion, which Korda calculated had reduced costs by 45 per cent. The following month, London Films showed a profit of £6,225 (March to August 1950). In October 1951 the NFFC loan to British Lion, due to be repaid, was extended with the expectation of added revenues from the 'Eady' Fund, but by May 1952 the NFFC admitted that at least £1 million of the loan would never be recovered.

1951 also saw the government's axing of the Crown Film Unit at Beaconsfield and the closure of Denham Studios, but fifty-three features and twenty-five second features were produced in the remaining sixteen major studios. Significantly for the film industry, by the end of January 1951, 657,950 television licences were current in Great Britain and Northern Ireland.

Coincidentally, on 25 January 1951 the NFFC announced a group production scheme, which was in operation within three months. This distorted the category of independent producer since many such producers accepted the financial and administrative protection of the group 'blanket'.

Three groups were formed within the scheme: the first in association with the Rank Organisation; the second with ABPC; and the third, somewhat different in conception, with ABFD. For the first group a holding company was formed, known as British Film Makers Limited. It engaged production companies on the following terms. The films made were owned by British Film Makers and the distribution rights were assigned to GFD, which gave a distribution guarantee for 70 per cent of the budget. This guarantee was used to obtain a bank loan on the usual terms. The remaining 30 per cent was provided by the NFFC, which also acted as the guarantor of completion. For security, the NFFC had a controlling interest in the share capital of the holding company. All production in this group was carried out at Pinewood Studios. Each production team in the group received an annual fee, which averaged about £5,000, and a percentage of the profits on any film that it made; this percentage was twenty-five on the first £50,000 profit, ten on the second £50,000 and five thereafter. After deduction of the producers' share, the remainder of the profit was divided between GFD and the NFFC in proportion to their shareholding. In accordance with the purpose of the scheme, these profits were not distributed until they had been used to cover losses on other films and to meet 'abortive story development costs' which were an integral part of any production programme.

The directors of British Film Makers were James Lawrie, representing the NFFC, and Earl St. John, representing GFD. Sir Michael Balcon was Chairman. The company considered propositions from its constituent production teams, determined which scripts were suitable, made changes, approved the budget and controlled expenditure. In a letter to the President of the Board of Trade asking for approval of the proposal to put the Group scheme into effect, Lord Reith claimed that the holding company would offer certain advantages to the producers:

> It will undertake, on behalf of all producers in the Group, the commercial negotiations which are usually an anxiety and distraction to the producer. It will arrange studio rentals, distribution terms, bank loans, completion guarantees, etc. It will provide certain common services. All this makes for efficiency and economy; for more artistic freedom for the producer; for the team spirit which is as desirable in this business as elsewhere.[14]

Taking into account its resources and the expected amount of repayments, the NFFC calculated that for the Pinewood Group alone, 'the initial experiment which we have in mind will provide for the production of at least six films.'[15] The first two films were *Appointment With Venus* (1951), produced by Betty Box and directed by Ralph Thomas for Action Films, and *High Treason* (1952), produced by Paul Soskin and directed by Roy Boulting for Conqueror Films. Other producers or production teams who had joined this Group included Anthony Asquith and Edward Baird, Thorold Dickinson and Peter de Sarigny, Anthony Havelock-Allan, Ronald Neame, Sergei Nolbandov and Leslie Parkyn, George Brown, Hugh Stewart, Jeffrey Dell and Julian Wintle.

Membership of the Group was not exclusive. It was open to anyone acceptable to British Film Makers. Those producers who started the Group were given a year's contract. For others, membership was terminable by three months' notice on either side. It was possible for a team to make a film within the Group, leave it to make another film outside, and then rejoin. British Film Makers operated for two years, during which time fourteen films were produced. The Group was terminated at the end of 1952 at the request of Rank.

The second Group was similar to the first except that it was run in association with ABPC and production was at Elstree Studios. In this case no formal holding company was formed, but the benefits to producers and their terms of contract were similar to those of British Film Makers. The scheme applied to most films financed jointly by ABPC and the NFFC, but, for this Group, ABPC made a cash advance instead of only giving a distribution guarantee.

Production control was vested in Robert Clark for ABPC and James Lawrie for the NFFC. This Group also included many well-established producers. The first two films from the Group were *So Little Time* (1952), directed by Compton Bennett for the Mayflower Pictures Corporation, and *Angels One Five* (1952), directed by George More O'Ferrall for Templar Productions. The Elstree Group produced five films. Like the first Group, it was also thought to have run its course by the end of 1952.

The third Group – Group 3 was its official title – was similar to the Pinewood Group in that there was a formal holding company, but its purpose was somewhat different. Group 3 existed to provide facilities, both technical and financial, for the producer who was not yet established in the main feature industry. Many of those working for the Group had extensive experience in short and second-feature film-making. They were not raw recruits, for whom the production industry was still largely impenetrable.

The leaders of the Group were executive producer John Grierson and production controller John Baxter. Both were on the Board of the company with James Lawrie and Chairman Sir Michael Balcon. ABFD provided a distribution guarantee for 50 per cent of the cost and the NFFC made up the balance. Production was at the small (7,500 square feet) Southall studio, which was leased to Group 3 for an initial term of one year.

The first film produced by the Group was *Judgement Deferred* (1951), produced and directed by John Baxter, which appears to have been more of a 'demonstration' film than a product of the Group's true potential. *Brandy for the Parson* (1952), directed by John Eldridge, provided a fairer assessment of Group 3 policy. The Group completed twenty-two features before it was wound up in 1955.

Despite the obvious advantages which it offered, the Group production scheme had its critics, not only among those who were not able to share its possible benefits. The strongest criticism was that both the Pinewood and Elstree Groups were linked to high-cost studios and that the NFFC's financial contribution, being 'end money', was taking the major part of the production risk from the two main combines. Effectively, the combines were having their production programmes and their quota films virtually subsidised by the state.

The NFFC claimed that the Group production experiment, which might 'show that such an organisation of production may give, with the other measures taken by the industry, the promise of stability which was so badly needed', could not be carried out in any other way. The Corporation's argument was that its purpose was to assist British producers and 'to help create conditions which would enable them to get finance in the ordinary commercial way',[16] but the speculative nature of film production inhibited stability and a steady supply of working capital unless a production programme was sustained long enough to allow the 'swings and roundabouts' principle to operate.

Part of the NFFC's responsibility was to contribute to this sustainment, but its resources were quite inadequate to finance such a programme completely. It had to make use of existing methods, including bank loans and their concomitant distribution guarantees. Because of the existing structure of the industry and the power of the main circuits, there was only a limited number of distributors who could risk an unbroken series of guarantees of sufficient size and number to make Group production practical. At the same time British Lion (with the help of the NFFC loan) was virtually operating Group production, which left GFD and ABPC. The terms under which these two companies would provide the assistance necessary for the implementation of the scheme was to be negotiated, but they would naturally insist that their allied studios should be used for production.

If nothing else, the Group production scheme had clearly raised a fundamental issue about the government's policy concerning the British film industry. As a statutory corporation without equity capital, the NFFC had to pay interest (to the government) on all the finance made available to it under the relevant legislation. From 1949 until the enactment of the Cinematograph Films Act (1957), the NFFC's loans tended to be of a non-commercial kind since the Act creating the NFFC laid down that loans could be made only in cases where the borrower was 'not for the time being in a position otherwise to obtain adequate financial facilities for the purpose on reasonable terms from an appropriate source'.[17] This condition was repealed by the 1957 Act. Interestingly, the loans totalling £3 million to British Lion were not covered by the NFFC's standard conditions, being subject to 'certain special arrangements' laid down in a document agreed between the NFFC and British Lion.

One other 'special arrangement', which originated in 1964, was the NFFC's retention of the Special Preference Share of £1 in British Lion Films. This 'golden share' was a means of depriving any new owner of the benefits of previous tax losses, which in 1972 was to be a major factor in the survival of Shepperton as a film production centre.

In retrospect, the £3 million loan to British Lion could be interpreted as a panic measure by the government and prompts speculation as to whether British Lion and Korda would have survived had the NFFC applied the criteria for assessment used when it was fully established. Despite criticism of the government's actions, without the loan to British Lion many producers, directors, actors and technicians would have been denied employment and the British film industry and cinema-going public would have been denied some of the finest films to come out of a British studio.

Inevitably, the government got cold feet about financing the film industry and the NFFC was asked to set up a consortium in co-operation with private interests to take over that responsibility. The NFFC issued a detailed Memorandum describing its consortium proposals and its new lending policy on 21 September 1971. By the end of November that year it had succeeded in obtaining commitments in principle from eleven groups in the private sector, aggregating £750,000.[18] Early in December the NFFC reported this to the Department of Trade and Industry, and on 8 May 1972 the government confirmed its decision to withdraw from film financing in a Written Answer to two Parliamentary Questions:

Advances of £7½ million within the total of £11 million authorised by the films legislation have so far been made to the National Film Finance Corporation. In June last year, the government stated that it was their intention to withdraw from the financing of the production of films.

They accordingly welcomed the proposal from the Corporation to set up a consortium in co-operation with private interests and had agreed to advance loans of up to a maximum of £1 million on condition that the private sector would put up £3 for every £1 from public funds. The Corporation have been able to raise £750,000 from private sources. The government have now agreed to contribute £1 million to the consortium to support its efforts to achieve financial independence. The government does not, however, intend to make any further advances in the future.

So ended the British government's direct involvement with film financing. Members of the new National Film Finance Consortium met for the first time on 31 May 1972 and the Consortium was formally launched the following day. To support the Consortium, the National Film Trustee Company was formed in 1971 as a wholly owned subsidiary of the NFFC for the legal protection and administrative convenience of Consortium investors and participants. The services provided by the Trustee Company included the distribution of revenues received among all those entitled to them as well as the protection of the investors' security position in relation to the film in question.

The NFFC loan to British Lion was a major factor in Sir Alexander Korda's post-1948 recovery. He reinforced his position by deciding, one month before the loan was announced, to remove his credit, 'Alexander Korda presents', from his films. This decision completed his retirement from producing and directing.

For his last seven years as an executive producer and studio administrator, Korda concentrated on promoting film projects and negotiating contracts and film rights. It was his ability to encourage and inspire filmmakers that, between 1946 and 1955, persuaded some of Britain's best filmmakers to transfer their allegiance from the Rank Organisation to Korda's British Lion/London Films set-up. Carol Reed, Michael Powell and Emeric Pressburger, Frank Launder and Sidney Gilliat, David Lean, Ian Dalrymple, John and Roy Boulting and Laurence Olivier were just some who were weaned away.

The Rank Organisation was run by businessmen like John Davis, who had no practical experience of film-making, and production controller Earl St. John. Korda's wealth of film-making experience created a bond of artistic sympathy and understanding between him and his associates in a way that Rank could not. Korda's major film-making experience covered the periods 1933 to 1948, when he presented, produced or directed fifty-eight feature films, and 1949 to 1955, when he was associated with thirty-seven films.

In 1949, thirty million British people visited a cinema each week. Sixty-six first features were produced in thirty studios offering eighty stages, the most features produced in one year since 1939. This production output was supported by twenty-one second features. Significantly, union membership had also increased – the Association of Cinema Technicians (ACT) to nearly 8,000 and the National Association of Theatrical and Kine Employees (NATKE) to over 34,000. The government tried to rectify its

Alexander Korda in conference with some of his producers, directors and writers. Left to right: Julien Duvivier, Carol Reed, Anatole de Grunwald, Leslie Arliss, Emeric Pressburger, Zoltan Korda, Alexander Korda, Vincent Korda, Ralph Richardson, Terence Rattigan, Michael Powell, Anthony Asquith, Bill O'Bryen, Herbert Wilcox and Anthony Kimmins.

earlier mistake by reducing the exhibitors' quota from 45 to 40 per cent. This was still too high, but it was the best the industry was to get.

When Rank sold its Lime Grove studios to the BBC in 1949, the long, slow demise of the British film industry began in earnest. Korda's influence on Shepperton Studios also declined over the following six years. Paradoxically, these six years saw Shepperton produce some of the most remarkable films to come out of a British studio. Unfortunately, this period also marked a classic confrontation between the creative element of a studio and the financial investment demanded by that creativity.

For the nine months ending 31 December 1949, Exchequer returns show that £4,130,000 of the NFFC's authorised loan capital of £5 million had been taken from the Treasury. No more than £6,000 had been returned. The NFFC claimed that since July 1948 it had directly or indirectly made forty-four films possible, at least thirty-five of them in 1949. For his part Korda had never been entirely happy with the £3 million government loan to British Lion. In April 1949 British Lion announced that even with this loan they expected to lose £700,000. By December 1949 London Films owed £1,350,374 to British Lion, which was repaid by London Films in June 1950 by transfer of assets and film rights by Korda. Because he had more independent and American producers working with him throughout 1949, Korda made fewer films of his own.

The Small Back Room (1949) was the first film for Korda by independent producers Michael Powell and Emeric Pressburger, under the Archers production banner, although they had collaborated for the first time on Korda's *The Spy in Black* (1939). Powell and Pressburger went on to make films including *One of Our Aircraft is Missing* (1942), *The Life and Death of Colonel Blimp* (1943), and *Black Narcissus* (1947), which was one of four films they made for Rank. But they could have returned to Korda earlier. In 1947 *The Red Shoes* no longer interested Korda, who before the war had commissioned Pressburger to write a starring vehicle for Merle Oberon in which she was to play a ballerina. Korda paid Pressburger around £2,000 for the script, which was never used. He eventually sold the script to Powell and Pressburger for £12,000, and they made *The Red Shoes* for Rank. It was both an artistic and a financial success. *The Small Back Room* was not, although Powell considered it his 'best film'.

Two commercial disasters for Powell were *Gone to Earth* (1950) and *The Elusive Pimpernel* (1950), both films resulting from Korda's wheeling and dealing with American movie moguls. *Gone to Earth* arose out of a deal Korda made with David O. Selznick, who, much impressed by the work of Powell and Pressburger, wanted them to make a film with his wife Jennifer Jones. The resulting film displeased Selznick, who tried to stop Korda releasing it, ostensibly on the grounds that the original story had been 'distorted'. Selznick's real objections had more to do with the inadequate amount of screen time for Jennifer Jones's close-ups.

Characteristically, Selznick announced that he was suing on deviation from the script. When Powell replied that they had not deviated, Selznick confirmed that that was why he was going to sue. Korda was perplexed, but he did understand Selznick's next move. Since Selznick's deal with Korda gave him control over the film's American release, he held up distribution until Rouben Mamoulian had recut the film and added some sequences more to Selznick's liking. This substantially different version was released in America in 1952 as *The Wild Heart*.

Samuel Goldwyn was the next to give Powell and Pressburger a hard time. Korda had made a similar deal with Goldwyn for *The Elusive Pimpernel*. Powell neatly summed up the situation: 'If you're making a film between Goldwyn and Alex Korda, you get ground to powder.'[19] The film had cost £450,000 to which extensive retakes added around £27,000, prompting Korda to match Selznick's perplexing line of reasoning regarding *Gone to Earth*. According to David Lewin of the *Daily Express*, at a news conference Goldwyn and Korda were questioned about the amount spent on retakes for the film. Korda quoted 2 per cent of the film's cost. When asked how much the film cost, he enigmatically replied that it cost 100 per cent.[20]

Two more successful producer/director teams worked with Korda at Shepperton at this time, Frank Launder and Sidney Gilliat with Individual Pictures and John and Roy Boulting with Charter Films. Unlike Powell and Pressburger, Launder and Gilliat and the Boultings stayed at the studio after Korda's departure and became an integral part of Shepperton's history, both creatively and financially.

Launder and Gilliat worked with Korda from 1948 until his death in January 1956, the first six years under contract, thereafter on an ad hoc basis. Their successful film partnership (in which they alternately pro-

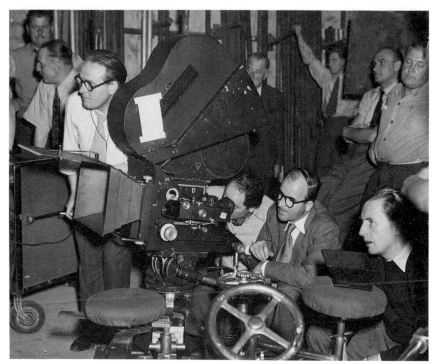

Frank Launder (bespectacled, behind camera), c. 1950

duced or directed for each other) started in 1933 with their first collaboration, followed by their first script together in 1935 for *Seven Sinners*. They formed Individual Pictures during the Second World War and produced several films for Rank which were, in order of financial success: *The Blue Lagoon* (1949), *The Rake's Progress* (1945), *Green for Danger* (1946), *I See a Dark Stranger* (1946), *London Belongs to Me* (1948) and *Captain Boycott* (1947).

When they moved to Korda in 1949, their first six films in order of success were: *The Happiest Days of Your Life* (1950), notable for the inspired casting of Alastair Sim, Margaret Rutherford and Joyce Grenfell, *State Secret* (1950), *The Constant Husband* (1955), *Lady Godiva Rides Again* (1951), *Folly to be Wise* (1953) and *The Story of Gilbert and Sullivan* (1953). The latter film had a higher gross than *Folly to be Wise*, but it also cost much more.

Their one box-office failure was with Korda's *The Story of Gilbert and Sullivan* (1953), London Films' 21st anniversary production. Korda's personal involvement with this one Launder and Gilliat film may have had something to do with it. His basic ignorance of music did not help. Music Director Muir Mathieson once summed up Korda's limited musical sense by claiming that Korda only knew the British national anthem was being played because the crowd stood up.

According to actor, George Cole, who worked often with Launder and Gilliat, they always had a good script although terrible money (for the St Trinian's films in particular). 'If Alastair [Sim] was in the film, it was even

72

Sidney Gilliat (behind camera), c. 1950

worse money because he got most of it! They were wonderful people to work with. Sidney Gilliat was very much the intellectual director and Frank was the down-to-earth one.... When you were doing a film with Frank, Sidney would go mad because, at the end of every take, Frank would say: 'That was lovely. Just do another one.' Sidney would say: 'Well, if it was so lovely, why are we doing another one?' It was just a habit Frank couldn't get out of.'[21]

Although the Boulting Brothers made only one film with Korda, the classic *Seven Days to Noon* (1950), which received an American Academy Award for Best Original Story, their subsequent comedies after the Korda period ran parallel to those of Launder and Gilliat, providing a rich vein of indigenous British humour through to the 1960s. Their best remembered comedy is *I'm All Right, Jack* (1959), a satire on labour relations in which Peter Sellers gave one of the best character performances of his career as Fred Kite, the shop steward.

Nine of the other British Lion Films made between 1949 and 1955 were also the work of established British film-makers. Jack Lee's *The Wooden Horse* (1950) and Anthony Kimmins' comedy *The Captain's Paradise* (1953) are probably the best-known productions in this group, but Kimmins' *Mr. Denning Drives North* (1951) and *Who Goes There!* (1952), George More O'Ferrall's *The Heart of the Matter* (1954) and *The Holly and the Ivy* (1952), Leslie Arliss's *Saints and Sinners* (1949), Guy Hamilton's *The Ringer* (1952) and producer Ian Dalrymple's *Three Cases of Murder* (1955) were all above-average efforts.

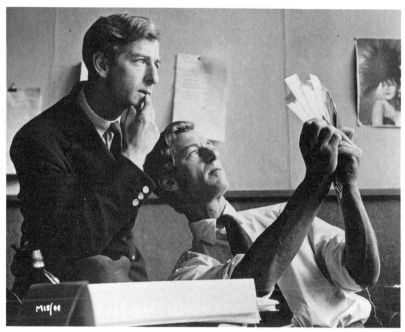

John and Roy Boulting

Four foreign producers – the Russian, Gregory Ratoff; German, Karl Hartl; Hungarian, Josef Somlo and Korda's brother, Zoltan – were responsible for an additional seven films. Ratoff produced and directed *That Dangerous Age* (1949) and *My Daughter Joy* (1950), Hartl produced *Angel With the Trumpet* (1950) and *The Wonder Kid* (1951), which he also directed, and Somlo produced *The Teckman Mystery* (1954, directed by Wendy Toye) and *The Man Who Loved Redheads* (1954, directed by Harold French). Zoltan Korda produced and directed *Cry, the Beloved Country* (1951), widely acknowledged as one of the finest statements about the necessity of racial understanding. It was a far cry from *Sanders of the River* and *The Four Feathers*.

Korda was only marginally involved with these films, but his presence was more evident in the remaining thirteen films of this period. Three of these were directorial debuts and ten were the work of Britain's most celebrated and individualistic film-makers, Carol Reed and David Lean.

The three directorial debuts were by three of Korda's favourite actors, Emlyn Williams, Robert Donat and Ralph Richardson. This trend by Korda, arising out of the NFFC/British Lion loan, also allowed actor Anthony Bushell to make his directorial debut with *Angel With the Trumpet*. Korda approved their scripts and budgets, arranged for these actor/directors to be guided by more experienced producers and assistants, provided the technicians and casts largely from his own stable, and gave freely of his time and advice when needed.

The first and best in this series was Emlyn Williams' *The Last Days of Dolwyn* (1949). The fine cast was headed by Edith Evans, Hugh Griffiths and a young Welsh actor, Richard Burton, whom Korda, three years later, put under a five-year, £500-a-week contract and promptly loaned him out to 20th Century-Fox for £150,000 for three pictures. As Williams and Korda feared, *The Last Days of Dolwyn* was not a commercial success.

Robert Donat's *The Cure for Love* (1950) also boasted a fine cast, including Donat, Renee Asherson and Dora Bryan. It was an unexpected commercial success. Sidney Gilliat believed this to be the major reason that Korda purchased *Hobson's Choice*, also with a Lancashire setting. He began shooting *Hobson's Choice* (1953, directed by David Lean) with Robert Donat who was later replaced by John Mills when he fell ill.

Ralph Richardson's *Home at Seven* (1952) was directed more by Korda than Richardson. It was the first of four experiments in the economical shooting of recent stage plays. The film was reportedly shot in 13½ days as against the normal eight weeks. Korda was pleased with the result and promoted three more similarly contrived films, *Who Goes There!*, *The Holly and the Ivy* and *The Ringer*.

Korda had hit the jackpot again in 1949 with *The Third Man*, widely considered a classic of the thriller genre and the most often revived production with which Korda was associated. Like his *The Fallen Idol* (1948), Carol Reed made *The Third Man* in collaboration with Graham Greene. The film derived from suggestions made by Korda, who had been gathering material for a film about the aftermath of war in a European city. Korda's tie-up with Selznick was still reasonably intact, so for American rights to the film, Korda was given Joseph Cotten to play the hero, Holly Martins, and Italian actress Alida Valli to portray Anna, Harry Lime's

Carol Reed (on ladder), c. 1950

Russian girlfriend. For Harry Lime, Korda hired Orson Welles, then in self-imposed exile from Hollywood.

Reed and Greene were forced to 'consult' with Selznick before production started, receiving forty pages of suggestions on their departure from southern California, but they stood their ground and made the film their own way. Its huge success prompted Selznick to admit:

> The creation of the film was almost entirely Reed's. I did a little work on the script with Reed and Greene, but nothing that contributed greatly to its success. I supplied the stars and I re-edited the film [for the US]. It was a substantial contribution to making me financially healthy again.[22]

Selznick had lost almost all of the $4.04 million investment in *Portrait of Jenny* (1948) and had a major failure with *The Paradine Case* (1947), which lost most of its $4 million investment.

Sidney Gilliat recalled a meeting with Selznick in 1950 during which Selznick attributed the success of *The Third Man* to Anton Karas's zither theme, for which Korda paid only £300 for all rights.

It is not widely known that *The Third Man* almost did not make its London premiere date. During editing, a cutting room fire at Shepperton Studios destroyed seven out of twelve reels of edited picture. Reed immediately drafted in an extra editing team to help reconstruct the missing reels, guided only by the soundtrack. The round-the-clock operation was successful.

Anton Karas recording the soundtrack to The Third Man

Perhaps the most unexpected addition to Korda's team was David Lean, whose career had been forged at Rank. In 1947, when Rank's industry monopoly was under fire, Lean had sprung to Rank's defence. Lean brought to Korda an impressive track record of films made with Rank. *In Which We Serve* (1942), which he co-directed with Noël Coward, *This Happy Breed* (1944), *Blithe Spirit* (1945), *Great Expectations* (1946) and *Oliver Twist* (1948). One possible reason for Lean changing studios was the less successful films made at Rank, *The Passionate Friends* (1948) and *Madeleine* (1949).

Korda told Sidney Gilliat that he had got Lean at a bargain price, implying that Lean had to take it or leave it. A meticulous craftsman, Lean took two years to make his first film for Korda, *The Sound Barrier* (1952). Made for comparatively little (£250,000), the film recorded a profit both in Britain and America, and won an Oscar for 'Best Sound Recording, London Films Sound Department'. The statuette was proudly displayed for many years in Shepperton's sound department, later seen alongside the second Oscar for 'Best Sound Recording, Shepperton Studio Sound Department', won for Lean's *Lawrence of Arabia* (1962).

Lean's second film for Korda was *Hobson's Choice* (1953), which gave Charles Laughton a chance to return to British films after a fourteen-year absence. Lean's third and last film for Korda, *Summer Madness* (1955), was less successful.

In 1950, Korda had formed a distribution company, Lopert Films Distributing Corporation, with American property investor Robert Dowling and his friend Ilya Lopert to promote better worldwide distribution for selected British and American films. This company provided Korda with production money in return for certain distribution rights, chiefly in America. In 1952, Robert Dowling's City Investing Corporation of New York invested $500,000 in London Films.

In July 1952, British Lion had asked the Board of Trade for financial assistance in building more stages at Shepperton in order to increase production. This was agreed and, in March 1953, stages 'E', 'F' and 'G' were ready. Two years later these stages played host to the then enemy – television. Producer/director Peter Graham Scott recalled this occasion in a letter to the author (12 November 1993):

When commercial television was planned early in 1955, I was snapped up by Associated-Rediffusion, who had gained the Monday to Friday London franchise, to direct major dramas. We were due to go on the air for the very first time on 22 September 1955, and as A-R hadn't a 'live' TV studio ready (they were still converting their recently bought derelict Fox-British Studios at Wembley), from May 1955 onwards we made a number of quickly shot films at Shepperton. I directed three scripts I was able to choose, *A Call on the Widow*, *The Guv'nor* and Bill Naughton's *All Correct Sir*. Others who made similar films at Shepperton were Robert Hamer, John Moxey, Charles Saunders and Peter Cotes. A-R had contracted Sir John Barbirolli of the Hallé Orchestra and one of his ideas was to record eighteen quarter-hour performances by young unknown soloists. I spent an enjoyable two weeks filming two of these programmes per day at Shepperton with pianists like Valerie Tryon and Robin Wood in their first public appearances. When A-R wanted six more programmes, clearly I was in danger of making a career in music. Luckily this was averted when the script for *A Call on the Widow*, adapted by Robert Irvine, became ready for production. I was expected to shoot this film in four studio days at the unheard of rate of twelve-and-a-half minutes screen-time a day (the average in film studios was only two minutes). However, I knew if I had a skilful cameraman and a swift and able operator, I could shoot as many as thirty-five setups per day. Planning ambitious camera movement and dramatic angles with care, I completed just on time with Jean Kent, Clifford Evans and Michael Craig achieving powerful low-key performances (usually in the first take), aided by Brendan Stafford's crisp black and white photography. *The Guv'nor*, by Tudor Gates, was shot in a hectic five days and *All Correct Sir* in six. It was a particularly lovely summer that year and stages 'E', 'F' and 'G' hummed with new activity. There was a great spirit of optimism as we gathered for drinks in the garden of the Old House at the end of each filming day.

Scott returned to Shepperton on three more occasions. In 1956 he directed *The Hide-out* for producer John Temple-Smith, in 1969 he produced *The Promise* with Ian McKellen and, in 1971, while waiting to produce and direct the television series *The Onedin Line*, he directed a series, *The Magnificent 6½*, for the Children's Film Foundation.

In September 1952, British Lion paid two years' arrears of Preference Share dividends, and a month later Korda loaned London Films £50,000 to finance the re-issuing of earlier London Films successes. By November 1952, alarm bells in the government were ringing. In a debate in Parliament on the Special Loans Bill, the NFFC's choice of Korda as beneficiary was called into question. Korda's admirers, including Harold Wilson, Sir Tom O'Brien and many Members on both sides of the House, defended him vigorously, but William Shepherd led a spirited and highly personal attack which was widely reported:

> I have reached the conclusion that it might be well and to the advantage of the British Lion Film Corporation if they had a new executive producer and someone other than Sir Alexander Korda should take on that job. Sir Alexander Korda was associated with the lush days of the film industry.... I understand from his recent public pronouncements that he is very interested, or more interested, in television and I think it might be to the advantage of both the Corporation and the country if someone else took over his job.... I do not think that containing Sir Alexander Korda can be done as a part-time job and, therefore, suggest a full-time Chairman.[23]

The last sentence was a dig at Harold Drayton, the City financier who had been appointed by the government to look after its interests in British Lion. According to Michael Korda, Drayton was a 'kind of corporate pluralist, with over fifty directorships to occupy his time, and was widely regarded as having been charmed, or misled into managerial impotence by Alex.' Drayton was removed and Sir William Lawson, the partner in chartered accountants Binder Hamlyn who had persuaded Wilfred Moeller to support Drayton, was put in charge of the company's affairs. According to Lawson, these would be government-controlled – but not government-run.

Despite receiving a telegram of 'whole-hearted support and continued loyalty' from the studio staff, Korda's days with British Lion were numbered. In December 1953, British Lion reported a net loss for 1952/53 of £150,330, taking the total debit to £2,217,035, over two-thirds of the original loan. In June 1954, British Lion was put out of its agony when the government finally called in the loan and applied to the courts for a Receiver to be appointed. The government had held off calling in the loan for two-and-a-half years in the mistaken belief that Korda would regain financial stability with the added revenue from the Eady Fund. The reality was that the Fund payments came in too late to be of any use to Korda and British Lion. Sir Wilfred Eady now called the bankrupt company 'a baby which was born of the unholy wedlock between public funds and private enterprise'.[24]

Korda had spent nine years building up British Lion, six of them in trying to adapt his film-making activities to the requirements of the loan, and getting involved in projects many of which were alien to him. In June 1954, Korda saw all his work wiped out. He was stunned by the loss of British Lion, having lost over £500,000 of his own money in the process. The holders of four million shares in British Lion saw their investment vanish overnight.

Lesser men than Korda, now 60, would have considered retirement. But within a week of the British Lion collapse Korda was back in business. He announced that London Films was to continue producing films under his guidance, having persuaded Robert Dowling to invest once again in the company, this time for £5 million. Korda himself had the final word on the British Lion disaster. After firing Korda, Sir John Keeling asked him who he thought should be appointed to succeed him as chief of production. Korda replied: 'Sir John, I do not grow on trees.'[25]

Korda's financial comeback was as impressive as it was swift. Although the British Lion Film Corporation was dead, the British Lion Studio Company and British Lion Films Limited continued respectively as a studio and a distribution company. Korda could still depend on the latter to release his films in the UK market. He had astutely maintained his international distribution agreements with 20th Century-Fox and Lopert Films, which he needed to continue promoting the 'international' film-making he had pioneered.

In 1954 John Woolf, now a producer, went to Korda after the collapse of British Lion to persuade him to invest in *I Am a Camera*, to be shot by Woolf's Romulus Films in Berlin. In 1932 Woolf's father, industry pioneer C. M. Woolf, had turned down the opportunity to help finance Korda's *Private Life of Henry VIII*. 'It's easy to be wise in retrospect,' Sir John Woolf recalled, 'but, at that time, costume films were disastrous. Louis B. Mayer used to say that he'd never make a film where they write with a feather.'[26]

John Woolf was not making a cold call on Korda. He had successfully distributed Woolf's *Moulin Rouge* (1953) in Germany through Deutsche-London Films and Woolf needed German marks to produce *I Am a Camera*. He went into Korda's Piccadilly office to discuss an advance of Deutsch-marks against the distribution of the film and came out having agreed to invest £500,000 in Korda's next four films: *A Kid for Two Farthings* (1955), *Summer Madness* (1955), *Richard III* (1956) and *Storm Over the Nile* (1956), a remake of *The Four Feathers*. Nevertheless, Woolf negotiated a 'tight deal' with Korda. All four films were cross-collateralised and Woolf got his money out first before the films went into profit.

John Woolf and his brother, James, were brought up in an atmosphere heavy with film talk and action. John started work for his father's original company, W & F Film Service, which in 1927 was absorbed by the newly formed Gaumont-British Picture Corporation and became Gaumont-British Film Distributors (GBFD). Woolf's father became managing director of Gaumont-British Picture Corporation, but left to form General Film Distributors (GFD) with part financial backing from J. Arthur Rank and Lord Portal. John Woolf was general sales manager of GFD until the Second World War, after which he returned to GFD as joint managing director following his father's death in 1942.

In 1948 he left to form Romulus Films as a holding company for a new film distribution company, Independent Film Distributors (IFD), which distributed its films through British Lion and Lion International overseas. Independent Film Distributors financed all the films it distributed through British Lion and paid all distribution costs, including prints and advertising, which enabled British Lion to distribute films at a low cost to IFD and gave it an important line-up of product. The films were financed 70 per cent by guarantees from IFD, 20 per cent from the National Film Finance Corporation and 10 per cent from Romulus Films.

Unfortunately, a dearth of good films from the various independent producers led to Independent Film Distributors losing most of its capital. It was never Woolf's intention to go into production, but so serious was his position that he had no alternative but to produce his own films. Under the umbrella of British Lion, Romulus Films, guided by the Woolf brothers, was to produce a string of high-quality successful films. Romulus financed its own films as an independent through Lloyds Bank against personal guarantees from the company's directors.

It was the McCarthy witch-hunts in America that led to the first Romulus production in 1950. Joseph McCarthy's infamous witch-hunt of alleged communists in America sent shock waves through Hollywood. The Woolf brothers, aware of the mayhem caused by the Un-American Activities Committee, sensed that some of Hollywood's production could be enticed to London. James was sent to America to see what might be available. He made a deal with director Albert Lewin to bring James Mason and Ava Gardner to London to make a film that had been cancelled by MGM because of the McCarthy influence. *Pandora and the Flying Dutchman* was produced at Shepperton Studios and, although not very successful, it enabled Romulus to recover its investment and subsequently to make a number of Anglo-American productions.

Alexander Korda had taken an avuncular interest in John Woolf, but

Pandora and the Flying Dutchman *(Albert Lewin, 1951)*

when he heard that *The African Queen* (1951) was to be the next film for Romulus, he begged Woolf not to make it. 'You will go broke. You can't make a film about two old people going up and down a river in Africa with a director whose last picture was a disaster.'[27] By that time John Huston had started the film. If *The African Queen* had failed, Romulus Films would have failed with it. But the film was a great success, securing an Oscar for Best Actor for Humphrey Bogart and nominations for Katharine Hepburn, John Huston and scriptwriter James Agee.

Huston was persuaded to stay in London to make *Moulin Rouge* (1952) and *Beat the Devil* (1953) for Romulus at Shepperton. The latter film was less successful, but *Moulin Rouge* received three Oscars for Colour Photography, Art Direction and Costume Design. Under a deal with Columbia, Romulus later brought Joan Crawford to Shepperton for *The Story of Esther Costello* (1957), directed by David Miller.

Concentrating mainly on British films, Romulus stunned British audiences in 1959 with *Room at the Top*, directed by Jack Clayton. This was the first British adult film to receive an 'X' certificate from the British Board of Film Censors, a classification Woolf did not welcome. The BBFC insisted on this classification in order to show that the 'X' certificate, which replaced the 'H' (for horror) certificate in 1951, could also apply to adult themes. To test this theory, *Room at the Top* was tried out before an audience in the Bruce Grove cinema in Tottenham, North London, where a horror double-bill – *Frankenstein* and *Dracula* – was being shown. *Dracula* was pulled out for one night and *Room at the Top* substituted. It was a

81

disaster. Everyone connected with the film feared the worst when it was generally released, but after its premiere at London's Plaza Cinema *Room at the Top* went on to be a major success, receiving two Oscars for Best Actress (Simone Signoret) and Best Screenplay (Neil Paterson).

In his book *What the Censor Saw*, John Trevelyan, Chief British Film Censor for thirteen years, commented:

> In retrospect one can see that Jack Clayton's *Room at the Top*, made in 1958, was a milestone in the history of British films and in a way a milestone in the history of British film censorship. Up to this time the cinema, with rare exceptions, had presented a fantasy world; this film dealt with real people and real problems. At the time its sex scenes were regarded as sensational and some of the critics who praised the film congratulated the Board on having had the courage to pass it. Ten years later these scenes seemed very mild and unsensational. Even in 1958 I found it difficult to understand what had justified the congratulations and even asked my colleagues at the Board whether we had missed anything. There was no nudity or simulated copulation, but there was rather more frankness about sexual relations in the dialogue than people had been used to.[28]

According to John Woolf, *Room at the Top* came about when he was watching the BBC's *Panorama* programme on television one night:

> Woodrow Wyatt was talking about a book read by a group of housewives and written by their librarian in Bradford, who was John Braine. They said it sounded quite exciting, so I got a pre-publication copy the next day and we bought the film rights very cheaply for £5,000. Of course, it hadn't been published and was quite a risk. Then John Braine wrote the sequel, *Life at the Top*, and we paid him a much fairer price for that.[29]

The film's younger leads, Laurence Harvey and Heather Sears, were under contract to Romulus but Woolf wanted Vivien Leigh to play the older woman. She was unavailable and since both he and his co-producer, his brother James, considered that there was no other comparable actress at the time in Britain, they introduced a foreign actress, Simone Signoret, rewriting the script to accommodate her role.

For lighting cameraman Freddie Francis, *Room at the Top* was the first of his 'kitchen sink' dramas, followed by *Saturday Night and Sunday Morning* (1960), directed by Karel Reisz, and *Sons and Lovers* (1960), directed by Jack Cardiff (for which Francis received an American Academy Award for Best Cinematography, Black and White). Francis had entered the industry in 1933 and, after a seven-year period in the army, joined Korda at Shepperton, working in the camera department:

> In those days, it was a huge camera department. I suppose we thought the industry was going to take off and so Korda got as many people as possible under contract. We didn't make a lot of films, but we got very good at football as we seemed to play that most of the time.[30]

Francis' career took off with The Archers (Michael Powell and Emeric Pressburger), and when their production output was reduced he continued as a camera operator with John Huston, working on *Moulin Rouge* and *Beat the Devil*. After photographing Huston's second-unit material for *Moby Dick* (1956), as well as the film's model work in the Elstree tank, he returned to Shepperton for his first feature as Director of Photography, *A Hill in Korea* (1956), for producer Ian Dalrymple. After Dalrymple's company, Wessex Productions, folded a year later, Francis was asked by Jack Clayton to photograph *Room at the Top*:

> I'd known Jack for many years. We were quite good friends. He used to run the film side of Romulus. John and Jimmy Woolf got the money, but Jack was really the producer. He was always giving me their second unit photography and then came *Room at the Top*. By this time, one got the feeling at Shepperton that all they wanted to do was make films. I'm quite sure that Korda created that atmosphere. The people working there were now making films all the time. It was a wonderful atmosphere.[31]

The success of *Room at the Top* and the whole programme of Romulus Films up to that time enabled John Woolf to buy out, at a profit, the NFFC's interest in the films they had helped to finance.

Jack Clayton had been production executive for Romulus at Shepperton before John Woolf gave him the opportunity to direct the Oscar-winning short *The Bespoke Overcoat* (1955), which was made for around £3,000. After *Room at the Top*, Clayton was offered other films by Romulus, which he was unable to make. He made *The Innocents* at Shepperton in 1961.

John Woolf had his biggest success with *Oliver!* (1968). Woolf had bought the matching rights to Lionel Bart's stage musical from Donald Albery, who had staged the original show, giving him the right to match any offer made. An offer was made by John Bryan and his partners to film *Oliver!* Woolf was in Cannes showing Clayton's *The Pumpkin Eater* (1964) when he received a telegram confirming Bryan's offer and his right to match it, which he did immediately. Lionel Bart refused to accept Woolf's offer, claiming that he had not matched Bryan's offer because Bryan had Peter Sellers lined up to play Fagin. Woolf countered by claiming that he could get anyone he wanted and the argument ended up in court for three days, at the end of which Woolf won the right to film *Oliver!*

James Woolf, sent to California to sign Julie Andrews, died from a heart attack. Having signed Ron Moody and Harry Secombe for the film, John Woolf suffered a further setback when the film's director, Lewis Gilbert, was pre-empted by his then contract with Paramount, leaving Woolf without a director three weeks before shooting was to begin. His inspired solution to his problem was Carol Reed. Woolf recalled:

> A musical is like making three films at once. We had Carol directing the actors, American Johnny Green doing all the music and Canadian Onna White the choreography. It's quite a thing to keep them all together. After all, none of us knew how to make a musical, but *Oliver!* was a great

Oliver! *(Carol Reed, 1967)*

success. We had wonderful weather at Shepperton, came in on budget and on time and it was one of those happy films to make.[32]

Oliver! received five Oscars for Best Picture, Best Direction, Best Musical Score, Best Sound and Best Art Direction, and a Special Award for Choreography for which there was then no Oscar category.

Between them, John and James Woolf left a legacy of films which include *The L-Shaped Room* (Bryan Forbes, 1962), *The Pumpkin Eater* (Jack Clayton, 1964), *King Rat* (Bryan Forbes, 1965), all produced by James; and *Oliver!, Day of the Jackal* (Fred Zinnemann, 1973), *No Sex, Please, We're British* (Cliff Owen, 1973) and *The Odessa File* (Ronald Neame, 1974), all produced by John.

John Woolf has fond memories both of Shepperton Studios and of Alexander Korda:

He was a great character. I lunched with him a couple of weeks before he died. After making the four films I was involved with, he used to ring me up and say he'd sent me a cheque and he'd made a bad deal with me. I would ask why he wasn't pleased to have a satisfied partner. He said that he wasn't because he'd never had one before. He was always very nice to me. He was the most brilliant man who has ever been in British film production.[33]

Korda's last programme of films made at Shepperton, before his death from a heart attack in January 1956, was ambitious and successful. He knew that

British films had to be exportable. In the 1950s, a British film had to earn at the box-office in the UK and from the rest of the world six to seven times its initial cost just to break even for the producer.

Five of the six directors involved with this programme of films were all previous Korda associates who remained loyal to him, as did the technicians and stars of the films. The films were as diverse as the talent involved. In 1955, Carol Reed directed *A Kid for Two Farthings*, David Lean directed *Summer Madness*, Terence Young directed *Storm Over the Nile* (using much action footage from Zoltan Korda's original *The Four Feathers*, and for which Alexander Korda paid £20,000), and Anatole Litvak, whose American films included *The Snake Pit* (1948) and *Sorry, Wrong Number* (1948), directed Rattigan's *The Deep Blue Sea*.

In 1949, Korda had encouraged Laurence Olivier to set up his own production company which, in association with London Films, produced Olivier's *Richard III* (1956), a worthy successor to his two other Shakespeare films, *Henry V* (1945) and *Hamlet* (1949). Also in 1956 Anthony Kimmins directed *Smiley*, which was shot entirely on location in Australia, supporting Korda's interest in producing films in foreign locations.

Korda was the first British producer to respond to the technical challenge provided by the wide-screen revolution. Three of his last six pictures, *Smiley*, *Storm Over the Nile* and *The Deep Blue Sea*, were filmed in CinemaScope, developed by 20th Century-Fox, and *Richard III* tried out Paramount's rival system, VistaVision. Korda pioneered the pre-sell principle of film financing when he pre-sold *Richard III* to American network NBC Television for $500,000. In 1948 he had sold twenty-four of his films to the New York Television station WIPX. In another interview, he predicted the widespread use of cable television and home box office 'devices'.

After death duties of £158,160, Korda left an estate worth £385,684. This surprised many people in the industry. As Korda had wheeled and dealed in millions of pounds and dollars over many years, it was thought his estate would be larger. David Cunnynghame, Harold Boxall and Korda's brothers Vincent and Zoltan were named as executors. They were instructed to pay £10,000 to Korda's son Peter, £2,000 to his first wife Maria, and £500 to his chauffeur Ernest Bailey. One quarter of the remainder of his estate and all Korda's personal belongings were to go to his then wife, Alexa.

No special provisions were made for preserving London Films. Korda's shares in it and his other companies and interests were liquidated on behalf of the estate, more or less guaranteeing that the London Films group of companies would cease to exist. However, today London Films is owned by a group of Swedish shareholders and the UK Leisure Group, Wembley plc, owners of London's Wembley Stadium. When Korda died, he had been negotiating a multi-picture deal with Columbia, who had already advanced him £15,000 for the script of *Arms and the Man*, supervised by Peter Glenville who was to direct the film. Korda was dissatisfied with the script and paid back the advance.

Korda once said:

> The job of the film-maker is to entertain as many people as possible. The
> questions of raising tastes and education are there too – but they are

asides. Entertainment counts and it is the most difficult thing of all. You can affect an audience three ways – you can make them laugh, make them cry and make them sit forward in their seats with excitement. You should never degrade them. We are in the show business now and we come from the fairground and the fairground barker. The barkers may have worn chequered coats and crude colours, while we are more elegant. But, never forget, we are the same. It is show business – and we should make it a good show![34]

Perhaps Alexander Korda and his work, both inside and outside Shepperton Studios, are best summarised by his choice of the Houses of Parliament clock, Big Ben, for the trademark of London Films. Big Ben was a monument known throughout the world, and in 1932, when the decision was made, Korda intended to be known throughout the world. But why did Big Ben always strike eleven in his films? Korda maintained: 'That was when the sun happened to come out. We'd waited three hours to get that shot.'[35] Whether true or not, it is the reply of a showman.

Notes

1. Author's interview with Sidney Gilliat, 27 February 1993.
2. Author's interview with Sir John Clark, 27 January 1993.
3. Harold Dunham. *The Life and Times of G.B. (Bertie) Samuelson*. Research document (unpublished).
4. *Sixty Voices*, edited by Brian McFarlane (London: BFI Publishing, 1992).
5. Ibid.
6. Pamphlet published by the ACT, 1939.
7. Report published in *Film and TV Technician*, May/June 1941.
8. National Film Finance Corporation Annual Report for year ended 31 March 1950.
9. Ibid.
10. Author's interview with Wilfred Moeller, 30 November 1991.
11. Author's interview with Sidney Gilliat.
12. Author's interview with Kenneth Maidment, 28 January 1992.
13. *Sixty Voices*.
14. National Film Finance Corporation Annual Report for year ended 31 March 1951 (extract from published letter from the NFFC Chairman to the President of the Board of Trade, 12 January 1951).
15. Ibid.
16. Ibid.
17. National Film Finance Corporation Annual Report for year ended 31 March 1954.
18. National Film Finance Corporation Annual Report for year ended 31 March 1972.
19. Karol Kulik, *Alexander Korda, The Man Who Could Work Miracles* (London: W. H. Allen, 1975).
20. Ibid.
21. *Sixty Voices*.
22. Ronald Haver, *David O. Selznick's Hollywood* (USA: Bonanza Books, 1985).
23. Michael Korda, *Charmed Lives* (New York: Allen Lane, 1979).
24. Ibid.
25. Author's interview with Sidney Gilliat, 27 February 1993.
26. Author's interview with Sir John Woolf, 12 August 1992.
27. Ibid.
28. John Trevelyan, *What the Censor Saw* (London: Michael Joseph, 1973).

29. Author's interview with Sir John Woolf.
30. Author's interview with Freddie Francis, 26 February 1993.
31. Ibid.
32. Author's interview with Sir John Woolf.
33. Ibid.
34. Korda, *Charmed Lives*.
35. Paul Tabori, *Alexander Korda* (London: Oldbourne Book Co., 1959).

4

LIFE AFTER KORDA

A Receiver's responsibility is to collect as much money as he can for a company's creditors and shareholders. Often the best way to achieve this is to allow the business to carry on working under his control. He takes responsibilities for any liabilities that arise after the Receivership, but prior liabilities are frozen while the Receiver does what he can to pay off the creditors. As the British Lion Studio Company, like its failed parent company the British Lion Film Corporation, was a public company, the Receiver allowed it to continue trading under that name, but in 1954, when the Receiver was appointed, British Lion was left without a nominal leader. The NFFC, which had never had anything directly to do with the daily operation of production, distribution or studio administration, had made no provision for any successor to Korda, or for any continuing production programme. According to Sidney Gilliat: 'Having wielded the axe, they found themselves having to rush forward to try to stop the trees hitting the ground. Indeed, those of us filming British Lion productions were warned that we might be in contempt of court if we carried on shooting.'[1]

The chairman of the NFFC at this time was Sir John Keeling (appointed on 28 July 1954), an industrialist with no experience in films but with a lively mind. A new company, British Lion Films Limited, was formed and an attempt was made to 'kick-start' it by putting in £600,000 of public money as capital and valuing the rights in the films already made on favourable (conservative) terms, bearing in mind the substantial tax loss against which profits could be charged. Then in September 1955 Lion International Films was formed under the joint ownership of British Lion Films and Independent Film Distributors Limited, to handle overseas distribution of those companies' films.

Sidney Gilliat recalled that while production continued on an ad hoc basis (with Korda unofficially making recommendations and providing ideas), Keeling appeared to have come to the conclusion that independent producers ought to have some kind of say. To that end he arranged two or three meetings, to which people like Launder and Gilliat were invited, to discuss the future of British Lion. Gilliat thought it likely that, had Keeling been able to continue with this task, a structure might have emerged and producers might have appeared soon afterwards on the British Lion Films Board. Unfortunately, on the very evening a large dinner had been laid on at the Ritz in London for producers and other film industry people, Keeling suffered a severe stroke and Sir Arthur Jarratt had to chair the meeting in his place. In such circumstances, no progress could be made and the idea of creating a consortium of producers foundered with the appointment on 20 June 1955 of Keeling's successor, Sir Nutcombe Hume, who also had no previous experience in the film world. In Gilliat's words, 'Nutcombe Hume was not so much a bull in a china shop as a mad elephant in a porcelain factory.'[2]

When Korda died in January 1956, British Lion was left altogether leaderless, although technically Jarratt continued as Head of British Lion Films to preside over a programme of films. It was hardly surprising that the new company did not flourish, even though Jarratt hired others to help him with decisions.

According to Wilfred Moeller, the only financial loser from the British Lion Film Corporation collapse was the National Film Finance Corporation, but he maintains that they recovered around £1.5 million over the following year or two and that all the other creditors, including the banks, were eventually paid. In those circumstances, the NFFC was now determined to keep a tight hold on the studio management[3] (which according to Gilliat they never did at any time after Douglas Collins resigned as Chairman both of the NFFC and of the studio).[4]

On 16 March 1955 the managing director of the NFFC (from February 1954), David Kingsley, was appointed a director of the studio company. With the resignation of Sir Arthur Jarratt in December 1957 (when he became President of the Kinematograph Renters' Society), Kingsley was appointed managing director of the studio from 1 January 1958. On 31 March 1958 another NFFC appointment saw Douglas Collins, a director of the NFFC from June 1955, replace Harold Drayton. Following Kingsley's appointment, Korda's original Board directors resigned (Vincent Korda had already resigned on 31 March 1953). Sir Arthur Jarratt resigned on 14 December 1957, David Cunnynghame on 31 March 1958 and Harold Boxall on 11 August 1959.

At the time, the share capital of British Lion Films was one million £1 shares and the company financed the 'A', 'B', 'C' and 'D' stage modernisation, secured by a second debenture. The company's net assets at 31 March 1957 were £912,330 and a profit was made for that year of £17,228. The following year saw a loss of £337,114, with a further loss of £153,354 being recorded for the year ended 31 March 1959.

In 1958 the composition of the British Lion Films Board of Directors changed, to include film-makers again, with the appointment of Sidney Gilliat on 31 March. Over the next eleven years, Gilliat was to be joined on the Board at various times by fellow film-makers Roy Boulting (22 January 1961 to 22 April 1964 and 31 August 1966 to 2 June 1972); John Boulting (7 December 1967 to 31 December 1972); Frank Launder (27 November 1969 to 23 June 1972); Hal Mason, an American who had been with Ealing Films since 1940 (22 April 1964 to 31 August 1966) and Italian-born producer Joseph Janni (22 April 1964 to 4 October 1967). Gilliat's appointment arose out of an NFFC report in 1957 which had effectively invited offers for the studio. Launder and Gilliat had been quietly working without interruption at Shepperton and, since the expiry of their original contract, had made (or, in one case, sponsored) five films, four of them for British Lion: *The Belles of St. Trinian's* (1954); *Geordie* (1955); *The Green Man* (1956); and *The Smallest Show On Earth* (1957), with producer/director team Michael Relph and Basil Dearden – all of them successful.

As a director of British Lion Films from 1958 to 1972 and Chairman of Shepperton Studios from 1961, Sidney Gilliat is best placed to record the sequence of events following that NFFC report:

> No one noticed this rather muted announcement concerning the possible sale of the studio. So Nut and his unmerry men found themselves without an offer, which would explain why a circuitous approach was made by a director of the NFFC to us, through our agent Christopher Mann. This approach advised us, in effect, that the company was for sale and that Frank [Launder] and I would be acceptable as purchasers. So far as we were concerned, this came at us out of the blue. Since Keeling's departure from the scene, little or nothing had been heard of the possibility of independent producers having a place on the British Lion Board. Yet now the company was being offered to the partnership of two producers with, initially, no mention of anybody else.[5]

The choice of Launder and Gilliat was not in itself remarkable since they had worked almost exclusively for British Lion since 1948 and had produced some ten or eleven pictures, of which seven had been profitable and over half developed from their own original stories. Both of them also had considerable experience of co-production of studio programmes and, to some extent, studio administration at Islington, Shepherd's Bush and Pinewood.

At first, they could scarcely believe the proposition that had been put to them, but if they were to dismiss it out of hand it was likely that British Lion would fade away and there might well be no independent middle-ground for British-financed production. Launder and Gilliat therefore decided to pursue the opportunity further:

> We agreed to investigate the possibilities on the condition that we advised certain colleagues of the progress of negotiations since, obviously, it would be both impractical and improper for us to try to take control of the company on our own. Interestingly, while the NFFC agreed to our consulting likely partners in the scheme, they at no time insisted, as they certainly ought to have done, on the necessity for bringing in other talents (as del Giudice used to call them).
>
> Rather to our surprise, matters advanced quite rapidly. Our representatives secured for us the promise of sufficient capital to purchase British Lion and an acceptable Chairman to go with it. Terms were agreed to buy out Arthur Jarratt and I think there is little doubt that the venture might well have gone ahead had not the British Lion results (with which, of course, our advisers had to be supplied) worsened every time they were put forward. Eventually, the financial picture of British Lion had declined so much in so short a time that our prospective Chairman's accountants advised him not to proceed. During these negotiations and discussions we never went so far as to discuss what

arrangements we ourselves might have with the company, had we been able to take it over. Our motives were, really, simple survival. It was pointed out to us and we agreed with it, that without British Lion we might have nowhere to go in this country, certainly nowhere where we could be independent. I suppose we imagined that if the deal had gone through we would have continued to make films, as in the past, on much the same basis.[6]

Unfortunately, it now looked as if not only had the chance of reconstructing British Lion Films departed but the whole future of the company was in doubt, with increasing losses the order of the day. Nothing happened for some weeks, then a fresh approach was made to Launder and Gilliat and to the Boultings at the same time. The deal offered was clearly a gamble, and not apparently a very good one.

For a very modest, indeed nominal, salary we were to join the Boards of British Lion Films and the studio and continue to make films, as well as help manage the companies. For the films, we would receive no production fees and no share in the profits other than in the event that two successive pictures collateralised showed an overall profit, in which case we would receive a modest percentage. As an inducement to increase the value of our association with British Lion a class of Deferred Shares would be issued, for which we would subscribe. If the affairs of the company improved, then so would the value of those shares. At the time I must confess that, speaking personally, I thought we would be mad to accept such an arrangement since the affairs of the company were definitely going downhill. The situation looked even worse when we saw some of the films awaiting release and looked at the latest figures.

John Woolf was also invited on to the Board at that time, though on a different basis. He left after a short time, apparently on some point of principle relating to the purchase of the shares. I have often wondered what he really thought of our prospects at that time.[7]

(Woolf says he left because he thought the purchase price to be paid to the NFFC for British Lion Films too low for a company in the public eye.)

Our pessimism was, however, confined to the past. The future looked more promising, and indeed proved so. This view was not shared by the NFFC, who produced a report on the prospects which was extremely downbeat and recommended an early sale of the company. (How the future could be judged when the new team had only been in position for a few months still totally baffles me.) As we were never allowed to read the report itself, I cannot comment further on its prognostications, except to remark that they were all wrong! On the strength of that report, we were told that unless we bought the company within a short space of time it would be offered to anyone who would care to buy it. In spite of our protests, this sort of harassment continued over the following eighteen months. Eventually we resumed some of our old contacts and managed to secure the promise of enough capital to cover the asking price, but the usual delays occurred when accountants and lawyers began drafting all the documents. Nearly a year had passed before the deal was complete.[8]

For once Launder and Gilliat found themselves in agreement with the NFFC, both on price and structure. The package was then submitted to the Board of Trade for its approval and turned down flat, on the grounds that the prospects of the company had improved so much under the management of Launder and Gilliat that the price was no longer sufficient.

> We all felt that the position was now quite intolerable. Through a chance encounter with the then President of the Board of Trade, Reginald Maudling, we were able to arrange a meeting with him at the Board of Trade to try to reach some kind of solution. Rather to our surprise he accepted most of the points we had made, agreed to give a guarantee that the company would not be sold during the remainder of our contract, providing we all extended the latter to a six-year term. In addition, he agreed that we might appoint our own Chairman, both of British Lion Films and the studio.[9]

As a result David Kingsley became chairman, as well as managing director, of British Lion Films, and Sidney Gilliat became chairman of Shepperton. The company continued to trade prosperously until the end of the six-year period approached. Launder, Gilliat, the Boultings and Kingsley were then made to feel that it was their obligation to buy the company; in that respect they were back to square one. On the other hand, it was made painfully clear to them that, should they be able to buy the company at an agreed valuation, the government would never agree to retain a financial interest in it, however small.

> The problem of the five of us was that although we had undoubtedly, between us, rescued the company and made it profitable under the most adverse circumstances, it had been very hard work at a yearly salary which any second-rank film director would have turned down as a fee for one film [£7,500, including expenses]. Under managing director Andy Worker, Shepperton Studios had been reorganised and considerably re-equipped. We had the right to buy the company, but obviously could never afford to work again under the same conditions. Also Kingsley, for instance, did not wish to continue in his office after six hard years and the rest of us felt that it would be wrong to continue without further partners. In our view, which was expressed both to the Board of Trade and to Sir Nutcombe, we would be prepared to continue ourselves, perhaps on the basis of a consortium involving other producers and a partial buy-out of our shareholdings.
> I can see now that, from 1957 onwards, the sole notion possessing the NFFC and the Board of Trade was to get rid of the company practically anyhow, so long as they could get an agreed price for it, and I think this had become an article of faith with Nutcombe. Moreover, the Board of

Trade refused to maintain even a very small shareholding in the company in spite of our protestations that even a small presence gave us a psychological lever when dealing with the circuits and others. Nutcombe came back at a small lunch party with a scheme that astounded us. He suggested, in effect, that the consortium should consist of Rank and ABC, in addition to ourselves. We pointed out that this cut right across the conception of the NFFC supporting the independent producer. What is more, production could get completely stymied if, as was very likely, Rank or ABC turned down film projects that we had put on the table.

That meeting developed into a very heated one. Perhaps some of us spoke too frankly about the shortcomings of the NFFC and other matters. Certainly, from that date onwards Nut continued his talks with David Kingsley and would not meet us. We did not wish to buy the company without the guarantee we had asked for, so they suddenly bought us out overnight and agreed to sell the company on immediately to Sydney Box, all of this coming conveniently as Parliament was on the brink of adjourning for the Christmas season. We insisted on seeing the Board of the NFFC and learned, at that meeting, that Box's was the selected bid. We felt this was outrageous and organised Questions in the House, public statements and so on, which eventually resulted in a general invitation from the government to any interested bodies to form groups to bid for the company on the understanding that the tax loss would be diverted to the NFFC by way of their single share and that the government would not renew their stake in the company. Between ourselves and Michael Balcon, we set up a group which was the only survivor among the contending parties, in fact the only group that would accept the special provisions and, on the last day, the only one left in the field. The NFFC appointed a director to the Board of the new British Lion Films as a representative of the single share, but after a year or two he ceased to attend.[10]

They had quite a successful period, in spite of the increasingly adverse trade conditions. During the latter half of the 1960s, American-financed productions were disappearing fast and Shepperton was having problems filling studio space. At the turn of the decade a scheme was devised for a reverse take-over by Star Theatres, which came to nothing. Meanwhile Barclay Securities, under John Bentley, stepped in with an offer which, as the new British Lion had become a public company, had to be recommended to the shareholders.

Whatever the ups and downs and frustrations of those fourteen-odd years, from early 1958 and into 1973 (because we were still looking after productions in the finishing stage after the Barclay Securities takeover in 1972), we and our colleagues had rescued an undoubtedly dying concern and given it a dozen or so years of prosperity and good management. The way the accounts were looking at the end of 1957, British Lion Films could have had little chance of surviving more than another eighteen months and I don't think this can be denied.[11]

By 1955, when the NFFC took over the running of the studio through the appointment of their own representatives to the British Lion Films Board, the old British Lion Film Corporation had ceased to pay interest on its loans from 21 May 1954 and from 1 October 1954 had been granted relief by the Cinematograph Film Production (Special Loans) Act 1954. However, the NFFC still had to pay interest to the Board of Trade in respect of accumulated losses in previous years.

Meanwhile yet another threat to British cinema was gathering pace. Commercial television was launched in September 1955 and there were now over four and a half million television receivers in the UK. Cinema admissions per week had plunged from the 1945 average of 31.4 million to 22.7 million. Ten years later, television's eclipse of cinema dramatically increased with 13.6 million television receivers in the UK, reducing the average cinema admissions per week to only 6.3 million.

Despite this reduction of interest in cinema-going by the British public, a new viewing theatre and twelve more cutting rooms were built at the studio in 1957, and in 1958 stages 'A', 'B', 'C' and 'D' were closed and modernised with increased height and overhead suspension of lighting. At an Extraordinary General Meeting on 22 October 1958, a Special Resolution of the British Lion Studio Company Limited changed the company name to Shepperton Studios Limited. This took effect from 29 October 1958, 95.8 per cent of the ordinary share capital being owned by British Lion Films Limited.

Throughout the 1950s, in addition to the output of regular producers such as Korda, John and James Woolf, the Boultings and Launder and Gilliat, many other films representing a wide cross-section of independent production were made. They included *The Wooden Horse* (Jack Lee, 1950); *The Mudlark* (Jean Negulesco, 1950); *The Gift Horse* (Compton Bennett, 1951); *The Intruder* (Guy Hamilton, 1953); *The Colditz Story* (Guy Hamilton, 1954); *Raising a Riot* (Wendy Toye, 1955); *Town on Trial* (John Guillermin, 1956); *A Hill in Korea* (Julian Amyes, 1956); *A King in New York* (Charles Chaplin, 1957); *Bonjour Tristesse* and *Saint Joan* (Otto Preminger, 1957); *Orders to Kill* (Anthony Asquith, 1958); *The Horse's Mouth* (Ronald Neame, 1958); *The Mouse That Roared* (Jack Arnold, 1959); *The Mummy* (Terence Fisher, 1959); *Our Man in Havana* (Carol Reed, 1959); *The Angry Silence* (Guy Green, 1960) and *Suddenly Last Summer* (Joseph Mankiewicz, 1960). It was this last film that gave Sydney Samuelson one of his most fearsome experiences:

> In 1959, I was a documentary cameraman shooting a film about Sam Spiegel, who had finally been pinned down by the director at Shepperton Studios with his Oscar-winning cameraman, Jack Hildyard. They were shooting *Suddenly Last Summer* and had just finished on a gigantic 'exterior' set on a sound stage. Designed by Oliver Messel, this huge set had trees, lake, exotic flora, a bridge across the water, all stretching as far as the eye could see, but was no longer lit as it was about to be broken down.
>
> I looked at the set, contemplated my 16mm sound-on-film Auricon camera, looked at the forest of arcs and 'inkies' suspended above and

decided it was time to seek expertise. The legendary 'gaffer' Maurice Gillette was working with Jack, so I asked if he would help me 'light the set' prior to Mr Spiegel turning up. Perceptively, I had decided that my own electrical facility (one man plus a kit of four little Colortrans) was probably not up to it. Maurice was not too happy about bailing out Sydney Samuelson and his miserable set of Colortrans, but wandered across to help me in my time of great need. In the vastness of this huge set, he said the following absolutely terrifying words, which have been imprinted in the part of my brain that handles frightening experiences ever since. 'Up there, mate, we have awaiting for you forty 5K's, forty 120 arcs, twenty 170's and six brutes. Where would you like to start?'[12]

The Angry Silence (1959) was a remarkable film for its time. It epitomised the true spirit of independent film-making in Britain and the courage and resilience of those involved with its production. Richard Attenborough (now Lord Attenborough) and Bryan Forbes were convinced that the original story by Michael Craig and his brother Richard Gregson had to be filmed. Despite its controversial subject of a man being 'sent to Coventry' by his workmates for refusing to continue supporting a strike, the film was finally made after Attenborough had persuaded everyone concerned to work for scale salary with a promise of more to come from the picture's profits.

At the time, Attenborough was unhappy with the direction being taken by the British film industry and had consciously decided to give up acting for a time. After that decision he found Craig's story and persuaded Forbes to write the screenplay. He deliberately avoided the Boultings in his search for financial backing for the film as he didn't want to 'go back into the nest', but failed to arouse any other interest. Finally, in despair, he did go to British Lion, the Boultings and Launder and Gilliat who agreed to support him if the budget of £142,000 was reduced to £100,000.

Two and a half weeks before the picture started shooting, I still couldn't persuade any actor to play the part of Tom for nothing. After keeping us waiting for weeks, Kenny More eventually said no. So I played in *The Angry Silence* because I couldn't get anybody else to do it. It was lucky for me because it permitted me to do something that had the contemporary social awareness I wanted so desperately. *The Angry Silence* changed, for what it's worth, my acting career. It was perhaps the best thing Guy Green ever did, I think, and it had wonderful performances. Pier Angeli gives a devastating performance in it, and Bernard Lee ... what a wonderful actor that man was. It really was, I think, a beautifully made movie.[13]

Bryan Forbes recalled that he was attracted to the story and wanted to make it very tough.

Not the usual thing of treating the British workman as if he were the salt of the earth. I felt there were two sides to the thing. Afterwards, Dickie and I were much attacked by the unions. The film was blacklisted by the miners' union and we had threatening letters sent to us. To this day, some people have never forgiven us, but I felt the film was just as hard on management as unions. I made management seem absolutely crass because it didn't see what was coming. The whole philosophy of the film is that if you can't be different, you are nothing. It's a plea for the individual. The character supports the strike in the first instance, then thinks it's gone stupid, which so many of the strikes in those days did. I mean, the film industry was in anarchy as a result. *The Angry Silence* was the beginning of a partnership between Dickie and myself, which resulted ultimately in Allied Film Makers.... It still makes money. It cost £98,000 and has made about £200,000 profit [up to 1989]. Now that's not a vast profit ... However, if you more than double your initial cost, it's not bad in business terms.[14]

Harold Boxall died in August 1959. On 1 January 1960 Adrian (Andy) Worker, an experienced production man, was appointed Managing Director of Shepperton Studios. At the end of March he and his fellow directors were able to announce a small profit for the year 1959/60 of £8,379, compared to a loss of £27,191 in the previous year and £200,232 in 1957/58.

The fortunes of Shepperton Studios changed dramatically throughout the 1960s. From the end of March 1960, British Lion Films had concluded an agreement with the Film Industry Defence Organisation (FIDO) for the granting of covenants in order to limit the number of films being shown on UK television. Subsequent payment of an agreed price for television showings of these films was spread over a number of years, giving British Lion Films approximately £300,000. By the year ended 31 March 1960, British Lion Films was back in profit (£126,771) and was attracting more independent producers' films for distribution. Bryanston Films and Britannia Film Distributors distributed through British Lion, as did the newly formed Pax Films and Wessex Film Distributors.

In March 1961 British Lion Films entered into a joint agreement to share, through British Lion Columbia (BLC), the cost of distributing films with Columbia Pictures (this agreement terminated in 1972), which contributed to the big increase in production at the studio in the early 1960s. Early in 1961, the resignation of Douglas Collins as Chairman of British Lion Films (and of Shepperton Studios since March 1958) saw a new management team created with the appointment of David Kingsley as Chairman of British Lion Films and Sidney Gilliat as Chairman of Shepperton Studios. John Terry, who had been the NFFC's solicitor in 1949, then its Secretary, and from January 1958 Managing Director, was appointed as a director of British Lion Films to represent the NFFC.

With British Lion's income from FIDO contributing to a profit of £576,800 (£316,610 of which came from FIDO) for the year ended 31 March 1961, this was the beginning of a boom period for Shepperton.

In 1950, the American government used existing Anti-Trust laws to break up the combined production, distribution and exhibition of films by integrated companies. The Hollywood majors lost their direct financial involvement in cinema ownership and, with this, their incentive to mass-produce films for exhibition in cinemas they no longer controlled. Up to 1950, Hollywood's annual turnover of features was between 350 and 500. Between 1952 and 1962, production declined from 278 features in 1952 to 211 in 1960 and 138 in 1962, largely because of the growing appeal of television.

A consequence was to increase the importance of independent producers, who often chose to work in foreign studios, such as those in Italy, Spain and Britain, where production costs were much lower. Between 1941 and 1961 the average cost for the Hollywood film rose threefold and costs continued to rise sharply during the 60s. It was hardly surprising that so many of the American independent producers moved to Europe.

In 1960, Stanley Kubrick ventured that 'the source of the supremacy of the majors was their power to make money. When they stopped making money, they sent for the independent producers.'[15] Other factors contributing to the rise of the independents were the successful court cases brought in 1960 by the Writers' Guild of America (Screen Section), who staged a strike in January for more equitable contracts and a share of profits from films sold to television, and by the Screen Actors' Guild of America, who in March demanded a raise in minimum salaries and a share of television residuals. Subsequently the studios became administrative centres organising finance and distribution, and the independent producer became the rule rather than the exception.

The fall-out from the McCarthy witch-hunt also led to some American independent film-makers leaving Hollywood for Europe, mainly because they were 'blacklisted' by the Un-American Activities Committee. Those who subsequently went to Britain included Carl Foreman and Joseph Losey, both of whom were to make major contributions to the development of Shepperton Studios. A second wave of American film-makers, including Stanley Kubrick, Joseph Strick, Charles Schneer, David Rose and Hal Wallis, came to Britain in the early 60s because they preferred to make films in the UK. Between 1960 and 1970, American financial investment virtually took over British production to the extent that over 90 per cent of capital tied up in production was American.

In the year 1960/61, a profit of £54,298 was announced by Shepperton Studios, but the new chairman, Sidney Gilliat (appointed in February 1961), warned that 'profitable studio operation is still dependent to a considerable extent on the continuance of American-sponsored production in this country and, secondly, that too much of our business is seasonal'.[16]

The latter problem was highlighted in 1960, when an almost unprecedented rush for studio space at Shepperton in the summer meant that some productions had to be turned away. Unfortunately, the reverse occurred during the following winter, causing Gilliat to comment rather testily:

There is really no good reason for the apparent tendency of the film-making season to become progressively shorter and every effort is being made to point out to producers the advantages, from their point of view, as well as ours, of spreading the load more evenly throughout the year, when, undoubtedly, we would be able to give them the benefit of special rates and even better service. The extension of the busy season by even as little as a month at either end could radically alter the position for the better and might even prevent the distressingly recurrent seasonal redundancies which plague studio operations in this country.[17]

In 1960, eighty-two first features were produced in the UK from twelve studios in use from the seventeen available, supplying over 3,000 cinemas operating in the UK. By July 1962, Shepperton Studios had a postwar high of 1,116 employees. Despite the high volume of production at the studio, this figure dropped dramatically to a mere 226 employees by September 1963, though by August 1966 it had climbed again to 315.

To cope with the rapid upsurge in production during the early 60s, the studio management, led by 'Andy' Worker, introduced in 1961 a series of improvements to the studio facilities. A new post-synch, music effects and dubbing theatre (RCA) was built alongside the scoring stage (today, stage 'L') and new wardrobe departments were provided for each block of stages ('A'/'B', 'C'/'D' and 'E'/'F'/'G'). The North Office Block, near the studio main gate, was reopened with eight extra offices, and more offices were created from rooms previously used for storage in the Old House. A new camera maintenance department and new cameras were provided and all sound channels were rebuilt, with two new ones added. The 'Robin Hood' stage (123 × 56 ft) – so-called because virtually all 165 episodes of the television series *Robin Hood*, for Sapphire Films and starring Richard Greene, were shot there – was bought from Walton Studios to become 'I' stage, and a new car park was built.

The studio restaurant was redesigned and a new bar, 'The British Lion', was opened. Sir Winston Churchill, no doubt remembering his past association with Korda, granted permission for his portrait to be used for the pub sign designed by art director Maurice Carter. The pub was officially opened by Bing Crosby, Bob Hope and Joan Collins when they were making *The Road to Hong Kong* (1961), directed by Norman Panama for United Artists.

At this time the studio suffered two fires, one destroying the general stores, plasterers' and paint shop. This setback was turned to advantage when rebuilding provided additional facilities of signwriters and art departments.

Arguably the most controversial development at the studio was the building of two new stages, 'J' and 'K', respectively 80 × 36 ft and 36 × 35 ft. The old stable block and clock-tower, whose history was so closely linked to the Old House, and the restaurant and bar in the Old House were demolished to make way for the two new stages. The adjoining conservatory, in which were shot the first films made at the studio, was and still is preserved as a reminder of those early days. The new stages were built specifically for 'tests' and the production of television commercials and series, reflecting the growing importance of television production.

In 1962 a new trademark for the studio was introduced, a symbol of continuity and growing vitality. These two elements were represented by the summer house, which has stood in the grounds of Shepperton since the days of King William IV and where Lady Caroline Wood helped the

The new pub sign being unveiled by Bing Crosby, Joan Collins and Bob Hope when making The Road to Hong Kong *(Melvin Frank, 1961)*

monarch find distraction from the affairs of state, and Shepperton's famous cedar of Lebanon, by then over 400 years old.

Also in 1962, Sidney Gilliat was able to announce increased profits of £114,032 for the preceding year, and for the first time for many years there were no seasonal redundancies at the studio. Profits rose again in 1962/63, enabling a dividend of 5 per cent to be paid to Ordinary Stockholders, who had received no payment since 1957. More important, after five years the deficit on the profit and loss account was transformed into a favourable balance of £22,998. Against this was an increasing trend for productions to require less space. Two pictures instead of one shooting on each production block effectively doubled the servicing required, but did not double the rent received.

Inevitably, the huge increase in production activity that had the studio working to capacity led to some mishaps. The most spectacular was the overnight collapse, prior to the first day's studio shooting, of a massive gun-cave set on the studio lot near the huge 'H' stage for *The Guns of Navarone* (1961, directed by J. Lee Thompson). For several days and nights, teams of riggers, carpenters, plasterers, electricians and prop-men worked round the clock to rebuild the huge set, victim of a heavy thunderstorm. Another mishap was a fire caused by a cannon accidentally backfiring on a gun-deck set during a sea-battle sequence for *HMS Defiant* (1962, directed by Lewis Gilbert).

Indeed, such was the pace of production that people were damaged more often than the sets on which they worked. Peter Finch, who suffered a heart attack on a set for *The Pumpkin Eater* (1964), was one of several actors who needed treatment of some kind during this hectic period. The accident victims were either treated on site by the studio's indefatigable nurse, Audrey Price, or ferried to the local hospital in Ashford by studio chauffeurs Len Goodson and 'Tubby' Whitcombe.

Len and 'Tubby' were two of the many studio 'characters' who emerged from the production mayhem. They were employees of the Anchor Garage in Shepperton village square. Through a judicious arrangement between the garage proprietor, Rex Thorley, and the studio management, they were permanently based in the studio garage near the main gate (which at that time opened on to Squiresbridge Road), from which they were summoned by the studio operating office, run by Harold Taylor, whenever a car was needed for studio business. Occasionally this definition was stretched when the business was collecting a budding starlet from London for an 'audition' by one of the management's directors in a secret room in the roof of the Old House, or driving a paranoid Judy Garland fifty yards from one stage to the next so that she could avoid being seen by anyone off the set of *I Could Go On Singing* (Ronald Neame, 1963).

The Reverend Harold Ironmonger, Rector of Littleton Church near the studio main entrance, had become part of the studio scene, acting as religious adviser to many producers, especially John and Roy Boulting. Ironmonger almost always based his studio operations in the bar, and could be found dispensing alcohol-based goodwill at most end-of-picture parties.

Special effects boffin Ted Samuels, who created the magnificent severed hand for *The Hands of Orlac* (Edmond T. Greville, 1960), decided one day to test the effectiveness of the tiny batteries in each finger joint of the hand. In the studio canteen he lined up the hand with an unsuspecting secretary's lunch, murmured 'Kill!' and sat back to watch the hand slowly crawl along the table and into her plate. During the resulting hysterics, he nonchalantly picked up the hand, slid it into his pocket and strolled off.

Characters stalked the studio. To many, they seemed worse than the creatures Ray Harryhausen was painstakingly bringing to life for *Jason and the Argonauts* (Don Chaffey, 1963) and *The First Men in the Moon* (Nathan Juran, 1964). The 'terrible trio' were Jack Bolam, Charlie Hillier and John Cox, respectively in charge of construction, electrical and sound departments. At daily production meetings, these cantankerous old hands produced a host of reasons why a production manager's requirements could not be met, before being persuaded to co-operate by studio manager Bill Rule, who could be as cantankerous as all three together.

The traditional end-of-picture party reflected the budgets of films produced at the time, ranging from the beer and nuts parties of producer Jack Parsons's 'B' pictures for the 20th Century-Fox second features unit, to the massive barbecue held on the studio lot for *Lord Jim* (Richard Brooks, 1964). This latter party was somewhat tarnished by a wild-eyed horseman, Peter O'Toole, galloping unannounced through the assembled crowd. Another unannounced visit highlighted the party for Walt Disney's *Greyfriars Bobby* (Don Chaffey, 1960). Disney made a personal visit to the party, much to the surprise of Arthur Knight, an ardent admirer of Disney's work, who whisked the white cloth from the table across which he was slumped and ran to Disney, imploring him to autograph it. Disney obliged by rapidly sketching Mickey Mouse. Knight promptly ran around the restaurant where the party was being held, whooping in ecstasy.

An end-of-picture party also reflected the current state of an actor's career. Even the humblest of 'B' pictures needed an American name to help sales in the US. Alongside popular stars of the day working at Shepperton – including Gregory Peck, Robert Mitchum, Vincent Price, Peter Cushing, Christopher Lee, Peter Finch, Jean Simmons, Cary Grant, Deborah Kerr, David Niven, Anthony Quayle, Peter Sellers, Ian Carmichael, Bob Hope, Bing Crosby, Peter O'Toole, Richard Burton and Dirk Bogarde (who, under Joe Losey's direction for *The Servant*, 1963, and *King and Country*, 1964, was producing some of the best work of his distinguished career) were stars of a decade before, whose careers were in decline and who agreed to appear in any film to keep the financial wolf from the door. Some, like Howard Keel in *The Day of the Triffids* (Steve Sekely, 1962) and Pat Boone in *The Horror of It All* (Terence Fisher, 1964), went on to find new success by adapting their talents to the changing world of entertainment. Others such as Dan Duryea, a popular 'heavy' in the 40s, failed to halt the slide to oblivion, ending his career as the obligatory 'name' in 'B' pictures, such as those produced by Jack Parsons.

Most of the 'B' pictures produced at Shepperton in the 60s were from Jack Parsons and his American partner, Robert Lippert. As well as *The Horror of It All*, they included *Witchcraft* (Don Sharp, 1964), *The Earth Dies Screaming* (Terence Fisher, 1964), *Night Train to Paris* (Robert Douglas, 1964), *Space Flight IC–1* (Bernard Knowles, 1964), *Curse of the Fly* (Don Sharp, 1965) and *The Murder Game* (Sidney Salkow, 1965). Shortly after this last film, Parsons committed suicide at his London home.

Hollywood stars were not the only ones active at Shepperton during this period. Disney's British production unit was briefly based at Shepperton, making *Greyfriars Bobby* and *The Horsemasters* (William Fairchild, 1961) there before moving to Pinewood in 1961. American producer Milton Subotsky filmed pop stars and jazz groups of the day in films such as *It's Trad, Dad* (Richard Lester, 1961). Later, with his partner Max Rosenberg, Subotsky's Amicus Productions made a string of low-budget horror films at Shepperton. Roger Corman was similarly engaged on adjoining stages, mostly in 'E'/'F'/'G' block, with American horror king Vincent Price.

The increasing influence of television in the 60s was evident in the production at Shepperton of television series such as *Danger Man*, *Sentimental Agent* and *Man of the World*. Two production companies specialising in television commercials elected to base themselves at Shepperton, Littleton Park Film Productions, run by Ronnie Spencer, and Film City Productions, run by the remarkable and courageous Jimmy Wright.

Wright had joined the Royal Air Force in 1942 to become a cameraman in the RAF Film Unit based at Pinewood Studios. His career ended on 23 February 1944 when the Martin Marauder aircraft in which he was flying crashed. His horrific injuries included permanent loss of sight and serious disfigurement. Following a long period at the world-famous Queen Victoria Hospital, East Grinstead, undergoing forty-six operations on his face and eighteen corneal grafts as one of surgeon Archibald McIndoe's 'guinea pigs', Wright was persuaded by Jim Davis, a fellow member of the RAF Film Unit who had worked at BIP before the war, to return to the film industry.

With Davis and Antony Squire, Wright became a founder member of Anglo-Scottish Pictures, based at Shepperton Studios. In 1951, he left hospital to live in Shepperton and administer the new production company. From small beginnings in an office in the Old House and in the park-keeper's lodge at the original entrance to Littleton Park close to the River Ash, Anglo-Scottish expanded, with the introduction of UK commercial television, to include office space in the North Office Block, near the studio main entrance. This block was in the house in which 'Poppa' Day, the brilliant matte artist whom Korda had brought to Shepperton from Denham Studios, had lived. Anglo-Scottish later acquired the old Plaza Cinema in nearby Addlestone for major animation and productions requiring special effects. The company also built Halliford Studios on a site close to Shepperton. This studio had two sound stages, one 60 × 40 ft and the other 60 ft square.

In 1961, Wright left Anglo-Scottish to form Film City Productions with Julian Caunter, again based at Shepperton in 'Poppa' Day's house; and in 1964 he left Shepperton to set up with ex-BBC producer/director Mike Leeston-Smith a small studio in London's West End under the banner of Cinexsa Film Productions.

Wright's courage comprehensively confounded the sceptics who maintained that it was impossible for a blind person to continue successfully a career in an essentially visual medium. Jimmy Wright, OBE, DFC, died, aged seventy, in February 1993.

Littleton Park Film Productions had been set up in 1961 by British Lion to produce television commercials and sponsored films for any and every market. Managing Director Ronald Spencer's fellow Board members included Frank Launder, Sidney Gilliat, Roy and John Boulting. Spencer had started in the film industry as a draughtsman in the art department, transferred to the camera department, then to the production department, working as assistant director on all four Independent Frame films at Pinewood in 1949: *Warning to Wantons* (Donald B. Wilson); *Poet's Pub* (Frederick Wilson); *Stop Press Girl* (Michael Barry) and *Floodtide* (Frederick Wilson). As assistant director he worked with many leading international directors, including Raoul Walsh, Edward Dmytryk, Carol Reed, Jack Clayton and David Lean. His advertising agency experience included two years as a producer/director with the London Press Exchange.

In 1969, Littleton Park Films became Lion Pacesetter Productions with the same Board. In 1973, after the purchase of Shepperton Studios in 1972 by Barclay Securities, Ronald and Adele Spencer bought Lion Pacesetter Productions and renamed the company Pacesetter Productions under a new Chairman, Lord Brabourne.

While based at Shepperton, Spencer had forged an important production link with the Children's Film Foundation (incorporated 18 July 1951 and, from 9 September 1982, known as the Children's Film and Television Foundation). Shepperton productions for the Foundation include *The*

Young Detectives (1964, Gilbert Gunn); *Project Z* (1968) and *The 'Copter Kids* (1975), both directed by Spencer.

Henry Geddes, from 1964 Executive Producer and from 1970 to 1981 Chief Executive/Executive Producer of the Foundation, recalled the special relationship the Foundation had with Shepperton Studios:

> Andy Worker, then Managing Director of the studio, was also on my Board. He was incredibly helpful from a practical point of view. We had a lot of inexperienced producers at the time, but Andy knew how to handle them. If we had any problems with our productions, Andy would do his best to slot us into the studio somewhere, often for the odd scene to be shot or to use the studio tank.

At times it seemed during the 60s that every nook and cranny of the studio was being used for production, making the daily morning production status check by the studio operating office manager a hazardous operation. On these occasions it was imperative to have efficient liaison with construction managers on sets being built or 'struck' (dismantled), production managers on sets lit and 'dressed' (ready) for shooting, and assistant directors on sets where filming was in progress. In addition to sets on stages, status checks were made on sets outside stages. Both small and large, these were spread around the studio's sixty acres, and the status check could take up to two hours each morning.

Often it was difficult to differentiate between a genuine classified set and a discarded piece of scenery, much of which littered the studio grounds. Daleks from the two Dr Who films produced at Shepperton, *Dr Who and the Daleks* (1965) and *Daleks' Invasion Earth* (1965), both directed by Gordon Flemyng, cluttered the studio for a time, as did Triffids of all shapes and sizes, a legacy of *The Day of the Triffids*.

On 6 November 1964 an unwanted dose of realism was injected into the studio's running schedule. An attempted armed payroll robbery by three shotgun-wielding men was thwarted by the cool courage of the studio cashier David Blues who, despite having a shotgun jabbed in his face, refused to hand over the money and pressed an alarm button. The men ran off in panic, and were later caught and sentenced.

A major source of production investment for Shepperton-based films during this period was Columbia Pictures, which was first registered in the UK in 1929. Columbia released its first British film in 1933, BIP's *The Song You Gave Me*, directed by Paul Stein and starring Bebe Daniels. In 1934, Columbia British was formed as an in-house British division. The company's inaugural film was *The Lady is Willing*, produced at Elstree B & D, directed by Gilbert Miller and starring Cedric Hardwicke, Leslie Howard and Binnie Barnes. For the next thirty years or so, Columbia British released dozens of low-budget films, mostly made by 'local' production companies for home-grown consumption; one of them was Sound City's *Youthful Folly* (Miles Mander, 1934). In 1937 the company produced London Films' *21 Days*, directed by Basil Dean and starring Vivien Leigh and Laurence Olivier, and in 1941 it released Anthony Asquith's *Freedom Radio*, produced by Two Cities.

Columbia British also produced comedies featuring the popular Lancashire comedian George Formby: *South American George* (1941); *Bell Bottom George* (1943); *Get Cracking* (1943), which also starred Dinah Sheridan; *He Snoops to Conquer* (1944); *I Didn't Do It* (1945); and *George in Civvy Street* (1946) – all directed by Marcel Varnel. The company also cornered the market for the British 'forces sweetheart' Vera Lynn, with *We'll Meet Again* (Phil Brandon, 1942) and *Rhythm Serenade* (Gordon Wellesley, 1943).

In 1947, Columbia started to move its British investment up-market with Two Cities' *The First Gentleman,* directed by Alberto Cavalcanti. Unfortunately the producer, Marcel Varnel, was killed in a car crash and the film went disastrously over-budget, a major contribution to which was the ordering of genuine antique furniture for the sets. Nevertheless, Columbia continued to distribute with *The Fatal Night* (1948), directed by Mario Zampi for Anglo Films; *Paper Orchid* (1949), directed by Roy Baker for Ganesh Productions; *Midnight Episode* (1950), directed by Gordon Parry for Triangle Films; and *Shadow of the Past* (1950, also known as *The Lady in Black*), directed by Mario Zampi for Anglo Films. This latter film was remarkable for two reasons: Charles Forte provided the completion guarantee, and Zampi repeatedly changed the camera sheet slate number to disguise the enormous number of takes for some scenes.

While most of Columbia British output at the time was for the UK home market, Columbia did distribute in the US two London Films productions: *My Daughter Joy* (1950; US title: *Operation X*) and Sidney Gilliat's *State Secret* (1950; US title: *The Great Manhunt*).

Columbia's first film at Shepperton Studios was *The End of the Affair* (Edward Dmytryk, 1955), which led to the company's subsequent long-term contract with Shepperton, agreed with Abe Schneider, then President of Columbia Pictures, who had found it increasingly difficult to find a studio home for his British productions. In addition to *The End of the Affair*, Columbia financed at Shepperton *Joe Macbeth* (Ken Hughes, 1955); *Port Afrique* (Rudolph Maté, 1956); *Seven Waves Away* (Richard Sale, 1956); *The Story of Esther Costello* (David Miller, 1957); *Bridge on the River Kwai* (David Lean, 1957); *Gideon's Day* (John Ford, 1958); *Night of the Demon* (Jacques Tourneur, 1958); and *Suddenly Last Summer* (Joseph Mankiewicz, 1959).

Columbia's British-made successes produced at Shepperton during the early 60s, under its long-term contract with the studio, include the action adventure *The Guns of Navarone* (J. Lee Thompson, 1961); David Lean's spectacular *Lawrence of Arabia* (1962); Stanley Kubrick's *Dr Strangelove* (1963); and the outrageous *Casino Royale* (1967), directed by Ken Hughes, John Huston, Robert Parrish, Joe McGrath and Val Guest. In addition to having almost as many directors as there were James Bonds, Ken Hughes remembers *Casino Royale* for using every stage at Shepperton for months, with 'H' stage in particular 'tied up for a long time for one sequence involving cowboys, horses, parachutists and all manner of madness.'[18] Indeed the film spilled over into MGM's studios, and at one time was being shot in three different studios.

Columbia hit the jackpot again with *A Man for All Seasons* (1966), directed by Fred Zinnemann, who in 1993 recalled his experience of working at Shepperton:

> One of the happiest experiences of my professional life was the making of *A Man for All Seasons* at Shepperton Studios, which was then managed by Adrian Worker. The crews and departments were top class and no request was too much trouble. It was a wonderful way of making a movie. There is still a glow twenty-five years later when I think of the lovely time we had.[19]

In 1968 Columbia had a further major success with Carol Reed's *Oliver!*

Columbia started its upsurge in British production with its active participation in Warwick Films, set up in 1952 by Irving Allen and Albert 'Cubby' Broccoli. Irving Allen had arrived in Hollywood in 1926 and through a high-school friend, Carl Laemmle Jnr gained employment as an apprentice editor at Universal Studios, where he worked on *All Quiet on the Western Front*. In 1940, he began producing films, investing $120 of his own money into a short subject on archery. His second production, *40 Boys and a Song*, made on a budget of $850, earned him an Academy Award nomination. He was one of the first American producers to shoot his films on foreign locations. On his return to Hollywood in 1965, he produced the first of four Matt Helm films, starring Dean Martin.

Albert Romolo Broccoli was a former coffin salesman. This experience was introduced into his later James Bond films – the flaming hearse in *Doctor No* (Terence Young, 1962), the funeral parlour of Nathan Slumber in *Diamonds are Forever* (Guy Hamilton, 1971), and the graveyard world of Baron Samedi in *Live and Let Die* (1973, also directed by Hamilton).

According to research carried out by Broccoli's wife Dana, he is descended from the Broccolis of Carrera, who first crossed two Italian vegetables, cauliflower and rabe, to produce the vegetable that took their name and, eventually, supported the family on their Long Island farm. 'Cubby' Broccoli, so named after a round-faced American comic-strip character, started his film career in Hollywood escorting Jane Russell to the Flagstaff, Arizona, location for Howard Hawks's *The Outlaw* (1943) and calling reveille for the reservation Indian extras. He quickly spotted a route to being a producer when, as Alan Ladd's agent, he teamed up with Irving Allen to take advantage of the British Eady subsidy. Allen and Broccoli made their partnership deal in New York's Warwick Hotel, so they named their company Warwick Films.

Warwick made three films at Shepperton: *The Red Beret* (Terence Young, 1953); *Cockleshell Heroes* (José Ferrer, 1955) and *Idle on Parade* (John Gilling, 1959). Warwick's output was an interesting, if undistinguished, mix of subjects which failed to find a successful balance between the content and the stars and directors employed to produce it. American stars – Alan Ladd (*The Red Beret* and *Hell Below Zero*, 1953), Rita Hayworth (*Fire Down Below*, 1957), Ray Milland (*High Flight*, 1957) and Victor Mature (*The Bandit of Zhobe*, 1959) – and directors – Mark Robson (*Hell Below Zero*), Tay Garnett (*The Black Knight*) and Robert Parrish (*Fire Down Below*) – failed to gel with their British counterparts. The resulting films were neither good enough to be very successful nor bad enough to be total failures. Although Warwick gave two excellent actors an opportunity to direct – José Ferrer (*Cockleshell Heroes*) and Nigel Patrick (*How to Murder a Rich Uncle*, 1957) – the company's last seven films, produced between 1957 and 1960, were directed by two workhorse British directors, John Gilling (five) and Ken Hughes (two).

Two years before Harry Saltzman met Ian Fleming, Albert Broccoli was given the opportunity to start a James Bond project, but Irving Allen rejected the idea outright. This incident contributed to the disintegration of their partnership in 1960 and Columbia bought out all the rights in Warwick Films. Two years later, Broccoli got his way with *Dr No*.

Until Pinewood built its first Bond film stage in 1976 (it was subsequently destroyed by fire and replaced in 1984), in total stage area Shepperton was the largest of the British studios, with 124,502 square feet from thirteen stages. Pinewood had 120,585 square feet from thirteen stages; ABPC Elstree, 97,300 square feet from nine stages; and MGM British, 91,260 square feet from ten stages.

In 1964 the Conservative government authorised the National Film Finance Corporation to sell Shepperton, but to retain its one Preference Share – the 'golden share' – in British Lion Films.

The NFFC's role in the film industry had always been that of a specialised bank, its statutory mandate being to make loans for the production or distribution of films. It was not intended that the NFFC should be directly concerned with production or distribution. The Corporation was established as a source of finance of last resort, but it failed to solve the problems of the British film industry.

Throughout the 1950s the NFFC was involved in the financing of a substantial proportion of feature films which qualified as British under the relevant legislation, usually with an investment of 'end money' which other investors were reluctant to provide. This was recoverable out of net revenues. The government provided this money through the Corporation to keep British film production going despite the dominant position of the American industry in the English-speaking market. 'Front money' was recoverable first out of net revenues.

During the 1960s the pattern of film financing in Britain underwent an important change. Attracted by the substantial box-office bonus for British films provided by Eady money from the British Film Fund, the wealth of British artistic and technical talent available and the lower production costs then prevailing in Britain, the American major distributing companies, through their British subsidiaries, increasingly took over the financing of British films. However, over-investment in film production by several of the American majors led to a crisis in the American industry and withdrawal of much of the film finance previously available from these sources.

During this period the NFFC, to improve its position, gradually persuaded distributors to allow its investments to become recoverable simultaneously with those of the distributors, instead of in last position. From 1949 to 1970, when the American financial withdrawal from Britain was almost complete, the NFFC conducted its business with a single revolving fund from the government of £6 million, with which it helped to finance 718 feature films and 170 shorts. From this fund it advanced more than £27.5 million. Up to March 1970, the NFFC lost £5,344,674 of the revolving fund available to it, over half of which (£2,969,000) was lost on the £3 million loan to the British Lion Film Corporation. This loss was partially offset through profit on the sale of shares in British Lion Films (£773,993) by the Balcon Group, of which the Boulting brothers and Launder and Gilliat were key constituents, and through dividends on the Special Preference Share in British Lion Films (£527,777) which essentially came from profits made under that same management.

Although the NFFC had acquired its equity interest in British Lion Films as the result of the collapse of the former British Lion Film Corporation and the acceptance by the NFFC of shares in the new British Lion in satisfaction of its loan to the old, the NFFC had never regarded that holding as one that it should retain indefinitely. In May 1957 the NFFC expressed the hope that 'in due course, the British Lion shares may be sold at a fair price to private investors willing and able to continue to finance and distribute independent British films.'[20] The opportunity for a sale arose at a time when the NFFC had become the owners of its entire issued share capital.

The five executive directors of British Lion – David Kingsley, John and Roy Boulting, Frank Launder and Sidney Gilliat – who had assumed control of the management in 1958, and Douglas Collins, chairman of the company from December 1957 to February 1961, had achieved the profitable exploitation of the large stock of films in which the former British Lion Film Corporation had considerable interests, acquired by British Lion Films on its formation in 1955. A substantial reduction in overheads had been obtained through the joint selling arrangement with Columbia which had operated since March 1961, its cost split between British Lion and Columbia. Profits arising from the films made by the Boultings and Launder and Gilliat, and an increasingly discriminating use of company resources, had resulted in the government finally recovering a far larger sum than at one time thought possible.

One factor which had operated to the benefit of British Lion was the activities of the so-called 'satellite' groups which began to emerge about 1958 with the company's active encouragement. Although British Lion participated to the extent of a contingent investment of some £200,000 in the funds which these groups set up in order to attract bank facilities, it was the groups themselves that took the major risks in providing 70 per cent 'front money' towards the financing of a large volume of product, whose UK distribution was handled on commission by British Lion. In many of these cases the NFFC provided loans of 'end money'. In this way, British Lion succeeded in attracting product as a distributor without providing the normal distributor-finance, or running the inherent risks.

In the first four years after its formation, British Lion Films invested (usually by way of guarantees discounted by a bank) an average of just under £1 million a year spread over thirty-seven films. Since the growth of the 'satellites', this average had fallen to about £300,000 a year, for the most part deployed in a small number of carefully chosen films for most of which no loans were sought from the NFFC and which had been extremely profitable to British Lion. Ultimately the number of 'satellites' rose to eight, but all were now inactive owing to shortage of funds. The NFFC's own losses on loans made for films sponsored by the 'satellites' had been more than offset by its profit from the sale of British Lion.

Although some of the films financed by the 'satellites' grouped around British Lion proved successful, most of them resulted in serious losses to the financing parties, particularly to the NFFC. The 'satellite' system, necessarily confined to modest-priced films owing to the limited funds available, became increasingly unsuited to the prevailing market conditions and to the changing public taste in films. The gulf between successful and unsuccessful films had widened considerably. It had become essential that any scheme for the financing of British films must be capable of supporting the more expensive type of film, which was beyond the financial range of the 'satellites'. British Lion, under its new owners, felt it necessary to return to the practice of providing direct finance for the films of independent producers and to become again 'the home of the independents', which Shepperton once was. To this end, in May 1964 there were discussions between the NFFC and British Lion designed to provide a new form of joint financing arrangement for the benefit of independent film-makers and suited to the needs of the day. This hope was not realised.

In June 1964, the Rank Organisation offered to participate in a joint financing scheme on the basis of a commitment by them of £500,000 and a similar commitment by the NFFC. Negotiations with the National Provincial Bank were lengthy, but eventually the bank agreed to provide the necessary budget finance for selected films up to a maximum sum of £1,500,000, on the understanding that this figure would be revised in the light of experience. The Rank Organisation, unsurprisingly, hedged its bets by insisting that the NFFC had the sole responsibility for the selection of films to be financed, for the negotiations and for the administration of the scheme. This withdrawal of the distributor/financier from any control over selection and administration was without precedent. Again unsurprisingly, Rank insisted that films selected should be made at Pinewood Studios and distributed worldwide by the Rank Organisation UK and Overseas Film Distribution Divisions, with processing and printing handled by Rank Laboratories except when films were made in Technicolor or Todd-AO.

Reservations were expressed from several quarters of the industry about the 'desirability of a public body [the NFFC] thus strengthening the position of one of the combines in a period when monopolistic practices in the industry were under review by the Monopolies Commission.[21] The NFFC defended itself, claiming that its concern was to strengthen the British film industry and that this scheme was a good way of doing it.

In May 1965 the first film under this arrangement was selected: *I Was Happy Here*, produced by Roy Millichip and directed by Desmond Davis. Two other films quickly followed: Paul Czinner's *Romeo and Juliet* (with the Royal Ballet, including Margot Fonteyn and Rudolph Nureyev) and *The Sandwich Man*, produced by Peter Newbrook and directed by Robert Hartford-Davis. Only three more films were selected under this scheme: *They're a Weird Mob*, produced and directed by Michael Powell in

Australia; *Maroc Seven*, produced by John Gale and Leslie Phillips and directed by Gerry O'Hara; and *Two Weeks in September*, a Franco-British co-production, produced by Francis Cosne and Kenneth Harper and directed by Serge Bourguignon.

The events leading up to the sale of British Lion had started in 1963 when, in the year ended 31 March, there was a reduction and reorganisation of the company's capital. This resulted in the NFFC receiving on 29 March 1963, in place of its 600,000 Preferred Shares in British Lion, 300,000 fully paid Ordinary Shares of one pound (one half of the total issued) and £591,000 in cash. Of this, £456,900 was paid by the NFFC to the Board of Trade in reduction of advances made by the Board to the NFFC and £134,100 was retained by the NFFC against an obligation to acquire from British Lion, at par, £134,100 6½ per cent Second Debenture Stock in Shepperton Studios. It was subsequently agreed that the NFFC's obligation in this respect should be cancelled on payment by the NFFC to British Lion of £3,352.50p, representing a discount of 2½ per cent on the par value, and the net balance then remaining in the NFFC's hands of £130,747.50p was paid to the Board of Trade on 10 December 1963, in further reduction of outstanding advances.

The cost of the NFFC's original investment in British Lion was £600,000. In preparing the NFFC's original accounts for the year ended 31 March 1963, the cash sum of £591,000 received in the capital reorganisation was deducted, leaving the investment then represented by 300,000 Ordinary Shares with a book value of £9,000. On 12 December 1963, £587,647.50p was readvanced to the NFFC by the Board of Trade for the purchase of the other half of the equity of British Lion, which, under the scheme of capital arrangement, had been allotted to the company's five executive directors and which, pursuant to the agreed options, the NFFC was entitled, or could be required, to buy early in 1964.

Sir William Lawson, of accountants Binder Hamlyn, was asked to make a valuation of the shares in British Lion. Based on figures as at 30 September 1963, he calculated their value at £1,590,000, or £2.65p for each of the 600,000 Ordinary Shares, half of which were held by the NFFC and half by the five executive directors.

On 17 December 1963 each executive director received £158,735 for the shares for which he had paid £1,800 less than six years before. The purchase price represented the valuation figure of Sir William Lawson and the NFFC benefited to the extent of one-half in the remarkable appreciation in the value of the shares.

Not surprisingly, would-be purchasers who could give the necessary assurances that British Lion would have the finance and management necessary to continue its role as a financier and distributor of independent British films were very thin on the ground, despite the options having been public knowledge since March 1963. At one time seven contenders (including Sydney Box) were in the field, from which three firm offers were made, only two of which were on the terms required by the NFFC. Of those two offers, only one stayed the course to finalise the purchase. This was Sir Michael Balcon's group.

A condition of sale imposed by the Board of Trade was that no purchaser should be entitled to benefit by any future tax relief obtainable by virtue of the losses (of which just over £2 million was outstanding, carried forward by British Lion from the former British Lion Film Corporation). The Board of Trade preferred to sell the share capital of the company rather than to sell its assets in a liquidation. To meet this requirement, the NFFC stipulated that it should retain one share (to be converted into a Special Preference Share), the main purpose of which was to ensure that it would receive, by way of dividend and on behalf of the government, a sum equal to the saving in tax to be obtained by British Lion, until the tax loss carried forward was exhausted.

In addition, certain veto rights were attached to this share, designed to ensure that British Lion would continue to be run as a going concern in the interests of independent production. These rights of veto applied to a voluntary liquidation of British Lion, the sale of its undertaking, or any part of it, or of Shepperton Studios, and any repayment of capital to shareholders. This single Preference Share also conferred on the NFFC the right to appoint a director to the board of British Lion. The purchaser of British Lion also signed an undertaking that the policy of the new owners would be to provide finance, distribution and studio facilities for British independent film producers and to preserve the company's independent trading position.

Contracts for the sale of British Lion to Sir Michael Balcon's group were exchanged on 31 March 1964, when a deposit of £160,000 was paid. On 7 April the remaining formalities were completed and the balance of the purchase price, £1,440,000, was paid. The agreed price was Sir William Lawson's valuation figure of £1,590,000 plus a £10,000 contribution towards the NFFC's disbursements. Out of this price, £1,575,000 was paid by the NFFC to the Board of Trade, who readvanced that amount back to the NFFC.

Balcon's group comprised five constituent production units: 1) Walter Reade Jnr (USA); 2) John Osborne, Tony Richardson, Oscar Lewenstein, James Isherwood, Border Television Limited, Brian Epstein and Karel Reisz; 3) Joseph Janni, John Schlesinger and David Kingsley; 4) John and Roy Boulting; 5) Frank Launder and Sidney Gilliat. Each unit had a representative on the board of British Lion Films. The other board members were Sir Michael Balcon (Chairman), David Kingsley (Vice-Chairman), James Isherwood (financial director), the Baroness Wootton of Abinger and Sir Lionel Heald, MP. Financial institutions supporting Balcon's group included Hambros Bank and the Edinburgh Investment Trust.

British Lion (Holdings) Limited was registered as a £100 company on 20 March 1964, the two subscriber shareholders being two partners from the law firm Goodman Derrick. The new British Lion went public on 16 October 1964, but in 1965 Sir Michael Balcon resigned as chairman, according to *Private Eye* magazine (5 May 1972) 'in rage and disgust at the film policy priorities of the company'. He was replaced by Arnold (now Lord) Goodman of Goodman Derrick.

Sidney Gilliat remembers 'the ride from 1964 onwards being quite a switchback':

We started indifferently, shedding other member companies at their request (thereby having to put in more capital ourselves than originally contemplated). A marked, but unexpected, upbeat period led to the Company going public as our financial advisers recommended. Unfortunately, this more or less coincided with a partly inadvertent change of policy, perhaps influenced by a fall-off in studio rentals on the one hand and renewed capital available on the other. We embarked on a more vigorous film-making phase, which, in the end, proved disastrous and which, from the standpoint of Frank Launder and myself, was directly opposed to our beliefs. In the end, it was agreed to limit the British Lion financial contribution to (I think) one third of the production cost in each case. This, for one reason or another, got out of hand. Four films especially cost us dearly, particularly *Loot* (1970), *The Three Sisters* (1970) and *Mr Forbush and the Penguins* (1971). All of these were made by other people, but financed by British Lion and others.

Loot was wrongheadedly produced and directed in our opinion, but British Lion's views were largely rejected by the makers. *The Three Sisters* (Olivier) went forward on the basis that an American art theatre group would not only put up a third of the cost, but would take any future National Theatre films that we could provide. Instead, they backed out at the last moment, leaving British Lion to fill the financial void. With their departure, the US art theatre market virtually died the death. *Mr Forbush and the Penguins* was agreed (with EMI) as a jointly funded project on the strict understanding that Michael Crawford played the lead, and certain revisions would be made to the script. In the event, neither undertaking was carried out, but British Lion was still left holding part of the baby.

The total results were disastrous, affording the lesson, learned too late, that unless you have the overall say and the authority to exercise it, it is a mistake to fund a series of expensive films. We had fallen into the trap that we had hitherto carefully avoided.[22]

The dramatic fall in profits for Shepperton Studios for the year ended 31 March 1964, from £119,225 to a mere £21,998, illustrated the aggravation caused by the uncertainty of British Lion's future. David Kingsley and Roy Boulting resigned by rotation from the board of Shepperton and were replaced by Joseph Janni and Hal Mason. In September 1964 Sir Nutcombe Hume retired as Chairman of the NFFC and was replaced by the Deputy Chairman, C. H. Scott.

The following year saw profits rise marginally to £28,443, despite the Scoring Stage (today, stage 'L') being completely re-equipped and, during the winter, the dredging of the River Ash, which flows through the studio grounds, to restore it to the condition in which it served as a location for *Sanders of the River* (Zoltan Korda, 1935) and *The Mill on the Floss* (Tim Whelan, 1937). 1965 and 1966 saw a massive leap in profits to £163,262, prompting chairman Sidney Gilliat to comment: '1965/66 produced the best results since the changes in the direction of British Lion at the beginning of 1958 when the new Shepperton Board was immediately faced with the necessity of re-roofing the principal stages and the prospects looked grim indeed.'[23]

The improving fortunes of Shepperton Studios in 1966 contrasted with the suddenly declining fortunes of the NFFC. The economic climate of the day forced a suspension on its lending in October. Only £750,000 could then be borrowed out of the £2 million which the NFFC could borrow from non-government sources under the Cinematograph Films Production (Special Loans) Act 1952. To compound the problem, no guarantees were forthcoming from the Treasury. However, the Films Act 1970 rectified the position, extending the NFFC operation until 1980. Indeed, had this extension not been granted, it is doubtful whether the NFFC could have continued, as only one lender, the NFFC's own bankers, Cox's and King's branch of Lloyd's Bank, agreed to provide the facility for £750,000 (increased to £1 million) without Treasury guarantee for five years.

The encouraging results for Shepperton for 1965/6 were the result of a major contribution from managing director 'Andy' Worker, who had implemented the new studio policy from 1958, aimed at giving a very special standard of service to film producers in general and independent producers in particular. This was a major factor in generating income, so that, in addition to bringing the Preference Dividend up to date in 1963 and paying the Ordinary Dividend every year from that time, £319,000 could be spent on redeeming Debentures and Notes, reducing the amount outstanding at April 1966 to £377,000.

Since 1958, over £500,000 had been spent on buildings and equipment, including bringing into service eleven new cameras with a complete range of lenses, three zoom lenses, eighteen Series 20 Moviolas, a new Westrex Theatre channel and a mass of the latest lighting equipment. On the debit side, the studio had to cope with the new Selective Employment Tax, which added some £40,000 annually to its overall bill.

In 1966, when Hal Mason retired as a director by rotation and did not seek re-election, Roy Boulting was elected to the board of Shepperton again.

Considerable satisfaction was felt at the studio when the ghost of the ill-fated *London Town* (1946) was finally laid to rest by Shepperton's 'big three' musicals – *Half a Sixpence* (George Sidney, 1967), *Oliver!* (Carol Reed, 1968) and *Scrooge* (Ronald Neame, 1970). Two other 'big' pictures, *Casino Royale* and the award-winning *A Man for All Seasons*, had helped boost profits again for the 1966/67 year to £198,796. Through the later 60s and the early 70s, the studio produced a number of costume pictures, including *Anne of the Thousand Days* (Charles Jarrott, 1969); *Cromwell* (Ken Hughes, 1970) and *Mary, Queen of Scots* (Charles Jarrott, 1971).

Profits dipped in 1967/68 to £152,514, reflecting the need to spend money on keeping the studio up-to-date. The vast silent stage 'H' was reroofed and a new cutting room maintenance workshop for servicing the Series 20 Moviolas was built. Electrical cradles for the shooting stages were redesigned and a six-track reversible ('rock and roll') dubbing system was installed. Work also started on a new multi-storey car park. Joseph Janni and Roy Boulting resigned their directorships of the studio board and were replaced by Max (now Sir Max) Rayne and John Boulting. Studio Manager Bill Rule's twenty-two years of service were rewarded with a directorship of the studio company (appointed 7 December 1967).

In 1968, to raise much needed cash, the studio's financial advisers, Hambros Bank, supported by British Lion directors Lord Goodman and Sir Max Rayne, recommended that British Lion Films went public. Over one million shares were offered at 16s 6d (82p) each. According to *Private Eye* magazine (2 June 1972), most of the company's new shares were owned by the directors. By 1969, John Boulting had 354,000 shares, Roy Boulting 366,000 and Lord Goodman 155,000. 'Since the 1968 splurge,' the magazine continued, 'there have been fewer and worse British Lion films every year and the profits have slumped.'

This may have had some bearing on why British Lion, on 22 December 1969, borrowed £750,000 from the Norwich Union Life Insurance Society, secured by a first mortgage on freehold property at Shepperton. Interest only was payable for the first five years. Thereafter, repayment of capital with interest was to be spread over twenty years by half-yearly instalments of £42,223. Coincidentally, in the Report of the Directors for the year ended 31 March 1969 it was felt necessary to have the studio's land and buildings independently valued, the resulting figure being approximately £500,000 in excess of that included in the balance sheet.

During this year, Shepperton Studios purchased 5,100 Ordinary Shares of £1 each in Bowie Films, a company engaged in special effects work, and 6,000 Ordinary Shares of £1 each in the Ravensfield Engineering Company, which was involved in sheet metal work, being the whole of the issued share capital of these two companies. In addition, Goodson Car Hire Limited was formed to operate a car hire service at the studio and the studio company acquired sixty shares at £1 each, being 60 per cent of the issued capital. These three new subsidiaries were added to another subsidiary, Island Film Company, acquired by the studio company in 1965.

The first public year saw profits slump to £63,334 and the first press speculation that the Americans were about to withdraw from film production in the UK. Sidney Gilliat remained optimistic. In his Chairman's statement for the year ended 31 March 1969, he commented:

> We cannot see any justification for it in the overall picture. It should be remembered that in some quarters there had certainly been a degree of over-commitment to production following on the dazzling success of a number of pictures made over here. In general, the inducements for American finance to continue to come forward remain very considerable – always providing that the government does not embark on yet another rash reduction of the Eady levy, the importance of which, in this context, cannot be over-stated, or wield some other unpredictable axe.[24]

Gilliat did acknowledge 'the changes that have been made to our benefit, however tardily, in the application of Selective Employment Tax, thus rectifying a serious anomaly and removing a truly Gilbertian absurdity.'

In 1993, Gilliat recalled another 'Gilbertian absurdity' which had a direct bearing on British Lion's fortunes:

> Somewhere between 1966 and 1969, when our principal bankers at British Lion were the National Provincial Bank (later merged with the

Westminster Bank into today's National Westminster Bank), who advanced the loans for almost every picture made under the aegis of British Lion, a cocktail party was held at the Bank's Green Street, Mayfair branch to celebrate the opening of a new strongroom system. In fact, the party actually took place *in* the strongrooms. On that occasion, I got into conversation with a Bank official who confided that things were going to be much more difficult for us all in the future. He indicated very firmly that the Bank was going to take a much harder look at the financing of films, since a producer had actually defaulted on an outstanding loan. I realised from what the official said that the Bank actually thought that *all* films paid their loans back wholly out of each film's revenues. Of course, the policy at British Lion and elsewhere was to repay loans the normal eighteen months after release and British Lion, like everybody else in an *overall* solvent position, had duly repaid every loan after eighteen months out of their resources whether the picture concerned was profitable by then or not. If our Bank official was right, therefore, the Bank must have been living for years under the delusion that *all* films got their loans back from revenue. When they examined the defaulting production company, it appears to have dawned on them that National Provincial Bank-financed films were not all profitable. The man finished our conversation by saying: 'I'm very sorry, but all you fellows, as a result, are going to find film funding from us much more difficult.' Not long after this event, National Provincial virtually ceased to finance new films altogether.

After that date, financing of any films became increasingly much more difficult. For instance, if I remember rightly, the last two films made under the old British Lion (which Frank Launder and I looked after) were financed by a consortium, the bank involved being the Bank of America. It may seem strange that one man's default on a single picture should have set alarm bells ringing to such an uncalled for extent, but I have always regarded financial bodies as possessing at least as much uninformed innocence as keen-eyed business acumen.[25]

In 1968, Shepperton Sound Department received an Oscar for the best soundtrack from any source for *Oliver!* At the time, Shepperton was the only studio in the country which could record six-track music and rerecord a six-track dub in the same premises.

Profits dipped again in the year ended 31 March 1970, to £46,848. This figure would have been higher but for the poor performance of the studio subsidiaries. In his Chairman's statement, Gilliat was philosophical about this downturn and, in particular, about the increasing problems regarding continuing American investment into the UK film industry.

Nobody can deny that, alas, quantities of Maryland chickens have come home to roost, some of them noticeably deficient in tail feathers, while the view on the ground is conspicuous for the numbers of hastily vacated bandwagons. For, however one mixes one's metaphors, there can be no doubt whatsoever that the regrettable tendency, so prevalent in our business, to seek success by slavishly imitating a pattern created by someone else, has led, not only to an almost ludicrous repetitiveness, but, also, in another direction, to an undisciplined inflation of costs. To paraphrase my old leader, the late and much-lamented Sir Alexander Korda, it is not enough to be trendy, one must also be entertaining and, one might add, professional.

The position has been further complicated by the fact that several major American organisations have recently changed hands, some of them having been taken over by so-called conglomerates, the dimensions of which are only exceeded by the extent of their unfamiliarity with show business. For them, at this moment, it seems a matter of licking wounds, recuperating fortunes and making up their minds.[26]

Gilliat was nearing the end of a ten-year period as Chairman of Shepperton Studios Limited, during which time he had attempted to steer the studio 'through some extremely choppy waters'. Many years later, he admitted that, as a film-maker, 'it had been damn difficult to run the business of a film studio, especially one with the problems of Shepperton. After all, Shepperton was the only major UK studio that had been financed by government, was answerable to government and was almost destroyed by government!'[27]

On 27 November 1969, Frank Launder was appointed a director of Shepperton Studios Limited, completing the involvement in the business affairs of the studio by the 'big four' British Lion film-makers, the Boultings and Launder and Gilliat.

Towards the end of 1970, the NFFC talked to John Boulting, of British Lion Films, regarding a new production financing structure. A new system was agreed between the NFFC, British Lion and Anglo-EMI Film Distributors, to take effect from 20 January 1971. Seventy-five per cent of the British distribution total receipts should belong to investors until they had received 1.35 times their principal investment. Thereafter, they would receive 50 per cent of total receipts with another 25 per cent to the producer in lieu of 'producer's share of profits' and the balance of 25 per cent to distributors. The NFFC was to set up a private consortium to put up 50 per cent of a film's budget, with the 50 per cent balance from British Lion, Anglo-EMI, or any other distributor who accepted the scheme, such as Scotia-Barber Distributors. Any investment of fees or cash from stars and directors or from overseas (including US) pre-sales, would be deducted from the budget first. This scheme was operated under Robert Clark, the NFFC's Chairman from January 1970, Sir Hilary Scott having resigned on 31 December 1969.

Although the studio's profits for the year ended 31 March 1971 rose slightly to £50,132, it would have been higher had not three American-financed films, which had reserved space at the studio, been cancelled. Another nail in the studio's coffin was the increasing number of films being shot as 'all-location' films. These were treated as location films by the unions, with far more flexible location agreements applying throughout, such as working a six-day week.

In his last Chairman's statement in 1971, before vacating his chair at Shepperton, Sidney Gilliat robustly defended the role of the studio in film-making and was openly critical of the cynical hypocrisy of the industry's unions of the day:

> While it is now fairly certain that location pictures are no longer any cheaper to make than a studio-based film (in fact, the costs today are similar and not so easy to control), the far more attractive film-making conditions help to entice almost one half of all producers away from the major studios and into other premises, which, often, are without satisfactory ventilation, proper sanitation, heating, welfare and security. Perhaps this position is tolerated by unions because of the solid material advantages that often accrue to some of their members, but they take no cognisance of the fact of the enormous studio overheads incurred by the major studios in employing hundreds of union members for fifty-two weeks a year. In this context, however, it is surely somewhat Gilbertian to promote a procession of film unionists, headed by brass bands and banners, to Westminster, for the purpose of deploring the sale of yet another major studio. Without the unions taking measures that would allow these institutions to engage, at least on equal working terms, with their 'location studio' competitors, such a gesture is not only hollow, but ridiculous. Meanwhile, the studios remain the repositories and centres of skilled craftsmen and technicians, indispensable to the prosperity of our business.[28]

In 1971, only eight films were made at Shepperton Studios, representing an ominous lull before the storm that was about to break in 1972. By that time, Sidney Gilliat was clearly disenchanted with the studio situation. In a letter to the author dated 3 February 1992, concerning his initial comments on this book, he justified his lengthy submission as 'partly venting my indignation when I think of the fourteen and a half years we gave to an ungrateful and hostile Board of Trade, not to mention the NFFC who, in my view, would have sold the company to a costermonger if they could put a good face on it.'

1972 was to be the year in which the studio faced its most desperate battle for survival.

Notes

1. Author's interview with Sidney Gilliat, 27 February 1993.
2. Ibid.
3. Author's interview with Wilfred Moeller, 30 November 1991.
4. Author's interview with Sidney Gilliat.
5. Ibid.
6. Ibid.
7. Ibid.
8. Ibid.
9. Ibid.
10. Ibid.
11. Ibid.
12. Author's interview with Sydney Samuelson, 2 December 1992.

13. *Sixty Voices*, edited by Brian McFarlane (London: BFI Publishing, 1992).
14. Ibid.
15. *Silver Screen – Strategy and Finance*, Autumn 1992. This was a quarterly magazine launched in 1992; one issue only was published.
16. Shepperton Studios Limited: Chairman's Statement for year 1960/61.
17. Ibid.
18. Ken Hughes, letter to author (undated), 1992.
19. Fred Zinnemann, letter to author, 8 February 1993.
20. National Film Finance Corporation Annual Report for year ended 31 March 1957.
21. National Film Finance Corporation Annual Report for year ended 31 March 1965.
22. Author's interview with Sidney Gilliat.
23. Shepperton Studios Limited: Chairman's Statement for year 1965/66.
24. Shepperton Studios Limited: Chairman's Statement for year 1968/69.
25. Author's interview with Sidney Gilliat.
26. Shepperton Studios Limited: Chairman's Statement for year 1969/70.
27. Author's interview with Sidney Gilliat.
28. Shepperton Studios Limited: Chairman's Statement for year 1970/71.

5

ENTER THE CITY

When British Lion Films went public in 1968 a new and ruthless breed of financier was emerging from the City of London woodwork. The era of the 'asset-stripper', which was to change forever the public's perception of the City, was being set in train by Slater Walker and Company.

In the early 1960s many British companies did not realise that their assets (buildings, equipment and land) were undervalued in their accounts, which meant that the share price of these companies often did not reflect their true worth. Slater Walker, as a takeover merchant, bought up a small company shell, sold off most of its assets and used the cash to begin a long series of takeovers.

The two partners in Slater Walker were Jim Slater and Peter Walker. Slater had qualified as an accountant in 1953–4. In 1955, he joined Park Royal Vehicles, transferring to Leyland Motors as deputy sales manager. In 1960 he bought his first shares with £2,000 savings. With a bank loan, the £2,000 became £50,000 and Jim Slater was on his way. In July/August 1964 he borrowed £325,000 and, with £50,000 of his own money, he and Peter Walker bought the company H. Lotery and changed the name to Slater Walker. By 1965 Slater Walker's pre-tax profits were £191,000. From 1966 to 1968 the company embarked on its infamous takeover spree, and by 1969 the company's pre-tax profits had risen to £10,704,640.

Peter Walker had run his own insurance broking business before becoming Deputy Chairman of Slater Walker. His political ambitions outstripped those he may have nurtured for the City and he left the company in 1970 to make a successful career for himself in the Conservative Party. Among the several senior ministerial positions Walker held over the years were the two key positions of Secretary of State for the Environment (October 1970 to November 1972) and Secretary of State for Trade and Industry (1972–74).

From British Lion's viewpoint, the danger man was to be neither Slater nor Walker, but Slater's first and most successful associate John Bentley, son of a Brighton insurance broker. A former stockbroker's messenger, Bentley had hated Harrow public school and had 'discharged' himself at seventeen to work for a speculator friend of his father on the Stock Exchange. He borrowed £100 and within six months had turned it into £2,000 in a series of shrewd investments copied from his employer. He emigrated to Australia, returned to Britain, married and had two children. Working from home, he started a launderette business, bought and sold properties and invested the profits. When he was twenty-seven, his wife ran off with a younger man and he was left with £250,000. Bentley vowed never to trust anyone again.

Bentley had worked closely with Jim Slater during the 1966/68 takeover spree, advising him on possible company 'shells' and, after purchase, going in to reorganise them. Dubbed by his enemies (and later, in a November 1972 House of Commons debate) as the nation's number one asset-stripper, Bentley was rewarded for his efforts with part of one of Slater Walker's 'acquisitions', the pharmaceutical firm Barclay & Sons. Bentley changed the name to Barclay Securities and set out to scavenge on his own, financed by Slater Walker who retained share interests in his purchases.

The *Investors Review* of 15 November 1971 described the company thus: 'As far as the City is concerned, Barclay is a simple asset-stripping outfit buying a company then releasing cash from its assets and reducing the purchasing price to three or four times its earnings.' A classic example of Bentley's method for Barclay Investments (Barclay Securities described itself as an Investment Holding Company) was the notorious case of the Erith, Kent, factory of D. Sebel & Company, which Bentley took over in 1970. Sebel had been making toys at Erith since 1947, employing 500 workers, mainly women, all union-organised. It was estimated that the firm would lose in the region of £100,000 in 1970 unless radical changes were made. Bentley urged the workforce to work harder and they co-operated. The estimated loss was turned into a £98,000 profit. One year later, the workforce's reward was Bentley's announcement, without warning or consultation, that the factory would close. He maintained that it was more profitable to move the Sebel plant to a Tri-ang factory at Merton in Surrey, which Barclay Investments had acquired, and sell off the Erith site. Five hundred workers lost their jobs. Asked why he had given no warning to the workers, Bentley replied: 'Apart from anything else, one could never expect an employer to say that a factory will be closing down – it would upset the employees too much.'[1] The Lines Brothers/Tri-ang/Pedigree operation was taken over by Barclay Investments in 1971. Six months later, the entire Merton complex was shut down and 1,200 people were thrown out of work, not long after vacancies at the complex had been advertised in the local press, stressing job security.

Against this background it was a black day for the British film industry when Bentley's roving eyes focused on British Lion – and Shepperton Studios. Bentley did not see past, present and future film-making at the studio. He saw sixty acres of under-utilised property in a London suburb valued at around £60,000 an acre and another £1 million or so of properties in London, a film library property worth around £3 million and a cinema advertising property worth whatever he wanted to value it at.

A major contribution to Bentley's success was the low profile he kept when planning his predatory moves for companies. He struck hard and fast, sometimes 'acquiring' a company before the true ramifications of his involvement were known to directors and shareholders. His strike for British Lion was typical. He had no reason to fear any opposition to his bid, or to his subsequent planned destruction of the studio for property redevelopment.

For the year ended 31 March 1972, one month before Bentley purchased British Lion, Shepperton Studios' turnover was £891,000 compared to £847,000 in the previous year. The group made a loss before taxation of £78,216, compared to £50,132 the previous year. The Shepperton accounts showed the value of freehold land and buildings at £1,727,954, but the annual report stated that 'In the opinion of the directors, the land and buildings have a value considerably in excess of that.' The report also showed that the average number employed during the year was 504, with a total remuneration of £1,054,156. None received emoluments in excess of £10,000. The highest-paid director received £8,410 and one other received £5,250 plus £250 in fees. Five received nothing.

British Lion's 1971/72 results showed a consolidated net loss of £1,221,000 against £143,000 pre-tax profit in the previous year. This loss was largely due to a £805,000 write-off for losses on recent British Lion films. This, then, was the British Lion lined up for slaughter by the City predator.

The circumstances surrounding British Lion's vulnerability revolved round two brothers, Derek and Rodney Eckhart, who were joint managing directors of the Star Group of Companies, a chain of ninety companies based in Leeds. The Group operated cinemas, bingo halls, discos and bierkellers in London, Yorkshire, Lancashire and Lincolnshire. The Eckharts' father, Walter, started the business in 1931, naming it after the first cinema he bought, The Star at Castleford, and his sons began their careers as cinema projectionists. Walter Eckhart also started at that time the system of fraud that was to be the downfall of his sons and their empire – and indirectly almost the downfall of British Lion and Shepperton Studios.

According to the then British Lion chairman, Lord Goodman, the Eckharts approached British Lion with a view to merging the two companies so that the Star Group could make its own films to show in its own cinemas, although their bingo activities accounted for 90 per cent of their business. Lord Goodman later recalled:

> It seemed to make sense at the time. They had plenty of income but little capital, and we had plenty of capital but little income. Our bankers, Hambros, supported the idea and we had no reason to think otherwise. Our shares were suspended pending the merger. During the negotiations, our accountants felt that something funny was going on and warned us of their fears, suggesting we check Star out with the Inland Revenue. This I did and was told of a pending investigation into the tax affairs of the Eckharts and the Star Group. Naturally, we withdrew from the deal, but, with our shares suspended, it left British Lion totally exposed. We were then approached by John Bentley of Barclay Securities who, again, was supported by our bankers, whose judgment we had to trust, and the rest is history.[2]

On 25 July 1975, Derek and Rodney Eckhart admitted at Leeds Crown Court to defrauding the Inland Revenue of £47,000. They were both jailed for two years by Judge Nevin and fined £14,000. EMI bought their bingo interests for £5,700,000. According to Sir Peter Rawlinson, defending, this was £2 million less than the amount that should have been paid.

In 1993 Gilliat recalled the circumstances of the Eckhart deal:

Frank Launder and I were never fully consulted over the proposal, partly because Star Theatres would only deal with principals. In fact, Frank and I never fully understood it, but what did become clear was that when that deal came off Frank and I would not be wanted. Our shares would be taken over at whatever the final price might be and there would no longer be a future for us at British Lion. Dealings in the shares were suspended for some months to allow time for production of accounts and other things like final adjustments. The price of the shares when suspended, if I remember rightly, was a good deal lower than the issue price when British Lion went public, so, had the Eckhart deal been consummated, our personal profit at best would have been relatively modest. Judging by the lack of adverse comment at the time, no particular objections were likely to be raised anywhere, although today it might be thought quite likely that the fate of company and studio would in fact have been no more secure under the Eckharts than under Barclay Securities.

Until the Eckharts defected, we were bound to accept a much smaller sum from Star and would certainly have done so had the deal gone through as planned. Long before, in fact months before Barclay Securities came on the scene, Frank and I were in no position to oversee, or much influence, British Lion's future. The Eckharts' defection left British Lion in a hopelessly vulnerable position, but I must say I find it difficult on any logical basis to detect any great difference between what happened under John Bentley and what *might* have happened under the Eckharts, which no one seems to have considered at all.

Mind you, had things continued to go downhill, which seemed likely, and the directors had lost their very substantial investments, we should have come out of it no better, since we would then have been derided as incompetents who deserved to lose their money. For that reason, amongst others, I have personally always regretted, in spite of the financial benefits that came in the end, that I went back into British Lion for the second time.[3]

According to both Sidney Gilliat and Roy Boulting, the British Lion board did not want to sell to Barclay Securities but their financial advisers, Hambros Bank, insisted that since they were a public company any bid must be placed before the shareholders. Gilliat recalls:

In any case from what I knew of the finances of British Lion as a whole in 1971–72, I cannot help wondering where the money would have come from to continue to keep Shepperton in operation with greatly diminished rentals and the likelihood of still fewer films from British Lion. I am no accountant, but I wonder how British Lion could have sustained the losses incurred for the years following. Pennies from Heaven, perhaps?[4]

Barclay Securities' offer was in cash at 137p a share, or in shares at two Barclay shares plus 370p in loan stock, for every seven British Lion shares. Bentley's offer was accepted by the British Lion board and on 25 April 1972 Barclay Securities Limited acquired British Lion (Holdings), British Lion's parent company, and Shepperton Studios for £5.5 million. The sixty-acre site was then valued at around £3.5 million and the studio employed between 350 and 400 people. Bentley claimed that Shepperton was losing some £12,000 a week, reinforcing his argument for replacing it with housing development.

According to calculations in *Private Eye* magazine (2 June 1972), if the British Lion directors took cash they could not make less than fifty pence a share. The magazine calculated that in 1971 the shares breakdown among the British Lion directors was: Lord Goodman (Chairman of British Lion Films since 1965), 190,111; Sir Max Rayne (a director since 1967), 589,164; Roy Boulting (1961), 366,304; John Boulting (1967), 361,218; Sidney Gilliat (1958), 271,388; Frank Launder (1969), 222,084. (The share totals for Lord Goodman and Sidney Gilliat include a number of shares held under non-beneficiary trust.) Translated into cash, Lord Goodman's shares would have made about £95,000; Sir Max Rayne, £294,000; Roy Boulting, £183,000; John Boulting, £180,000; Sidney Gilliat, £135,000; and Frank Launder, £111,000. If they had accepted Barclay shares, at the time worth £2.13 each according to that company's Annual Meeting, they stood to make considerably more. These are minimum figures based on the theory that the directors bought their shares at the 1968 asking price of 82p each.

Whether or not *Private Eye*'s figures are realistic, British Lion's directors, at the time of Bentley's acquisition, would not have resigned empty-handed. By the end of 1972, all the second group of postwar British Lion directors had resigned, with the exception of Bill Rule, a director from 1967, who resigned on 30 November 1973 with an extra payment of £10,000 and a Rover car, and Wilfred Moeller, a director from 1949, who resigned on 31 December 1973.

Within a month of purchasing British Lion, Bentley was planning the demise of the studio. In an interview with David Lewin for *Cinema TV Today* (20 May 1972), he outlined his plans for the studio which, in the light of his record of asset-stripping, had an ominous ring. According to Bentley, British Lion constituted the following parts: a production and distribution company; a film library; a property company; a studio-owning company and an advertising company, these total assets estimated at £20 million.

It may be necessary to move some of those parts into other areas of our operation where they would be more suitable. The advertising side, through Pearl & Dean, for example, to our poster company.... At the moment, we have a programme of films at Shepperton until September [1972], with John Boulting in charge, and no changes will be made until then. It has been suggested that Shepperton could occupy less space than it does. That is one hypothesis. Another hypothesis is, why should not Shepperton be merged with Pinewood? We have four hundred people at Shepperton earning high salaries and not being used through the year. Pinewood is the better studio but Shepperton has excellent equipment and it could be that the men and equipment could be moved there. I am not saying this will happen but it has to be considered a possibility.[5]

[For Shepperton, read Erith, and for Pinewood, read Merton.]

The stage was now set for one of the most remarkable survival battles in the history of the British film industry. Whereas the British film industry had always been its own worst enemy, the battle for Shepperton Studios was now against an outside predator whose admitted aim in life was making money. Bentley's many victims could testify to his single-minded ambition in that respect. Yet Lord Goodman, as Chairman of British Lion Films, was persuaded to reassure delegates at the 1972 NATTKE Annual Conference in Bournemouth that Barclay Securities had given him 'the firmest undertaking that they intend to remain in film-making. They have asked me to say so as Chairman. Unless they intended to remain in film-making, I would not stay there for one minute.'[6]

When John Bentley acquired British Lion and Shepperton Studios, he also inherited the restriction of the National Film Finance Corporation's one Preference Share in British Lion Films Limited, created in 1964. On 4 February that year, Edward Heath, in his then capacity as Secretary of State for Industry, Trade and Regional Development and President of the Board of Trade, had spelt out in Parliament the terms under which this 'golden share' would operate:

It is intended that, probably by the device of holding a single special share in the company, the NFFC should retain certain rights. These rights will include the right to veto the company's voluntary liquidation, the right to veto the sale of its undertaking, the right to veto the repayment of any capital to shareholders and any disposal of its interests in Shepperton Studios Limited, except in defined circumstances which would be in the judgment of the special shareholder.

It will also be ensured, probably by the same device, that a sum equivalent to any tax relief enjoyed by the company as a result of the use of the present accrued tax loss, will revert to the National Film Finance Corporation. The Corporation will also have the right to nominate a director to the Board, so that the Corporation and the government will be fully apprised at all times of the conduct of its affairs.

These provisions, which will be permanently effective, should ensure that no purchaser of British Lion shares can strip it of its assets, or do anything but continue to operate it as a going concern. It will also mean that no cash made from an authorised sale of any assets can be removed from the business without the agreement of the NFFC.

In addition, the purchasers will be required to give positive assurances to the National Film Finance Corporation that British Lion will continue to provide the facilities for independent producers which it now gives and continue to maintain an independent position.[7]

The 'defined circumstances' referred to by Mr Heath were clarified in an assurance given by the NFFC to British Lion Films on 31 March 1964:

> While any sale, or disposal, of British Lion's interest in Shepperton Studios Limited, or of the Company's interest in any real property shall require the consent of the holder of the special Preference Share of British Lion, our intention is that such consent will be given if:
> a) assurances are given which satisfy the holder of the special Preference Share, that there are satisfactory alternative studio facilities available to British Lion (to which similar restrictions would then subsequently apply) or
> b) it can be shown, to the satisfaction of the holder of the special Preference Share, that the Shepperton Studios can only be operated at a critical loss and that there is no reasonable prospect of their being operated as Studios for cinematograph film production on a profitable basis in the foreseeable future.[8]

It would be naive to believe that John Bentley was not aware of these studio defences erected, not by the company, but by the government. It would be equally naive to believe that he could not breach them. It was public knowledge that Bentley was seriously considering a political future within the Conservative Party. It would not be unreasonable, therefore, for him to anticipate practical support from the Party for his endeavours, logically through the Department of Environment, at the time headed by Peter Walker. Not surprisingly, Bentley's first attack on these studio defences was against their weakest point, the need to show the commercial unviability of the studio. For someone of Bentley's business pedigree this objective was simple to achieve, but he quickly discovered that people who work in the film industry are radically different from those who work in the pharmaceutical and toy industries. He was also to discover a radically different attitude to adversity than he had previously experienced in the rarefied atmosphere of the City.

In August 1972, almost four months after acquiring British Lion and Shepperton Studios, Bentley also acquired the unwelcome attention of the Shepperton Studios Action Committee, comprising representatives from the studio workforce and from the Shepperton Residents' Association. The committee was formed on 11 August, appropriately in 'The Bull' public house, Shepperton village, following a *Daily Telegraph* article by Stella Shamoon on 1 August, highlighting the studio sale. I was the committee's chairman, having worked at the studio in management, based in the studio operating office nerve centre, from 1960 to 1965.

Before opening the committee's public campaign, I took out 'insurance cover', requesting clarification from the Urban District Council of Sunbury-on-Thames, the local authority, of the tree-preservation status of a large oak tree in the studio grounds. The committee did not underestimate the task before them. It was necessary to launch the campaign from a positive platform with some form of action that would stick from the beginning. The signs were that Bentley's planned development of the studio site, once he had successfully disposed of the irritation called film-making, was for high-density housing. The committee reasoned that to achieve this would mean the removal of several trees from the studio site. An attempt to obtain tree-preservation orders on all the trees in the studio grounds, if successful, would provide a valuable holding operation so that the committee could organise for the battle ahead.

The gamble paid off. On 28 September, Mr H. Smith, Engineer and Surveyor to the Council, confirmed the following:

> I have to inform you that it is anticipated that all the trees at Shepperton Studios will, eventually, be the subject of a review with the object of obtaining a Tree Preservation Order. When this is done, the Oak Tree will be included in that review. In the meantime, should it become known that the tree in question is likely to suffer damage, I should be grateful if you will inform me so that the necessary action can be taken.

Armed with this information, the committee swept into action, opening its campaign with a publicity broadside aimed at John Bentley's Achilles heel – his desire to avoid publicity relating to his activities.

This opening skirmish was largely ignored by Bentley, but not by the local newspapers, who all headlined the story on their front page. In Bentley's view, this action by the committee was a predictable, spontaneous reaction to his purchase of the studio and without funds or resources the campaign would not be sustained, whereas he had at his disposal the financial muscle and resources of some of the City's sharpest operators.

Events began to move swiftly to the advantage of the committee. By the end of August, the story had been taken up by the national press, spearheaded by a follow-up story by Stella Shamoon in the *Daily Telegraph* of 21 August. Both national and local radio covered the story and film industry personalities began publicly to rally to the cause. Spike Milligan, Sir Alec Guinness and lighting cameraman Freddie Young were the first to pledge support.

Incredibly, by October support for the campaign both in the UK and abroad enabled the committee to mount its own bid for the studio, backed by financial group Global Participants (Eire). The euphoria was short-lived. Global Participants introduced new but onerous terms for their continuing support, forcing the committee to discontinue its association with the company and withdraw its bid. Despite this setback, the committee continued with its campaign against Barclay Securities and John Bentley, forming a fragile alliance with film industry trade unions both in the UK and abroad.

Throughout John Bentley's involvement with British Lion and Shepperton Studios, the British trade unions had been predictably active, in particular the Association of Cinematograph, Television and Allied Technicians (ACTT), which from March 1956 had superseded the Association of Cine-Technicians (ACT). The ACTT had most to lose if Shepperton was closed. The Federation of Film Unions – comprising the ACTT, EETU/PTU, Equity, FAA, the Musicians' Union, NATTKE and the Writers' Guild of Great Britain – had convened a mass meeting of members at the Criterion Theatre, Piccadilly Circus, on 16 April 1972, to protest at the imminent

Barclay Securities takeover of British Lion. On 24 August a mass meeting of workers was held at Shepperton Studios, with a further mass meeting at the studio on 13 November. The latter meeting endorsed an FFU Resolution agreed at an FFU meeting on 10 November 1972. The Federation pledged itself to:

1. Endeavour to maximise the number of studio-based films in Britain.
2. Contest strenuously any further restriction in film studio production facilities at Shepperton.
3. Rally the support of all construction unions to guarantee that Shepperton Film Studios will not be developed for any other purpose than film production.

The membership also adopted seven points which the ACTT Executive had adopted. Predictably, these points emphasised the ritual union demands of the day – 'No redundancies'; 'Occupation until these demands are met'; 'Nationalisation of all studios in financial difficulties without compensation and under workers' control', etc. The Federation of Film Unions convened a further mass meeting at the TUC headquarters in London on 3 December 1972, to endorse these seven points.

The action committee took a different approach to the problem. Whereas the trade unions tended to attack Bentley personally, the committee's view was that it would be more effective to attack Bentley's company, Barclay Securities, referring to him on a personal level only in his capacity as chairman of that company. It was also becoming clear to the committee that more was going on behind the scenes at Barclay Securities and British Lion than was publicly apparent. Minutes of meetings held by the local council, at which key decisions were taken concerning the future of Shepperton Studios, were mysteriously unavailable when I asked to see them. A 'fifth column' of selected studio workers representing all the major studio departments was set up by the action committee to secretly monitor the studio operation and to feed back to the committee any evidence of a deliberate run-down of the studio by management. Often this information, hurriedly scribbled on a piece of paper, was surreptitiously dropped through my letter-box a few hundred yards from the studio entrance, in the early hours. This was the safest time for an 'agent' to deliver information without being recognised. However, most of the committee's plotting and planning was done in its unofficial headquarters, 'The Bull' public house, where the public campaign was born.

In a letter to the *Daily Telegraph* (11 September 1972), Shepperton's managing director 'Andy' Worker had concluded that 'the studios are no longer a viable proposition without a subsidy of some kind.' Not surprisingly, the timing of this public confession was viewed with some cynicism within the industry. It seemed to presage Bentley's public announcement in the *Cinema TV Today* interview with David Lewin that 'no changes will be made until then [September]'. Coincidentally, on 10 September the NFFC announced that it was prepared to allow forty of the studio's sixty acres to be sold. Inexplicably, this decision was rescinded one month later.

Barclay Securities' original plan was to sell off fifty-five acres of the studio site, preserving the remaining five acres on a 'care and maintenance' basis, with film production carried on elsewhere. According to valuers Healey and Baker, the fifty-five acres of residential land was then worth around £2.5 million. This valuation was based on the sale, for £330,000, of 3.23 acres of residentially zoned land and 4.3 acres of Green Belt land close to the studios. The valuation was well below estimates that had reached as high as £5 million. Even so, on this basis Bentley would have recouped almost all his investment in British Lion, considering that, according to the London *Evening Standard* (6 September 1972), he had spent only £3 million on Barclay's majority shareholding in British Lion because holders of 40 per cent of the company 'decided to stay along for the ride'.

Throughout this hectic activity, John Bentley had restructured his organisation. At the time of his purchase of British Lion his parent company was Barclay Securities Limited, under which was the Mills & Allen poster advertising group, at the time the largest in the UK (accounting for approximately 30 per cent of the industry's annual turnover), and various other interests in toys and pharmaceuticals. British Lion (Holdings) Limited was parent company to British Lion Films, Shepperton Studios and Pearl & Dean, then one of the two largest cinema advertising groups in the UK.

On 9 November 1972 brokers Joseph Sebag and Co., on behalf of Barclay Securities, publicly offered shares for sale in a new company, Lion International. The new company comprised British Lion Films, Shepperton Studios, Pearl & Dean (at the time operating a franchise agreement to exhibit advertising films in about 850 UK cinemas, the largest franchise being with the 240 cinemas run by Associated British Cinemas), Mills & Allen and Leonard Ripley and Co.

Mills & Allen had started life in 1928, as Mills and Rockleys, and had adopted its later name on 30 October 1964. Leonard Ripley and Co. was founded in 1927 as lithographic and general printers, took over Hampton Press in 1946 and in turn was taken over by Barclay Securities in 1970. Producing and printing posters represented over 80 per cent of Ripley's turnover. The pre-tax profit for this new group for the year ending 31 March 1973 was £1,800,000.

Peripheral companies – Lion Pacesetter Productions, producers of sponsored advertising films for cinema and television; Davis-Poynter, publishers; and Pearl & Dean Publications – lost £128,730 before taxation for the year ended 31 March 1972, and were sold. Lion Pacesetter (formerly Littleton Park Films) was sold to Ronnie and Adele Spencer, and under new chairman Lord Brabourne changed its name to Pacesetter Productions. Davis-Poynter was sold to a consortium of former British Lion senior management and shareholders. Pearl & Dean Publications was sold to a subsidiary of St Ives Press for a nominal £1, though the agreement provided for participation in future profits.

British Lion's distribution arrangement with Columbia Pictures, through BLC under managing director Victor Hoare, was not renewed on 1 October 1972, being terminated by mutual agreement with each of the parties retaining their respective distribution rights. British Lion's principal source of revenue at that time was its film library, which consisted of over

300 feature films. A major contract with the BBC covered 136 films, providing a gross annual revenue for British Lion of approximately £210,000 for a seven-year period, ending 31 March 1975.

Directors of the new company, Lion International, were Lord Goodman (Chairman), Sir Max Rayne (Deputy Chairman), Jeremy Arnold (Managing Director), John Boulting, Beverley Ripley, John Bentley and Charles Holden (Finance Director of Barclay Securities). The Managing Director of British Lion was Peter Snell, a Canadian independent film producer, and 'Andy' Worker remained Managing Director of Shepperton Studios. Lord Goodman, Chairman of British Lion, and British Lion directors Sir Max Rayne and John Boulting remained on the board of Lion International after the acquisition of British Lion by Barclay Securities, in order to deal with an application to the Department of Trade and Industry and the NFFC relating to the future use of Shepperton Studios.

Early in March 1972 British Lion had approached the Department of Trade and Industry with representations designed to show that both sets of circumstances in which the NFFC would be permitted to sell the studio had arisen. British Lion claimed that satisfactory alternative studio facilities were available to the company on a short-term lease at Pinewood Studios, and that Shepperton Studios were, or soon would be, operating at a critical loss. A cynical observer could be forgiven for thinking that the timing of such a move – just over a month before Barclay Securities' takeover of British Lion – was more than a coincidence. Perhaps it was rough justice when the ploy failed.

On 28 March 1972 the DTI sought advice from the NFFC, which on 14 April reported that it considered that neither of the sets of circumstances had been satisfied. On 3 May, after Barclay Securities' purchase of British Lion on 25 April, the DTI asked the NFFC to open direct discussions with British Lion, with a view to investigating the position in detail and reporting back. Just why the DTI should have felt the need to reopen this subject so soon *after* Bentley's purchase of British Lion, when the NFFC had clearly advised the DTI that there was no case to pursue remains a mystery.

On 2 June the NFFC had a meeting with representatives of British Lion at which the latter agreed that, owing to the type of tenure available at Pinewood Studios, the 'satisfactory alternative studio facilities' could not be said to exist.[9] As to the claim that the studio was, or would be, operating at a critical loss, the NFFC requested replies to a number of questions concerning the British Lion claim, answers to which were given on 8 June. The NFFC, apparently unconvinced, submitted further questions to British Lion on 3 July, and replies were given on 25 July. Nevertheless, on 16 August, the NFFC reported to the DTI that it was not satisfied that Shepperton Studios could only be operated at a critical loss and these conclusions were notified to British Lion, by the DTI, on 21 August.

There was now a stalemate. On the one hand, the management of Shepperton Studios had been prevented by the NFFC's decision from selling, or disposing, of all or any part of the studio property. On the other hand, the NFFC had no power to prevent the closing of the studio, which its new owner, Barclay Securities, threatened to do. Clearly a compromise solution had to be reached if Shepperton was to be maintained as a major film studio and if the spirit of Edward Heath's assurances to Parliament was to be preserved.

After a series of meetings, an exchange of letters (dated 2 and 3 November) between Lord Goodman, then Chairman of the British Lion Group, and R. A. Clark, Chairman of the NFFC, produced a compromise which was publicly announced in a joint statement by the NFFC and Lion International on 7 November. This compromise allowed for a studio complex of about fifteen acres, based on the existing stages 'A', 'B', 'C' and 'D'. Included were the associated workshops, dubbing theatre and other existing facilities, plus an area outside the Old House to be used as a back lot. Development permission was to be sought for an additional five-acre plot between the studio complex and the main road for the purpose of offices and other facilities ancillary to the studio operation. The remaining area of land, approximately forty acres, could be used by the owners for its own purposes subject to planning permission being obtained.

Lion International undertook to maintain facilities at Shepperton as a self-contained and independent studio capable of sustaining the production of two major films simultaneously. The initial staff to be employed at the studio under the new arrangements would be no fewer than 200, but it was hoped that other existing staff would be absorbed in arrangements then under discussion with other film interests. The statement did not disclose details of these other interests. It was left to Lion International to decide whether the studio remained under their individual control, or whether it would be operated in conjunction with studios elsewhere.

The twenty acres comprising the new Shepperton Studios would be subject to a restrictive covenant similar in intent to the existing restriction operated by the NFFC, the 'golden share', but subject to suitable clarification of wording. However, these proposals had been approved by the NFFC in principle only. Detailed arrangements had yet to be agreed. On 14 December 1972, Jeremy Arnold, Managing Director of Lion International, made detailed proposals which the NFFC regarded as generally acceptable. Plans were made, with the approval of the DTI, to announce the detailed implementation of the arrangements, already agreed in principle, at a conference to be held and organised on the initiative of Lion International at Shepperton Studios on 16 January 1973, and terms were agreed for a press statement. The conference failed to materialise, since Jeremy Arnold resigned in January as Managing Director of Lion International, and it was back to the drawing-board for all concerned with Shepperton Studios.

By November 1972 a rift over strategy had developed between the action committee and the film industry unions, notably the ACTT. The committee was not convinced that the rhetoric of the unions was helpful to the campaign and, for a time, went its own way. It was during this period that one of the more bizarre episodes of the campaign occurred.

On 14 November 1972 John Bentley arranged to address a meeting of the studio Joint Works Committee, to which he also invited me as action committee chairman. On entering the studio, I was promptly escorted out again on the order of Managing Director 'Andy' Worker. Within minutes of returning home, I was telephoned by studio security, requesting my return to the studio to meet Bentley in the Old House. Still ruffled by the indignity of being unceremoniously thrown out of the studio for whose preservation I had been fighting, I reluctantly agreed to return and was escorted into the studio boardroom. To my further surprise, instead of witnessing Bentley's proposals to the Joint Works Committee, I was asked by Bentley to remain in the boardroom until the meeting was finished. To reinforce his request, Bentley positioned a very large gentleman on the door. After the meeting, Bentley returned and informed me that his proposals had been accepted, but did not elaborate. An aerial photograph of the studio adorned one wall of the boardroom. On this, Bentley then drew a line with a chinagraph pencil around those parts of the studio which, he claimed, could now be disposed of. Effectively, only four stages would remain: 'A'/'B' and 'C'/'D'.

With some disbelief, I studied Bentley's artwork for a few minutes. Then, with another chinagraph pencil, I drew a further line on the photograph. Outside of this line were those parts of the studio which I thought the committee and its supporters would be prepared to sacrifice as a compromise. Within this second line were all the studio stages and buildings (including the Old House) but not the studio back lot and lawns to the rear of the Old House. Twenty years later the studio and adjacent property development precisely reflect the parameters of that second line I drew in 1972.

Within five months of its formation, the campaign of the action committee and of the Shepperton Residents' Association persuaded John Bentley – at a private meeting in his London home between him and myself as committee chairman – finally to admit that he was 'bottled up'. Confrontation slowly gave way to consultation.

Plan of the battleground in 1972. The solid black line shows the old studio boundary, the broken line shows the boundary proposed by Barclay Securities.

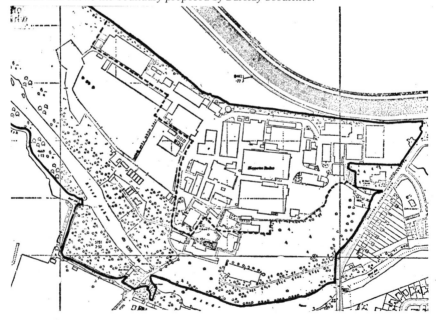

Despite this, the studio management continued to emphasise, as it had done throughout 1972, that the studio was operating, or was about to operate, at a critical loss. Yet eighteen films were made at the studio during 1972, the most produced in one postwar year since twenty-one were made in 1965, during the boom years. Therefore it was not unreasonable to assume that either the 1972 films had badly drafted contracts or the studio management was inefficient. How else could a major studio operate in such a financial mess when that number of films were being produced? Perhaps it was a combination of both assumptions that led to the persistent pessimistic assessment of the studio's future. But the imminent financial failure seems extraordinary in the light of some of the films made in 1972. They included *Asylum* (Roy Ward Baker), *Alice's Adventures in Wonderland* (William Sterling), *Day of the Jackal* (Fred Zinnemann), *Hitler – The Last Ten Days* (Ennio de Concini) and *The Wicker Man* (Robin Hardy), films made by experienced producers most of whom were Shepperton 'regulars'.

In January 1973 a brief flurry of rumours concerning the BBC's interest in purchasing the studio proved to be unfounded. These rumours were based on the BBC's need for a studio to replace Ealing Studios, which they were shortly to vacate.

Also in January, the Shepperton Residents' Association further undermined Bentley's plans for disposing of the studio site when they publicly confirmed their opposition to development on the site, astutely introducing Green Belt and Public Open Space arguments into the controversy. In a written statement dated January 1973 the Association's chairman, C. E. Wenman, spelt out their position:

Since the Action Committee for preserving Shepperton Studios was formed, the Shepperton Residents' Association has had representation on that committee. Our concern has been, and still is, not who owns the studio, but what may happen to the sixty-acre site. Quite naturally, we wish it to remain a studio because:
  1. No development problems would arise.
  2. Many jobs would be safeguarded.
  3. The studios are known throughout the world and form part of the Shepperton heritage.
The last point is, no doubt, of little interest to people outside Shepperton, but it is a fact.

A lot has been published during the past year [1972], in the national and local press, stating that various bodies intend to develop certain acreage as though this were a fait accompli. In other words, a kind of conditioning process. We would point out that this is not so. Our latest enquiry at the offices of the Sunbury Urban District Council has revealed that no application has yet been submitted. If and when it is, the voice of Shepperton residents will surely be heard.

The latest press reports suggest a likelihood of the studio remaining but covering a much smaller area, with the major portion hived off for potential development. We would be delighted to see the studio continue, but feel sure our members would oppose development of the remaining land.

On the Staines and Sunbury town map the sixty-acre studio site is designated as Film Studios and is enclosed on the south side by Green Belt land and Public Open Space and on the north side by the Queen Mary Reservoir. Planning attempts have been made in the past for development on the adjoining Green Belt land and my committee feels that, should housing take place on the studio site, a real danger exists of further attempts being made to develop on the Green Belt land, with the subsequent sprawl joining Shepperton and Laleham [the next village].

It is our understanding that such urban expansion into open areas between communities on the London periphery is contrary to government policy. This view was strengthened by statements made by Lord Sandford (Joint Parliamentary Secretary, Department of the Environment) on a recent visit to the district, following representations by this Association.

A 'mini-poll' was conducted by us recently in the vicinity of the studio which shows a five to one opinion in favour of the site being either Green Belt or Public Open Space. It is now our intention to take further action to establish more fully the residents' wishes on this subject.

It is the view of my committee that any land on this site not required for studio use should be redesignated Green Belt, or Public Open Space, and shown accordingly on the Staines and Sunbury town map. If necessary, this should be ensured through a Compulsory Purchase Order by the Local or County Authority.

On 19 January 1973 Bentley countered by offering the studio workforce a 50 per cent stake in a new company, Shepperton Studios (1973) Limited, if they agreed to forty-six acres being sold for development and retaining the remaining fourteen acres for production, plus a further fifteen acres to be leased from adjoining land owned by the Metropolitan Water Board. This plan involved 106 redundancies, but guaranteed that film-making could continue at the studio for at least one more year. The workers' 50 per cent stake would come out of whatever was left of Shepperton Studios once the land was sold.

The action committee insisted on another five acres of studio land being made available for production, to include all existing studio facilities and to avoid the power house, 'E', 'F' and 'G' stages, the timber store and most of the preview theatres from disappearing, as planned under Bentley's proposal.

On 31 March 1973 agreement was reached for a twenty-acre studio site, retaining all production facilities and stages but losing the studio backlot. The action committee asked for a voluntary redundancy scheme for studio workers and a three-year guarantee of work for those not taking voluntary redundancy. Barclay Securities agreed in principle to these proposals despite the fact that they had been taken over by the financial group J.H. Vavasseur and Co., for £17.5 million, on 19 March. Once again, it was back to the drawing board.

John Bentley had been fighting the Vavasseur take-over since January 1973, when he had ensured an eternal place in City mythology by asking

'Vava-Who?' when telephoned in New York and told of the bid for his company. As a take-over expert himself he had rapidly assessed his chances of survival, which may have contributed to his suddenly accommodating nature regarding the future of the studio. Also in January, Bentley had lost the services of his right-hand man Jeremy Arnold, who had resigned as Managing Director of Lion International, allegedly over a disagreement with Bentley concerning the future policy for British Lion. Eventually, Bentley gave up the fight for Shepperton Studios and Vavasseur became the new owner. As part of the deal Bentley collected some shares in Vavasseur, which he then sold to the National Coal Board Pension Fund. In later years he continued to be successful with his diversified business interests.

Interestingly, Bentley's business associates from his Shepperton Studios escapade, Jim Slater and Peter Walker, both resurfaced into the public eye in 1992. Slater, building on a successful career as an author of children's books, achieving sales of more than two million, wrote an incisive guide on how to invest in the stock market, *The Zulu Principle – How to Make Extraordinary Profits from Ordinary Shares*. Peter Walker (now Lord Walker) was appointed by Prime Minister John Major to head the enquiry into the government's controversial pit closure plan which had led to huge demonstrations of public support for the coal mining community.

The campaign to save Shepperton Studios had been successful in respect of John Bentley and Barclay Securities but now the threat to the studio's future remained with its new owner, Vavasseur. These fears were confirmed when Jeremy Arnold was reinstated by Vavasseur as Managing Director of Lion International. He immediately reopened negotiations with the NFFC regarding the future of the studio.

These negotiations, and representations made to the NFFC by the Federation of Film Unions, resulted in yet another set of proposals for the NFFC to consider. On 19 July 1973, Anthony Grant, Parliamentary Under Secretary of State for Industrial Development, announced to the House of Commons in a Written Answer:

National Film Finance Corporation Limited, Lion International Limited and Shepperton Studios Limited, announce that, pursuant to the agreement in principle announced on 7 November 1972, they have now agreed detailed arrangements concerning the future of the facilities at Shepperton Studios.

The present arrangement ensures the continuation of Shepperton as a major British film production centre, improves its commercial viability and in no way impairs existing facilities. In due course, however, the unused land which will not form part of the revised Shepperton facilities will be released from NFFC's veto restrictions.

Of the eleven film stages currently available at Shepperton, eight will be retained under the new arrangements. These eight stages account for over 90 per cent of the existing stage space there and they include the silent stage (H), the largest stage in Europe. Apart from the three surplus stages (I, J and K), the only facilities excluded from the revised studio layout are a scene dock and the Old House, which is currently used for administration purposes. The scene dock facilities will be provided within the scope of buildings existing within the reorganised studio. Although the Old House is excluded from the new studio boundaries, this building and the lawn in front of it are expected to remain available for studio administrative purposes and for occasional filming.

Because there are no film lot facilities within the revised studio boundaries, Lion has obtained from the Metropolitan Water Board an agreement to grant a lease for a term of twenty years of five acres of open ground adjacent to the existing studio area and these five acres will be used as a lot. The Metropolitan Water Board will have the right, in certain special circumstances, to determine the lease on twelve months' notice, but, in that event, Lion would anticipate no difficulty in arranging alternative lot facilities. Additionally, arrangements have been entered into which will make available further facilities in the close vicinity of the studio for shooting river scenes and wooded areas.

The Board of Lion states, with the full support of J. H. Vavasseur and Co. Ltd, majority shareholders in Lion:

As a matter of firm policy, Lion has determined that it will continue to operate a major film studio at Shepperton for so long as this activity may be maintained on a basis of commercial viability.

The Board of Lion is therefore prepared:

A. To agree manning levels with each of the unions represented amongst the work force at Shepperton and to enter into all reasonable undertakings as to future employment in the light of these agreements.
B. To take active steps to optimise the long-term trading position within the boundaries agreed with the NFFC as the new studio complex.
C. To finance a programme of re-equipment currently being planned.

As a result of this plan, within eight months the planned stage capacity for Shepperton's survival had been doubled from four (as proposed by Barclay Securities in November 1972) to eight, as now proposed by the new owner, J. H. Vavasseur and Co., through Lion International.

On 2 November 1973 agreement was reached between Shepperton Studios Limited and the Federation of Film Unions for no redundancies on a studio site of around twenty-two acres. A further undertaking was given to preserve the Old House and lawns for at least five years. Planning permission was to be applied for to rebuild 'H' stage between the boiler house and the adjoining reservoir. This latter, rather desperate move did not materialise and today 'H' stage is still firmly ensconced where Sir Alexander Korda put it in 1948.

The Shepperton Studios Action Committee was officially disbanded on 9 November 1973, but as its chairman I continued to keep a watching brief on subsequent developments at the studio, and on more than one occasion was persuaded publicly to voice my concern over some of those developments.

The production upsurge of 1972 did not continue into 1973, with only six films produced at the studio, including *The Internecine Project* (Ken Hughes) and *The Beast Must Die* (Paul Annett) from studio stalwart Amicus Productions.

Christmas 1973 saw the first of several developments which fore-shadowed more trouble for the studio. Security, or the lack of it, was an unwelcome topic of conversation in and around the studio early in 1974. It is debatable whether this disquiet was known to the studio's insurers (at that time the Prudential), but certainly the studio had entered what one employee described as 'a really mucky phase'. Allegedly, the studio bar was raided over the 1973 Christmas period with, uncharacteristically, little fuss being officially recorded.

The subject of security came to a head on 8 March 1974 through a labour dispute involving the Shepperton Security Shop represented by the industry union, NATTKE. As with many union disputes of the day, the issue was so-called 'blackleg' (non-union) labour and cheap labour (also non-union) being employed in place of union labour. The issue was the introduction of labour from a private firm, Securicor, whose workforce in the studio was being paid fifty pence an hour, 10.52 pence per hour below the NATTKE 'rate for the job'. When told of the studio management's intention to supply Securicor guards under a contract labour clause, the chief NATTKE steward and the studio organiser had taken the view that under the Contractual Labour clause in the NATTKE/FPA Agreement it was permissible to have contracted labour of this sort if NATTKE labour was not available. This dispute subsequently led to a hard-hitting statement by the NATTKE Security Shop steward in the studio, which outlined the union's view of security arrangements at the studio:

> The result is that all sorts of persons are being introduced to the premises and the security arrangements. Master Keys are given over to single individuals who are allocated to this work in place of two NATTKE ... Since they work singly at below the rate, it is quite apparent that they are a much cheaper proposition than NATTKE grades on standard time, or on premium time, plus half or double time.[10]

According to NATTKE, the company had reaffirmed its policy as recently as 26 January 1974, that no one would patrol the studio unaccompanied during the hours of darkness, yet Securicor members were patrolling singly, not doing their job efficiently and were failing to ring the main gate at each half-hour interval of a patrol to verify their position and time, as required of NATTKE members.

Management had assured NATTKE that Securicor guards were all trade union members, trained in security, fire-fighting and first aid. Again, the NATTKE statement presented a different picture:

> Generally speaking, the Securicor members have maintained a silence upon their training background, their status as trades unionists, or

professional standing. On Tuesday 26 March, a single Securicor guard admitted that he was a regular soldier quartered at Aldershot camp and doing this work in his spare time to earn fifty pence an hour. This confirmed other remarks about fifty pence an hour and a general suspicion that the work was being sub-contracted to personnel 'moon-lighting' from other jobs.

The department feel, as they have always felt, that this is a pure case of a 'black-legging' operation, unscrupulously organised by the company, through their policeman – Mr R. Field [an Inspector with Staines Police before he joined the studio in 1963] – with the dregs of industry being exploited by the Securicor to turn a swift 'buck' in dispute conditions and by the connivance of the FPA and Shepperton Studios to blunt action by the NATTKE Security Shop to a claim for proper basic rates of pay in return for a whole range of multi-function expected from and hitherto given by the Security Shop to the management.[11]

If the tone and style of this statement had a familiar ring, emanating from the studio that made the Boultings' *I'm All Right, Jack*, then more of the gospel according to Fred Kite followed. Having warned the management of the dire consequences of continuing to employ Securicor guards on the current basis, the statement concluded:

The department now insists that the Securicor be withdrawn from the studio forthwith or a vicious campaign will be conducted against them and the studio management with no holds barred. The insurers of the studio will be informed of the inadequacy of the arrangements and the risks being taken by the management to avoid facing their financial responsibilities.[12]

Securicor guards were rumoured to have been in the studio on 19 March and 16 and 17 April 1974, but providing no night cover. Apparently, there also was no full security cover for the studio after 21 April until the problem was resolved after the studio management decided to go 'four-wall' later that year.[13] As if the security problem were not enough, the 1973 'winter of discontent', brought about by the paralysing conflict between the Conservative government of Edward Heath and Arthur Scargill's miners, produced another local difficulty for the studio. The infamous 'three-day week' produced by this confrontation and the resulting power cuts under government emergency regulations persuaded the studio management that it could not keep the premises open and lit at night. From 2 January 1974 studio night cleaners were told to work only during the day. For reasons best known to herself, 56-year-old Mrs Charlotte Squib of Shepperton, a night cleaner at the studio for twelve years, thought otherwise and refused to transfer to day-work cleaning, claiming her right to work, under the terms of her contract, as a night cleaner. The management terminated her employment, giving her six weeks' money in lieu of notice. Supported by her union, NATTKE, she took her case to an industrial tribunal and won a redundancy payment of £498.63.

Clearly these local difficulties were becoming an irritation to manage-

ment – and to the studio's owner, Vavasseur, who were having considerable difficulties of their own. In the first six months of 1974 Vavasseur
made an attributable loss of £8,869,000 after writing off £9,145,000 in
provisions for unrealised losses. This was the last unhappy chapter in the
group's history before the revamp operation that took effect from 1 July that
year.

In March 1974 reports that the Greater London Council's plans for 700
houses on thirty acres of studio land had been dropped were strenuously
denied by the GLC who, it was reported, were 'still talking to Surrey
County Council about the possibility of acquiring the studio for housing
purposes'.[14] Their cause was not helped by the continuing opposition of
the Shepperton Residents' Association to housing development on the
studio site. The Association's chairman, Arthur Williams, claimed that if
the GLC did build on the studio land they would be turned into the 'slums
of tomorrow' by high-density housing.

By early April 1974 losses of £155,000 in the first six months to 30
September 1973 were £55,000 over the yearly limit set by Lion International to save the studio from closure, although for the same period Lion
turned in profits of £1.1 million, and in February 1974 had sold an office
property for £1.9 million. Jeremy Arnold, Managing Director, announced
that the studio would close after June 1974 and a phased rundown would
be carried out leaving only maintenance staff. The twenty-acre studio site
would be retained with its buildings in the hope that the studio would
reopen a few years later. Of the studio's 300 staff, 265 accepted voluntary
redundancy, but according to Alan Sapper, General Secretary of the ACTT,
early in May that year four different production companies had approached Vavasseur offering to move into the studio to film. All four offers had
been rejected. Industry observers believed that this decision was strongly
connected with the deteriorating fortunes of Vavasseur. Behind the scenes,
Vavasseur was in deep trouble.

Barclay Securities had been bought for its cash and assets. The studio
represented a small part of Vavasseur business and the company had been
led to believe that it would not be troublesome. At the end of April 1974
Vavasseur had asked for dealings in its shares to be suspended. The share
price had plunged from 246p in 1973 to 18p. The company's head office
near London's Tower Bridge was sold to the National Provident Institution
for £1.68 million and on 13 June 1974 Vavasseur's Chief Executive, David
Stark, confirmed to shareholders at the Annual General Meeting that, with
reference to the bid for Barclay Securities, 'It looks awful – it is awful!'

Stark also confirmed that some £4 million had been paid for goodwill but
after unravelling Barclay's assets it was discovered that 'lots of assets did
not reach the price at which they had been evaluated.' He revealed that the
unauthorised action of an employee who had bought 1.1 million shares in
William Whittingham, a Wolverhampton building group, had led to Vavasseur losing more than £1.5 million. In 1992, Stark admitted: 'It [Barclay
Securities] was a bad deal.'

1974 had started badly for Vavasseur. In the first three months of the
year, the studio lost £250,000. Dealings in the shares of J.H. Vavasseur, the
financial group at the top of the pyramid which owned Lion International

and Shepperton Studios, crashed to a new low from 254p in 1973 to 24p, reducing the group's market value from £30 million to £3.5 million. Dealings in the shares were suspended at lunchtime on 19 February 1974, but by evening a misunderstanding with the Stock Exchange had been resolved and dealings were reinstated next morning.

The trouble had started with a loss of confidence in Vavasseur Life Assurance, an insurance subsidiary, which had written most of its business in the form of a Money Back Income Bond. Vavasseur Life had been founded as the Annuity Assurance Society in 1964 and was acquired by Vavasseur in 1972. It was reported to have had a life and annuity fund of some £25 million. In December 1972 the fund had stood at £984,333, but with this loss of confidence Vavasseur admitted that Vavasseur Life 'had become a possible source of worry to the group'[15] and eventually sold it to the Prudential for a nominal amount.

Although Vavasseur held 49 per cent of Lion International shares, Lion International and Shepperton Studios had not been affected by this situation. But it rapidly became clear that, should anyone make a suitable cash offer for the film side, Vavasseur would grab it with both hands. On 23 March 1974 Kenneth Courte, writing in the trade weekly *Cinema TV Today*, confirmed that 'the dominant 49 per cent (in Lion International), held by J.H. Vavasseur, is up for sale at the right price.'

After the collapse of Vavasseur early in 1974, the group was revamped by Hambros Bank. From 1 July 1974 J. H. Vavasseur and Co. became a subsidiary of J. H. Vavasseur Group, the company which resulted from the revamp operation. Sir Gordon Newton, former editor of the *Financial Times* and chairman of Vavasseur, announced a loss of £17.9 million for 1973 (1972 profits were nearly £3 million). He blamed the run on the secondary banks in 1973, on the collapse of the property market, 'which made one unable to get liquid', and the fall in stock market prices which meant that 'one had to write off a massive amount'.

When Vavasseur bought Barclay Securities, it had seemed a perfectly sensible decision. However, Barclay Securities had a lot of investments in the company, and with the fall in the stock market the investments were worth less. Vavasseur accounts disclose a £7.2 million write-off for the Barclay Securities deal.

After shares were suspended at the end of April 1974, pending the capital restructuring of the company, the setting up of a new holding company (complete with new Board) and a rights issue, Sir Ian Morrow took over from Sir Gordon Newton as Chairman of the new company and Clive Hollick from Hambros Bank became Managing Director. Other Board members were David Probert, Finance Director of Lion International, and Ian Wasserman of Slater Walker Securities. Jeremy Arnold told *Cinema TV Today* (4 May 1974):

> I have been given personal assurance by the new management of Vavasseur that it would not oppose Lion's continued production programme. I am now more relaxed than I have been for the past three months when Vavasseur was in danger of crashing. It has been saved by a scheme of reconstruction and this means that, where before the

position of JHV was perilous, it is now a great deal more secure. It is under much less pressure now to realise its assets and the prospect of Vavasseur parcelling off their shares to someone disagreeable to us has receded. It is a mark for stability. We are as anxious as ever to remain in film production. We are making money out of it and I am confident we can go on making money out of films.

The restructuring involved shareholders participating in a £1 million rights issue. This was to be underwritten by Slater Walker (who would become the largest shareholder), Hambros Bank and Jessell Securities.

The rights issue flopped. Only 35 per cent of the shares were taken up and the remainder were left with the underwriters. The shares closed at thirteen pence each on the first day of reopened dealings, placing a value of only £2.6 million on the company as against £28 million in 1973. Films Minister Eric Deakins, in a speech to NATTKE members in Bournemouth reported in *Cinema TV Today* (4 May 1974), had described Shepperton Studios as 'the most treasured jewel in the crown of the British film industry'. At the end of May the jewel in the crown became somewhat tarnished when Spelthorne Council advised British Lion to submit two planning applications for forty acres of the studio site, excluding Green Belt land belonging to the Metropolitan Water Board, which adjoined the studio. In June the first steps were taken to move the studio into its present 'four-wall' operation.

The new Chairman of Shepperton Studios and Deputy Managing Director of British Lion Films, Barry Spikings, announced that a major reorganisation would be completed by the end of September 1974: 'We are tailoring the facilities we have to the demands of today's cost-conscious industry.'

In July 1974 Jeremy Arnold announced at a press conference that Shepperton Studios would now be known as The Shepperton Studio Centre and would operate on a 'four-wall' basis, available for hiring to any film or television concern.

In August, Vavasseur purchased another 2 per cent of shares in Lion International for around £75,000, giving them a 51 per cent controlling interest. Spikings claimed it was just coincidence that Vavasseur had bought more Lion shares at the same time as their own had flopped (five million Vavasseur shares had been put on the market and fewer than two million had been bought). Of importance to Vavasseur was that, with a controlling interest in Lion International, Lion's profits could now count in Vavasseur's annual accounts.

Lion had a satisfactory year. Turnover for 1973–74 jumped from £12 million to £15.6 million and trading profit was up from £1,887,000 to £2,522,000. This was after allowing for a £159,000 trading loss on the US operations of Pearl & Dean. These profit figures excluded losses at Shepperton Studios, which were £469,000 on trading account, well up on the £16,000 deficit recorded in 1972–73. Even when the studio was not being used, it was estimated to cost around £17,000 a week to run. In addition to the trading loss of the studio, Lion also had to bear redundancy costs of £360,000 as a result of cutting back the labour force from over 300 to just eight. By August 1974 the revamped studio operation was bringing in rental income from normal five-year leases on what was basically industrial space, at the rate of £115,000 a year. Lion supplied the buildings at fixed rents on normal commercial terms, with the studio services subcontracted.

As part of the restructuring of the studio, a clear-out of studio equipment and props (costumes were sold separately) was organised by Shepperton Studios Limited. A five-day public auction was held in the studio, beginning on 30 September 1974. Over 3,000 lots were listed in a 168-page catalogue, and the auctioneers claimed to have received over 2,000 enquiries from abroad before the auction opened.

To thousands of film fans and industry workers this auction reflected a hypocrisy on the part of studio management and signalled the end of an era in British film industry history. Long-serving prop man Bobby Murrell was not one of the eight employees retained in the studio, but having spent nearly thirty years in the prop business, the last few years as half of the famous Shepperton prop duo Chuck and Bobby, he had one last card to play before his death soon after this event. Bobby was the only person left from the studio who knew which star used which prop and in which film. Armed with this knowledge, he became the 'star' of this episode of the studio's history. 'These props have been my life's work,' he told the *Surrey Comet* (14 September 1974) before the auction. 'I'm heartbroken to see them going. I haven't got any future employment lined up, but I expect I'll find something. If not, I've always got my redundancy money.'

Oliver's begging bowl from *Oliver!* was knocked down for a paltry £28. According to Murrell, it seemed hardly worthwhile removing it from under

'The big sell-off'

CATALOGUE
OF THE
FILM STUDIO EQUIPMENT
AT
FILM STUDIOS, SHEPPERTON, MIDDLESEX
FOR SALE BY AUCTION
ON
MONDAY 30th SEPTEMBER 1974
And Following Days at 10-30 a.m. precisely each day

On View: From 16th September 1974, Monday to Friday from 9-30 a.m. to 4-30 p.m.
(On Wednesday & Thursday 25th & 26th viewing will be extended until 7-30 p.m.)

AUCTIONEERS:
FULLER, HORSEY, SONS & CASSELL
IN CONJUNCTION WITH
EDWARD RUSHTON SON & KENYON

---

his bed where he had hidden it since 1968; allegedly, some twenty other Oliver begging bowls were also in circulation at the time. A Surrey man paid £55 for a twelve-foot high triffid, and the BBC programme *Dig This* paid for a number of mini-Flying Fortress aircraft, after bidding for the wrong lot number – they wanted a triffid. According to Studio Manager Graham Ford, 'The auction probably did more harm than good, knowing that, coming on top of the redundancies, one then had to convince the industry that we were still in business.'[16]

A further blow to industry confidence in the studio was the removal of Adrian 'Andy' Worker after fifteen years as Managing Director, steering the studio through the boom years of the 60s and the traumatic early 70s. According to Barry Spikings, Worker's removal in October 1974 was 'amicable', but Worker had threatened legal proceedings over his claim for compensation for the remaining three years of his contract.[17]

Twenty-eight year-old Charles Gregson took over as Managing Director of Shepperton Studios. Gregson came from Lion International, where he had specific responsibility for British Lion Films.

> The job I was given was very clear. I had to strike a balance between running the studio at a profit, while at the same time investing as much as we could afford in upgrading facilities. The trouble with Shepperton was that, over the loss-making years in the late 60s and early 70s, the studio hadn't got any money and had made no investment in the place. [This is disputed by Sidney Gilliat, who claims some time had been spent on services and repairs during his ten-year Chairmanship.] It just looked awful in terms of facilities. The drains were blocked, the wiring was wrong, the dressing rooms were tatty and unloved and weeds were everywhere. It was very run-down.
>
> We invested the money we were generating from the studio operations into rebuilding the infrastructure. We put in a completely new heating system for the entire studio, which was one of our first major projects; we completely redid all the roads; we completely rewired most of the stages and refurbished them because of the asbestos problem and we redid a lot of the roofs. There was considerable reinvestment into the studio.[18]

The new-look Shepperton Studio Centre was officially launched at the beginning of November 1974. The management team was Barry Spikings as Chairman and as Studio Manager 29-year-old Graham Ford. (In July 1976, Ford resigned over a basic policy difference with Mills & Allen. His successor, was David Munro, who fared little better, being dropped from the team after a year.) The first film to be produced on a 'four-wall' basis was *Conduct Unbecoming*, directed by Michael Anderson and produced by Robert Enders. Only one other film was made at Shepperton in 1974 – Ken Russell's *Lisztomania*.

According to Graham Ford, the new 'four-wall' Shepperton spent the first two-thirds of its first year of operation 'proving there was no wind-up, as people thought it was a front and we were setting up the Centre to cover up the fact that we'd given people the elbow'.[19]

Conduct Unbecoming *(Michael Anderson, 1974)*

In 1975 only four films were made at the studio: *Sinbad and the Eye of the Tiger* (Sam Wanamaker; released in 1977), *The Pink Panther Strikes Again* (Blake Edwards), and two films for 20th Century-Fox, *The Adventure of Sherlock Holmes' Smarter Brother* (Gene Wilder) and *The Omen* (Richard Donner).

By the end of March 1975 outline planning permission for 253 houses, 234 garages and 237 parking spaces to be built on forty acres of the studio site was given by Spelthorne Council, despite continuing opposition from the Shepperton Residents' Association.

In June 1975 it was reported that Lion International was selling, for £1.24 million, its remaining interests in feature film production and distribution to a company backed by five banks and controlled by the Managing Directors of British Lion Films, Barry Spikings and Michael Deeley. Of the two, Deeley had the greater experience in the film industry, having produced films as wide-ranging as *The Case of the Mukkinese Battlehorn* (Joseph Sterling, 1956), *One Way Pendulum* (Peter Yates, 1964), *The Italian Job* (Peter Collinson, 1969) and *Murphy's War* (Peter Yates, 1970).

This move coincided with the resignation of the Managing Director of Lion International, Jeremy Arnold, who stayed with the company as a director and consultant. He was replaced by Clive Hollick, Managing Director of Lion International's parent company, J. H. Vavasseur Group.

The reported deal was denied by Spikings within a week of it becoming public knowledge:

No negotiations have been entered into and no arrangements have been

142

agreed between British Lion and Shepperton Studios, other than those set out in a circular, despatched on 7 June to the shareholders of Lion International, parent company of Shepperton Studios.[20]

This circular laid out proposals whereby Spikings and Deeley would acquire Lion International's film production interests, leaving Lion International with businesses in the media field – and Shepperton Studios.

Spikings and Deeley dropped off the board of Shepperton Studios because of a 'conflict of interests'. David Gourlay, a Vavasseur man, took over as Managing Director, assuring everyone that he intended 'to get his hands dirty in the process'[21] – an unfortunate turn of phrase, given Shepperton's previous experience of City financiers.

On 30 June 1975 Spikings and Deeley bought British Lion from Vavasseur/Lion International for £1.2 million. British Lion Limited owned the entire share capital of British Lion Films Limited. Shortly after this purchase, Lion International changed its name to Mills & Allen International (MAI), which had, in Vavasseur, a 76 per cent shareholder.

As from 1 July 1975 British Lion was once again a totally independent film-making and distribution company.

Notes

1. Roger Smith, 'The Big Stripper', *Film and Television Technician*, July 1972.
2. Author's interview with Lord Goodman, 19 March 1992.
3. Author's interview with Sidney Gilliat, 27 February 1993.
4. Ibid.
5. *Cinema TV Today*, 20 May 1972.
6. Ibid.
7. National Film Finance Corporation Annual Report for year ended 31 March 1973.
8. Ibid.
9. National Film Finance Corporation Annual Report for year ended 31 March 1973.
10. Extract from copy of document (undated), 'Labour Dispute – Shepperton Security Shop', reporting on negotiations between NATTKE and management on 8 March 1974.
11. Ibid.
12. Ibid.
13. 'Four wall' was when a producer rented studio space and facilities, but provided his or her own labour force and equipment.
14. *Surrey Herald*, 29 March 1974.
15. *Cinema TV Today*, 23 February 1974.
16. *Screen International*, 17 January 1976.
17. *Cinema TV Today*, 28 June 1975.
18. Author's interview with Charles Gregson, 10 January 1992.
19. *Screen International*, 17 January 1976.
20. *Daily Telegraph*, 12 June 1975.
21. *Screen International*, 17 January 1976.

6

MORE LOCAL DIFFICULTIES

When Spikings and Deeley bought British Lion, a company called Head-home became the new holders of British Lion Films' shares in Shepperton Studios (except for the minority shares). One Special Preference Share in Headhome was created and issued to the NFFC. This share had rights attached to it similar to those of the NFFC's Special Preference Share in British Lion Films.

On 15 March 1976 the exact boundaries of the revised studio complex and of the surplus land were finally determined and agreed between Mills & Allen International (through Headhome) and the NFFC, providing about twenty-one acres of revised studio complex and surplus land of about thirty-six acres. Later, Mills & Allen agreed to add to the studio complex another four acres, adjacent to the agreed boundaries, to act as a studio lot.

Under the same Agreement, Mills & Allen, Headhome and Shepperton confirmed to the NFFC that it was their intention to use every reasonable endeavour to ensure that Shepperton should continue to operate the revised studio complex as a Studio Centre for film production on a 'four-wall' basis. The Agreement also provided that if at any time within the following twenty-one years Shepperton could not continue its business, or could only be operated at a critical loss, or a Receiver was appointed, then the NFFC had an option to purchase the freehold of the revised studio complex at the highest open market value (with a minimum of £750,000), and the land could be used either for film production or for any other purpose for which planning permission could be obtained. (This option, due on 15 March 1997, is no longer valid following the demise of the NFFC in 1985.)

This Agreement was made in the knowledge that on 26 January 1976 an Agreement between Shepperton Studios and Spelthorne Council had restricted the use of the studio site to film production, with the exception of studio tenant Peteric Engineering. However, if the studio closed, it was agreed that housing could be built on the site.

Only three films were made in the studio in 1976: *The Marriage of Figaro*, directed by Jean Pierre Ponelle; *Queen Kong*, directed by Frank Agrama; and *Jabberwocky*, directed by Terry Gilliam.

This sad state of affairs presaged yet another upheaval in the studio's turbulent history. In a dramatic move, EMI bought British Lion Limited on 25 August 1976. Most industry observers gave Spikings and Deeley the benefit of the doubt over this deal, but cynics argued that their purchase of

British Lion in 1975 had been a stepping stone to the more rarefied atmosphere of the huge EMI conglomerate. Certainly, both men were rapidly elevated in position and power. They joined the parent company, EMI Film and Theatre Corporation, whose Chairman and Chief Executive was Sir Bernard Delfont. They also became joint Managing Directors of EMI Film Distributors, whose Chairman and Chief Executive was Nat Cohen.

Spikings and Deeley were British Lion's main assets. EMI had purchased their production ability, the price for which was £730,000, paid with £230,000 cash and by the issue of 235,850 Ordinary Shares in EMI Limited. 'We are not actually buying up British Lion,' said EMI, rather tongue in cheek, 'but rather, Mr Deeley and Mr Spikings have the controlling shares, so they are bringing the company with them.'[1]

EMI told the NFFC that it was the intention of the EMI Group to retain the name of British Lion in some significant form within the context of the EMI Group's film financing and distributing activities, having regard to British Lion's long history and the goodwill attached to its name, both at home and abroad. EMI also told the NFFC that the acquisition of British Lion would add substantially to EMI's management strength and lead to a stimulation and enlargement of EMI's support for, and financial involvement in, British film production and distribution. In these circumstances, the NFFC was asked by British Lion and EMI to sell to British Lion its single Preference Share in British Lion Films.

The NFFC, after consulting the Department of Trade, agreed that the retention of the rights attached to this Special Preference Share, in this new situation, were no longer relevant. On 25 August 1976, when EMI bought British Lion, the NFFC sold its Special Preference Share in British Lion Films to British Lion for £90,000.

Some in film circles supported the EMI purchase of British Lion, hoping it would provide a boost for the industry now that British Lion was once more in the hands of entertainment people, albeit a huge conglomerate, which inevitably meant a risk to employee security. Despite this, it was thought that Sir Bernard Delfont, who had committed himself to full employment at Elstree Studios, may have found Shepperton Studios more attractive in the longer term. Critics of the purchase pointed to the committed internationalism of Spikings and Deeley, along with EMI's tendency at the time to invest their money in international projects that might not be made in the UK. British production, it was thought, might be relegated to low-budget domestic films such as EMI's *The Likely Lads* (Michael Tuchner, 1976).

The NFFC itself came under fire in the House of Commons when Trade Secretary Edmund Dell told John Gorst, MP for North Hendon and Chairman of the all-party Parliamentary Films Committee, that in reaching their decision to sell the Special Preference Share the NFFC had kept in touch with his Department and he had not raised any objection. 'The price at which the sale took place was decided in negotiation between the NFFC, who had the benefit of professional advice, and EMI, taking account of any rights which might arise from the tax loss.'[2]

Gorst believed that the way in which the transaction had been carried out called for immediate investigation since it enabled the profitable EMI company to purchase a tax loss of £720,000 for the 'paltry sum' of £90,000, thus avoiding nearly £750,000 of tax on profits. The 'dubious' role of the NFFC in this matter should be investigated. He wanted to know why the NFFC had failed in its annual report to make it clear that this was the sale of a tax loss and why EMI should have been accorded a tax loss benefit which the previous proprietors of British Lion had been denied and which, had they also enjoyed such a benefit, might have significantly altered their fate. Gorst's concern was the all too familiar tale for Shepperton of seeing the studio gates shut long after the film has been released, so to speak.

The subject of the EMI purchase of British Lion surfaced again in the House of Commons in 1978 when former Arts Minister, Hugh Jenkins, asked the government whether it thought EMI had fulfilled its undertaking in retaining the name of British Lion in some significant form when it purchased the NFFC's Special Preference Share in British Lion. Films Minister Michael Meacher replied that half the films being released by EMI over the following few months would appear under the British Lion banner and EMI's policy for this pattern was to be maintained. This assurance was given despite the fact that on 13 May 1977 British Lion had announced that it had ceased to trade. EMI then changed the company name to Berwick Films Limited.

Concern over EMI's purchase of British Lion seemed to be justified when, within a short time, British Lion and EMI worked together, sharing distribution rights outside the UK and the US as minority partners in Columbia's *Nickelodeon* (1976), produced by Deeley and directed by Peter Bogdanovich.

In June 1976 yet another twist to the Shepperton saga occurred. Producer Harry Saltzman made a bid, estimated at £8 million, for the entire sixty-acre site. Unfortunately for Saltzman (and arguably for the British film industry), a deal had already been agreed between the studio board and the local authority, Spelthorne Council, for the council to purchase fourteen acres of the studio site for housing development and a further twenty acres for open space amenity. The price was £473,000, of which £348,000 was payable on completion and the balance on 30 June 1977. In a statement, the studio board said:

> Shepperton has succeeded in retaining approximately four acres adjoining the studios for use as a back lot, so that the studio lot now comprises an area of approximately twenty-five acres and a further five acres of back lot is already leased by Shepperton, resulting in a totally available back lot of nine acres. This transaction was an improvement in the arrangements previously approved by the NFFC and should considerably strengthen the commercial and film position of Shepperton.[3]

Saltzman made it clear that he wanted the whole sixty-acre site, comprising forty acres of lot and twenty acres of studio kernel, and in particular 'H' stage (then the largest silent stage in Europe). Canadian-born Saltzman had amassed a fortune from his co-production (with Albert 'Cubby' Broccoli) of the James Bond films. He had moved his office from Pinewood to Shepperton the previous Christmas in anticipation of a programme of films to be produced at the studio, the first of which was to be *The Micronauts*. According to Saltzman's Publicity Director, Tom Carlile:

> Basically, the purpose [of Saltzman's bid] is to stimulate American finance in England. Mr Saltzman feels that there had been a healthy pick-up at the box office world-wide. He was waiting for a response to his bid and was hopeful it would be accepted.[4]

Sir John Terry, Managing Director of the NFFC, had given Saltzman's bid the NFFC's blessing:

> This would be excellent for the British film industry. Mr Saltzman is known to believe that, with the rapid decline of the British pound, American film companies will seek the relatively cheap facilities for film production here.[5]

(Sir John Terry, who chose not to co-operate with research for this book, retired from the battle on 31 December 1978.)

Unfortunately, none of this enthusiasm for Shepperton Studios again to be run by film-makers seeped through to the studio board. Their decision to sell land to Spelthorne Council further underlined the scepticism about their repeated assurances of a film-making future for the studio. Managing Director Charles Gregson claimed: 'Owning a studio is rather like owning a racehorse. There are always punters, but Saltzman was the only other serious interested party.'[6] Saltzman's bid failed.

Others at the time interested in buying the studio included Ladbrokes, the bookmaking and hotel group, and the entertainment company Pleasurama. In due course interest waned and the studio remained in the hands of Mills & Allen.

1976 ended with yet more controversy. Despite denials from both Clive Hollick, Chairman of Shepperton Studios, and Charles Gregson, the industry trade paper *Screen International* insisted that a firm bid of around £1 million had been made for the studio by an (unnamed) businessman who had plans to go into film production himself and who was willing to make substantial investment in the studio. *Screen International* claimed it had documents indicating that at one point the offer was being considered 'favourably' by Mills & Allen. Like Harry Saltzman's earlier bid, this mystery businessman's bid also came to nothing.

Throughout 1976 the studio's tenants had become increasingly restless, complaining about the deteriorating state of the site. A director of BBRK, a commercial design company renting permanent space in the studio, summarised in *Screen International* on 27 November 1976 his views on the tenants' feelings:

> The place seems to have deteriorated greatly in the past few years and liaison between management and tenant and incoming clients is really abominable. We have had so many changes of management, we don't know who's who any more and the studio staff seems to be too small to run the place properly.

Of particular annoyance to the tenants was the sudden closure of the restaurant in the Old House, replaced by an 'executive' eating area next to the canteen. Clive Hollick had reacted angrily to these accusations. He agreed that the studio was 'old and antiquated' and 'needed a coat of paint', adding:

> Shepperton is just one of the companies competing for resources from the Mills & Allen Group. It has to show that investment is justified. The company will have to trade profitably and secure contracts. Once we can see the trend developing, as it has done increasingly in the past years [the studio made a small pre-tax profit of £28,461 in its previous financial year], we will be prepared to spend some money.[7]

Hollick also denied that the closure of the Old House restaurant constituted an important loss in studio amenities:

> It makes more sense to move it where our other restaurant is. If people want to hire the Old House, they can, but the people who use the studio are increasingly young and no longer subscribe to the Grade 'A', Grade 'B' eating place theory. If Brando and Gene Hackman come to the studio in *Superman*, and want to eat in the officers' mess, they can do so because there is an officers' mess available. What we all want to do is recognise what we've got. It's not part of the national heritage, or anything like that, but we are attracting international business and we are going to try and develop that foreign earnings potential to the full.[8]

Despite Hollick's bravado, parts of the studio continued to be sold off. On 7 January 1977 part of the original Sound City lot, the studio main entrance, was sold to become part of the subsequent development of housing on the studio site.

On 1 July 1977 Shepperton agreed to lease part of the studio site to Ramport Enterprises for a term of 999 years, for a premium of £350,000. Ramport was also granted an option, exercisable within twenty-one years from the date of the lease, to purchase the freehold for £1. The NFFC approved this lease on the basis that Shepperton would spend a minimum of £200,000 over the following two years on improvements to the studio premises, fixtures and fittings. Shepperton agreed this condition and on 1 November 1977 the NFFC confirmed its approval of the deal.

What upset many people at the time was an anticipation that this deal would signal an invasion of pop stars and groups into the studio. Pop groups had been filmed in the studio on many occasions during the 60s, but they were minor entities compared to the group who now owned six acres of the studio, including the Old House, 'J' and 'K' stages and adjoining offices.

Ramport, incorporated in 1967, owned the rights to the entire income of the pop group The Who and each of its individual members – Roger Daltrey, Pete Townshend, John Entwistle and Keith Moon. Coincidentally, The Who had been created by Kit Lambert, who had been an assistant director at Shepperton Studios. The Who's reputation for destroying the public stages on which they performed did not extend to the studio. Indeed Ramport's management, under Managing Director Tony Prior, kept a firm control on discipline during their short tenure of the studio. (On 9 July 1981, Ramport, now The Who Group Limited, surrendered the land and buildings from their lease.)

Despite this, it was noticeable to older members of the studio staff and to ex-studio employees who visited the Old House during Ramport's tenure that scant respect was shown both to the historic nature of the Old House and to the stars, producers and directors who had resided there. The narcissistic world of pop had no time for the broader appreciation and preservation of those talents who had been major contributors to this British 'dream' factory.

To their credit, The Who did go out of their way to preserve the studio's 400-year-old cedar of Lebanon which overlooked their Old House offices. This tree had been seen in over fifty films, but was to be felled by the local council to make way for forty-seven housing units on the site. A concerted and well-organised campaign, involving David Hemmings, Roger Daltrey and Spike Milligan, persuaded the council to redesign the site to trade off the loss of six housing units within the area occupied by the tree for some extra land.

From the dismal production record of 1976 business improved with eight films produced at the studio during 1977, including the sequel to *The Guns of Navarone*, *Force 10 from Navarone* (Guy Hamilton), *The Revenge of the Pink Panther* (Blake Edwards), *The Boys from Brazil* (Franklin Schaffner) and *The Medusa Touch* (Jack Gold).

Throughout 1977, which saw the resignation of Sir Robert Clark as Chairman of the NFFC (he was replaced by Geoffrey Williams), the twists and turns in the studio ownership were reflected in the convoluted affairs of Vavasseur and Mills & Allen. J. H. Vavasseur Group, victim of the fringe banking collapse in 1973/74, had been bailed out by the Bank of England 'lifeboat operation' set up to help companies caught up in the collapse. Vavasseur had hoped that by the end of 1976 it would no longer need to be considered a special case and would be able to operate under more normal banking arrangements.

Vavasseur owned 78.9 per cent of Mills & Allen, but in a bizarre move bid for a further 19.3 per cent, after which it adopted that company's name, becoming Mills & Allen International (MAI). On the announcement that the two Boards (both under Sir Ian Morrow) had broadly agreed this third capital restructure of Vavasseur since the secondary banking crash, shares in both companies were temporarily suspended, Mills & Allen at 62p and Vavasseur at 8p. 1977 preliminary figures showed that Vavasseur had increased its pre-tax profits from £1.2 million to £2.6 million and Mills & Allen from £1.1 million to £2.5 million.

The reconstruction was complicated. Instead of three classes of capital, there would be only two – 8.2 million Ordinary Shares and 4.1 million Preference Shares. The largest shareholder was to be Britannia Arrow, the former Slater Walker Securities (which had set up John Bentley in business), with 22.7 per cent; Hambros Bank would have 7.8 per cent and

London Indemnity 6.3 per cent. Other institutions were to hold 13 per cent, with the remainder spread among 12,000 shareholders.

Throughout 1978 Mills & Allen International continued to recover, and over the next six years, until it sold Shepperton Studios in 1984, it gradually improved its position in the market place. Paradoxically, the studio became more isolated within the Mills & Allen corporate structure, though it continued to operate, if precariously. This situation was not helped by the fire which destroyed the *Oliver!* set in 1979. The set was being demolished by contractors when wind blew rubbish onto a bonfire; the resulting fire was brought under control by the joint efforts of the studio fire crew under Fire Officer Percy Maskell and the local fire brigade. This was the second time the *Oliver!* set had caught fire, the first blaze destroying half the set. Maskell was no stranger to studio fires. He worked on over forty fires with *Superman* (1977), and extinguished a spectacular fire on *The Medusa Touch* (1977) when a special effects sequence simulated a jumbo jet crashing into a skyscraper.

In October 1980 the Agreement between the studio and Spelthorne Council, which restricted use of the studio site to film production, was varied. For a five-year period rent obtained for 'H' stage was to be divided 70 per cent to the council and 30 per cent (net) to the studio. In May 1981 a further exchange of land with the council, agreed with the NFFC, saw outline planning permission given for new buildings on the studio site, plus space for 907 cars and three trucks.

At the 1981 studio Annual General Meeting, held on 2 November, a Special Resolution was passed for Shepperton Studios Limited to be registered as a private company, which took effect from 12 May 1982.

Over the next two years a series of Agreements was made between the studio and outside contractors for work and services within the studio. These Agreements were negotiated on behalf of the studio by Clive Landa, who took over from Charles Gregson as Managing Director in 1980. Landa, who chose not to co-operate with research for this book, was to be the last of the 'City' executives to run Shepperton Studios before its acquisition in August 1984 by John and Benny Lee's Lee Electric (Lighting) Limited.

Notes

1. *Daily Telegraph*, 19 May 1976.
2. *Screen International*, 6 November 1976.
3. *Screen International*, 12 June 1976.
4. *Guardian*, 4 June 1976.
5. Ibid.
6. Author's interview with Charles Gregson, 10 January 1992.
7. *Screen International*, 27 November 1976.
8. Ibid.

British Screen Finance
Consortium Ltd
1985

Lee International Film
Studios Ltd 1985

Media Technology International plc
1984

Mitchell Camera Corporation
(US) 1985

Mitchell Camera UK Ltd
1985

Meddings Magic Camera Company Ltd 1987

Film and Television Workshop Ltd 1987

Moores and Griffin Ltd 1987

Delta Sound Services Ltd 1987

Lee International Ltd
1985

Lee International plc
1986

Shepperton Studios Ltd 1988

Lee International Film Studios Ltd

Lee International Inc 1991

Lee Lighting Ltd 1991

Humphries Film Laboratories Ltd 1985

Advertising Films Ltd 1985

Creative Images Ltd 1985

Readifoto Ltd 1985

Humphries Holdings plc 1985

CTS Studios Ltd 1985

Humphries Video Services Ltd 1985

Humphries Film Financing Ltd 1985

Filmec Laboratory Projects Ltd 1985

Mole-Richardson (International) Ltd 1985

Mole-Richardson (England) Ltd 1985

Mole-Richardson (Ireland) Ltd 1985

Mole-Richardson (Vienna) Gmbh 1985

Mole-Richardson (Deutschland) Gmbh 1985

Mole-Richardson (Iberica) SA 1985

Mole-Richardson (France) SA 1985

Mole-Richardson (Cote d'Azure) SA 1985

Mole-Richardson (Espana) Ltd 1985

Mole-Richardson (H.H.) SA 1985

Joe Dunton Cameras Ltd

Lee Filters Ltd

Lee Panavision International Inc 1988

Panavision International LP 1991

Panavision France SA 1990

Panavision Moscow Ltd 1990

Panavision Europe Ltd 1990

Panavision Ireland Ltd 1987

Panavision Italia SRL 1989

Westward Communications plc 1987

Ewesham Investment Company Ltd 1985

Lee International Aquisitions Inc 1987

Panavision Inc 1987

Panavision Overseas Inc 1987

Colortran Inc
1985

Shepperton Studios

London Films

British Lion

7

LET THERE BE LIGHT

In 1961 two film lighting electricians, John and Benny Lee, incorporated Lee Electric (Lighting) Limited. The company was primarily involved in the rental of lighting equipment for commercial and documentary productions, all major film and television studios having their own lighting equipment.

Although the lighting rental market in the UK grew throughout the 60s, largely due to the impact of commercial television, the market was dominated by a single manufacturer of lighting equipment, Mole-Richardson, which was also the largest rental house.

In 1967 Lee Electric started to purchase lighting equipment from the Italian manufacturer Ianiro, which was itself trying to establish a foothold in the international market. In addition, Lee Filters Limited was formed to design, market and, from 1974, manufacture lighting filters. Also in 1967, BBC2 started to transmit in colour, with BBC1 and ITV following in 1969.

The introduction of colour transmission entailed a substantial increase in the amount of lighting needed in studios, as well as on location. With a major increase in the amount of equipment available to it as a result of purchasing Ianiro equipment, Lee Electric was able to win a five-year contract with the BBC for the supply of lighting equipment for UK television outside broadcasts. This contract necessitated further substantial investment in equipment and also guaranteed high utilisation of that equipment, which established Lee Electric's leading position in the lighting rental market. More important, this contract was won from Mole-Richardson.

In 1968 Lee Electric expanded by buying a three-acre site in North Kensington, London, which was converted to provide premises for the lighting equipment rental business and a three-stage film studio, operating on a 'four-wall' basis. Significant features produced at this studio include *Ten Rillington Place* (Richard Fleischer, 1970), *A Touch of Class* (Melvin Frank, 1972) and The Who rock opera *Tommy* (Ken Russell, 1975). In the same year Lee Electric acquired Telefilm Lighting Services, a competitor, thereby expanding its range of marketing contacts.

Over the following six years Lee Electric made further inroads into the industry's servicing sector. In 1969 it formed Lee Scaffolding to service television outside broadcasts (from 1984 Stagemate provided the same service for film production companies); in 1972 Lee Electric (Northern) began servicing the lighting requirements of the BBC in the north of the UK, and in 1974 Lee Enterprises started business as a bulk buyer of consumable items, principally for the rest of the Lee Group but also as a wholesaler to third parties. In 1975 Joe Dunton Cameras was established to provide a camera rental service to the industry. In 1977 Lee Electric moved to Lee International Film Studios in Wembley, North London which, over the following two years, was completely refitted for film and television production and commercials.

By 1979 Lee Electric had established good working relationships with a number of American film production companies, servicing their lighting requirements outside the US. The companies also used Lee's studio at Wembley. The same year Lee Electric took the strategic step of opening a lighting rental house in New York. The establishment of Lee Lighting America was coupled with the acquisition of Belden Communications, a New York-based distributor and selling agent for film and television equipment, which had been the exclusive distributor of Lee Filters since 1976 (ten years later, Lee opened a second rental house in Los Angeles). But John and Benny Lee wanted to get into the big league of film production. Their chance came in 1984.

By 1980 Shepperton's Managing Director, Charles Gregson, on his own admission had worked himself out of a job. 'There just wasn't enough for me to do. By the late 70s and early 80s the studio was full. I wasn't needed, so I became redundant.'[1] Having held this position for over five years, Gregson felt that Studio Manager Paul Olliver was quite capable of running the studio, which Olliver is still doing.

From a high of eighteen productions in 1972, production at Shepperton had declined by the end of the decade to between six and eight features a year, including *Alien* (Ridley Scott, 1978), *Murder by Decree* (Bob Clark, 1978), *Saturn Three* (Stanley Donen, 1980) and *Dracula* (John Badham, 1978). Only two films were made in 1979: *SOS Titanic* (William Hale) and *Flash Gordon* (Mike Hodges). Production picked up again in 1980 with seven films, including *The Elephant Man* (David Lynch) and James Cagney's swansong, *Ragtime* (Milos Forman).

Although the Films Act 1980 had allowed the NFFC to continue its operations until 1985, under its terms the National Film Development Fund (set up in 1976) ceased to operate. The NFFC staggered on, using industry consultants and a full-time employee, but its days as an integral part of the British film industry were numbered.

In 1981, as part of a tidying-up exercise, Shepperton Studios asked the NFFC (as holder of the Special Preference Share in Headhome) to use the studio for television production in addition to film production. Approval by the NFFC brought its last significant involvement with Shepperton Studios and British Lion, before the sale of the studio to Lee Electric in 1984 and Lee's purchase in 1985 of the NFFC's Special Preference Share in Headhome.

By 1984 Shepperton Studios represented the only part of the feature film world that Mills & Allen owned, and produced a very small contribution to their business. According to Gregson:

Having a super film studio, which always looked good in the Annual Report, was a luxury we could no longer justify in terms of business.

Also, it didn't make sense any more to own a film studio on its own. One surely should also be in film production, which we are not. So it really made sense to find an owner for the studio who had an interest in the studio relative to its other interests.[2]

Paramount and Handmade Films had been major contributors to the studio's well-being during the three-year lead-up to the decision by Mills & Allen in 1984 to sell the studio, with films including *The Missionary* (Richard Loncraine, 1982), *Privates on Parade* (Michael Blakemore, 1982), *The Keep* (Michael Mann, 1982), *Lords of Discipline* (Franc Roddam, 1982) and *Bullshot* (Dick Clement, 1983). Other productions during this period included Richard Attenborough's *Gandhi* (1982) and *The Company of Wolves* (Neil Jordan, 1983).

The Lee brothers had been studio tenants since 1974 and had casually discussed with Gregson over two or three years the possibility of purchasing the studio. When Mills & Allen decided to relinquish the studio, in Gregson's view the Lee Group was the ideal buyer.

On 16 August 1984 Lee Electric (Lighting) acquired the entire share capital of Headhome (other than the Special Preference Share held by the NFFC) and its 99.5 per cent-owned subsidiary, Shepperton Studios Limited. The eighteen-acre studio site was acquired for £3,365,746. An important part of this Agreement was that, in addition to confirming that they would endeavour to continue using Shepperton for film and television production, the Lee Group granted the NFFC an option to acquire certain land known as 'The Ramport Land'. On 9 October 1984 an Agreement between Mills & Allen (Holdings), Cordellina Holdings and Rathcoole Investments enabled Lee to purchase from The Who Group, for a further £550,000, the Old House and stages 'J' and 'K'.

In that month it was also decided by Lee that the allied, but self-contained, activities of Lee Filters and Joe Dunton Cameras (which had established an American subsidiary in June that year) could be more successfully developed under their own management and with direct access to the capital markets. To this end a new holding company, Media Technology International (MTI), was formed to acquire these two companies and admission to the Unlisted Securities Market was obtained.

In 1984, Sir David Lean made a welcome return to the studio when he completed *A Passage to India*, his final film before his death in 1991 and arguably the most important of the nine films hosted by the studio that year.

In May 1985 Lee International was formed as a holding company for the Lee Group, and in November acquired the entire share capital of Lee Electric in exchange for shares.

1985 continued to be a hectic year for acquisitions by the Lee Group. In June, Lee Electric acquired Colortran, a US manufacturer of lighting products, through which the Lee Group secured an international network of distributors and agents: in November, MTI acquired Mitchell Camera Corporation, the Los Angeles-based manufacturers of film cameras. This acquisition reduced the Lee Group's interest in MTI from 59.3 per cent to 53.9 per cent (which was further reduced to 29.9 per cent as part of the

A Passage to India *(David Lean, 1984)*

reorganisation that took place prior to the flotation of Lee International in 1986.

On 13 November 1985 Lee International made a recommended offer of 33.5p in cash per share for Humphries Holdings, which rented lighting equipment in Europe, manufactured low-voltage lighting, operated music recording studios (CTS Studios) and duplicated videotapes. The offer was declared unconditional on 5 December 1985, at which date it had been accepted in respect of shares representing 94.2 per cent of the issued share capital (subsequently increased to 97.5 per cent), with the outstanding shares compulsorily acquired.

Through the acquisition of Humphries Holdings for £2,680,000, Lee International also acquired competitors Mole-Richardson and its European subsidiaries. Another division of Humphries Holdings was the film processing laboratory in London, Humphries Films Laboratories, which at its peak was one of the three major UK film processing laboratories (the other two being Rank Denham and Technicolor). On 29 November 1985 the London laboratory leasehold premises in Whitfield Street and North Court were sold to the Saatchi & Saatchi Compton Group for £987,500 against a book value at 31 March 1985 of £1,082,000. There were now no competitors with a significant market share compared to that of the Lee Group in the UK.

1985 saw two major films at Shepperton Studios: *Absolute Beginners*, directed by Julian Temple, and *Out of Africa*, directed by Sidney Pollack.

With its purchase of Shepperton Studios in 1984, the Lee Group now owned more film stages in the UK than either of its principal competitors, the Rank Organisation (Pinewood) and Screen Entertainment (Elstree). Some four months prior to the Shepperton purchase, Lee had ensured its domination of north of England independent film studios with the purchase of land in Kearsley, Greater Manchester, from Pickford Removals for £185,000. This provided Lee with a Manchester-based studio offering 6,400 square feet of sound-proofed stage.

Lee began to take immediate steps to revitalise the Shepperton studio complex. The major work was begun following the Deed of Release, dated 30 September 1985, between the Secretary of State for Trade and Industry, Lee International and Shepperton Studios. This released Shepperton Studios, Lee Electric (Lighting), Headhome, Ramport Enterprises and Lee International Film Studios from all their obligations under the NFFC Agreement (and under eight earlier Agreements) in exchange for the transfer to Lee International of the Special Preference Share in Headhome. For their part Lee International agreed to provide finance for the redevelopment and extension of the studio as a premier studio complex, unless otherwise agreed with the Secretary of State. The removal of the Special Preference Share from Headhome made it possible for Headhome, on 19 December 1985, to change its name to Lee International Film Studios, a wholly owned subsidiary of Lee International, which in turn was an intermediate holding company of Shepperton Studios.

According to Lee Group Company Secretary Nigel Hurdle, the share structure of the company was far from straightforward:

> It is complicated because there were lots of stock issues during the Sound City and British Lion periods. When we bought the company, there were a number of shares that were originally issued to Mills & Allen and there were a number of minority outside shareholders. Since acquiring the studio, some members of the company have died and those shares have not been traced, although we know where they were originally issued.[3]

Despite these corporate complications Lee International continued to expand. Branches of Lee Electric and Lee Scaffolding were established at Shepperton as part of the overall plan to provide a 'total package' facility company for film and television producers. That 'package' included the appointment, on 25 March 1986, of Lee employee Denis Carrigan as Managing Director both of Shepperton and of Lee's Wembley Studios.

Delta Sound Services, a long-time resident of Shepperton, was acquired by Lee International on 6 October 1986 for £300,000 and the issue of 375,000 fully paid Ordinary Shares.

1986 saw production at Shepperton levelling off again. Two contrasting productions in that year were the ill-fated *Shanghai Surprise*, directed by Jim Goddard, and *84 Charing Cross Road*, directed by David Jones.

In 1987 Lee International finally acquired the rest of the studio for £950,000, bringing the total purchase price of the entire twenty-six acre site to £5.2 million. This last purchase was of land comprising 'H' stage, by that time scheduled for demolition by Spelthorne Council, and some housing development land on the studio site. The return of ownership of the studio to a company in the film industry, coupled with the management style of the Lee Group, served to lift morale and to attract substantial prestigious new business.

A massive £15 million refurbishment programme was introduced. New stages, 'L' and 'M' (respectively, the old Scoring Stage and the Special Effects Stage), came into operation in 1985 and new workshops servicing stages 'A', 'B', 'C' and 'D' were built.

John Renton of the Renton Welch Partnership had been commissioned to streamline the studio facility, on the basis of the many practical lessons learned at Lee Studios Wembley during the seven previous years:

> Lee International had the foresight to commission a Masterplan Study to establish an efficient framework for their development strategy. This even included our expressing their corporate image by colour co-ordination of materials, whilst blending new and existing buildings with strong graphic signage and imaginative landscaping.[4]

Certainly, visitors to Shepperton Studios during the 'honeymoon' period of Lee's ownership could not fail to be impressed by the many visual improvements to the studio's infrastructure. In addition to these essential cosmetic touches, the entire complex was rewired, providing – as well as an upgraded electrical system of 28,000 DC amps – a seven megawatt AC ring which made Shepperton the first major UK studio complex to have high-powered AC all the way round the site. As a failsafe precaution, this power was connected to two separate sections of the National Grid, enabling crews to work on 'H' stage without 'brutes' (the largest standard studio lamp). Communications ducts for video and satellite links were also installed around the site.

Coincidental with the 1985 surge of studio activity was the demise of the 'Eady' Levy, which was phased out (as recommended by the Cinematograph Films Council in 1984), and of the National Film Finance Corporation and its subsidiary companies, the National Film Trustee Company, the National Film Finance Consortium and the National Film Development Fund. The undertakings, assets and liabilities of these companies, under the terms of the Films Act 1985, were transferred to the British Screen Finance Consortium.

The often stormy history of the NFFC had produced approved loans totalling £43,201,176 for 596 television films, 189 shorts and 780 features. (This total loan figure includes the infamous £3 million loan to British Lion.) Of the loans approved, £37,975,552 had been advanced and £21,710,063 repaid. At 31 March 1985 the NFFC's final accounting period showed an overall loss of £3,377,297.

In 1986 the industry was further decimated by the Conservative government's removal of tax incentives in the form of 100 per cent capital allowances, and by changes in the Independent Television exchequer levy, which reduced available funds for film production. Yet no one anticipated the chain of events which, in 1987, were to enmesh Shepperton Studios once more in a net of uncertainty and threatened extinction.

When Lee formed Joe Dunton Cameras Limited in 1975 to provide a camera rental service to the industry, it was a logical move relative to the then overall Lee Group strategy. In 1984, it also seemed logical to establish a subsidiary in the US for Joe Dunton Cameras. JDC America was established in North Carolina in premises within a film studio set up by a major Lee customer, producer Dino de Laurentiis. Principal competitor to JDC America was Panavision, whose cameras were rented to film producers outside the US both through its own outlet in Tarzana, California, and through exclusive rental agencies worldwide. When MTI bought Mitchell Camera Corporation in 1985, it enabled Joe Dunton Cameras to begin manufacturing camera bodies and to take on repair and modification work. It also enabled them to compete with Panavision in the US. In 1987 Lee International went one better – it bought Panavision.

Panavision was founded in 1954 as a supply company for innovative wide-screen lenses and became a market leader in 1968 with the introduction of the PSR Studio Reflex Camera. In 1972 Panavision introduced the world's first silent portable sound camera. The Panaflex and its successor models became the industry standard in ease of use, quality of manufacture, silence and optical perfection.

In 1985 Frederick W. Field acquired Panavision from Warner Communications, where Panavision had been a trading division since 1968, and engaged John Farrand, formerly President and Chief Executive Officer of the coin-operated products division of Atari, in the same capacity for Panavision. In 1986 Panavision acquired a 50 per cent interest in Aaton, a French company known for its innovative technology. Aaton manufactured and sold 16mm advanced technology cameras, primarily used for television and documentaries. A year later Panavision generated 80 per cent of its operating turnover in the US and Canada. During the previous two and a half years it had invested approximately $40 million in research and development and was ready to expand its operations outside North America.

From the Lee Group's point of view, the acquisition of Panavision could be interpreted as the 'icing on the cake' and would substantially increase their activities in the US. This was in line with the Lee International Group policy. Certainly the price would be high and the financing of this deal would be the most ambitious attempted by the Lee Group. Indeed, the Offer Document sent to the Lee International shareholders stressed the high price being paid for Panavision, in consideration of its short history as an autonomous trading entity:

> It was clear to Lee that a full price would be required in order to secure the goodwill of a company of the quality and reputation of Panavision. Lee believes, however, that there are substantial commercial benefits which will arise in the medium to long term on the merger of the two businesses and which justify the price to be paid.[5]

The Offer Document further warned:

> Although Panavision offers Lee a unique chance for a major expansion in the US, the apparent high price for Panavision and the short-to-medium-term impact on Lee led your Board to recognise that some shareholders may not wish to hold an investment in the Enlarged Lee Group (the Lee Group after the purchase of Panavision), for a number of reasons:

The Stock Exchange have indicated that the Enlarged Lee Group, after the Acquisition, would not be suitable for listing in view of Panavision's short independent trading record and its size relative to Lee.

Whilst there are substantial commercial benefits which will arise on the merger of the two businesses, it is likely that these will only impact on profitability in the medium to long term. As a result, there will be high earnings dilution in the short to medium term. The Enlarged Lee Group will have a high level of borrowings, which shareholders may find unacceptable. This would be the case even if a large part of the consideration was satisfied by way of an issue of Lee shares.

Consequently, the Independent Directors (John T. Davey, FCA, and Colin S. Wills, FCA) have sought to ensure that the Lee shareholders representing the minority should be given an opportunity, if they so wish, to realise their investment in Lee shares. The rather complicated approach to financing the Acquisition results from the desire to afford the minority shareholders the opportunity of Cash Consideration.[6]

Clearly, it was apparent to the Lee International shareholders that such an acquisition was fraught with financial uncertainty. Nevertheless, it was announced on 2 September 1987 that Lee International had conditionally agreed to acquire Panavision, but the size of the transaction needed the approval of the company in a general meeting. Prior to the Extraordinary General Meeting for this purpose, held on 21 September 1987, 61.8 per cent of the members of the company had given irrevocable undertakings to vote in favour of the Resolution to implement the acquisition and to accept the offer.

Financing for the purchase of Panavision was provided by Citicorp, who agreed to make available to the Lee Group loan facilities totalling $220 million. This was used to purchase Panavision for $100 million, to refinance Panavision's then existing debt of $47.6 million, to refinance Lee's then existing debt of $50 million, to provide additional working capital for Lee and partly to finance the expenses of the Acquisition. The loan facilities were to be made available no later than 1 November 1987, and were repayable over seven years, the final payment being due not later than 1 November 1994.

The vehicle through which Panavision was acquired was Westward Communications, which was incorporated on 6 August 1987 specifically to acquire the whole of the issued share capital of Lee International at the same time as Lee International acquired Panavision. It was intended that Westward Communications be floated in the autumn of 1988, to reduce the borrowings incurred by Lee International in acquiring Panavision and to refinance the Lee Group. Citicorp also financed Westward's purchase of Lee International shares when, on 1 September 1987, it agreed to provide Westward with a facility of $116 million and a related interest facility of $6 million. These facilities were to be repaid by 2 September 1989. Security for the financing of the Panavision purchase included the underlying assets of the Enlarged Lee Group – one of which was Shepperton Studios.

The high level of borrowing associated with the acquisition of Panavision led the Stock Exchange to inform Lee International that it should make a Cash Offer to its minority shareholders. The £3.60 per share offered by Lee International represented a 100 per cent increase on its original Offer price of £1.80 per share in 1986. 'Had we held back just one week,' said Nigel Hurdle, 'we could have offered the shareholders a much lower price and saved the company a substantial sum in loans.'[7] The commercial reality of the situation was quite different. The failure to delay that operation by seven days was to prove costly to the Lee Group and to everyone connected with the company.

'Black Monday', 19 October 1987, rocked the City as the Stock Market crashed, wiping millions of pounds off share values. 'Black Monday' was the catalyst for a chain of events that, ultimately, brought down the house built by John and Benny Lee.

The American Scriptwriters' strike, which paralysed American film production in 1988, also paralysed Panavision. For the first few months under the Lee Group ownership, Panavision was unable to generate the income originally projected to assist in financing the debt incurred in its acquisition and the privatisation of the Lee Group. An investigation into the Lee Group by the Serious Fraud Office did little to help matters, although a year later the SFO confirmed that there was no substance to their investigations and withdrew from the scene.

'Black Monday' occurred only days after Lee completed the acquisition of Panavision. Up to that time it was envisaged that the Group would be able to finance the deal over a short term and refloat the company in the US, with an enhanced organisation, including Panavision, and increased profitability. But at the end of 1988 the Lee Group was in breach of the various banking covenants associated with the loan documents, and this was to prove their downfall.

A 'White Knight', American investment bankers Warburg-Pincus Capital Company LP, acquired the Lee Group in December 1988 for some $60 million. From that time, the Lee brothers ceased to have any management responsibility for the Lee International Group of Companies.

Throughout this traumatic period, production at Shepperton had continued, with eight films in 1988, including *Bert Rigby You're a Fool* (Carl Reiner), *How to Get Ahead in Advertising* (Bruce Robinson), *Mountains of the Moon* (Bob Rafelson), *Eric the Viking* (Terry Jones), and Kenneth Branagh's powerful *Henry V*.

Warburg-Pincus wasted no time in restructuring the Group, doing so again in 1989 when the lighting activities of the Group were divisionalised. May 1991 saw a further restructuring, with cameras and filters transferred into a separate company under Panavision Europe, leaving Lee International holding Lee Lighting and Shepperton Studios.

Throughout this reorganisation the production emphasis at Shepperton moved to television, with films made for Scottish Television (*Killing Dad*); BBC Television (*The Choice*); Central Television (*Free Frenchmen* and *About Face*); Central Television/Home Box Office (*Shell Seekers*) and TVS (*Back Home*). The only feature film produced in 1989 was Handmade's *Nuns on the Run*, directed by Jonathan Lynn. In 1990 feature films were

Henry V *(Kenneth Branagh, 1988)*

again prominent with *Hamlet* (Franco Zeffirelli), *Robin Hood – Prince of Thieves* (Kevin Reynolds), *Three Men and a Little Lady* (Emile Ardonilo), *A Kiss Before Dying* (James Dearden) and *The Rainbow Thief* (Alejandro Jodorowsky).

Lee Group Company Secretary Nigel Hurdle is philosophical about the Warburg-Pincus influence on the Group:

> A year after the Lee Group went public in 1986, the economic climate was in the heyday of the Margaret Thatcher years. Everyone was motoring at a considerable rate. The Group had been acquisitive for a two-to-three-year period and was moving along very quickly. We had made a number of acquisitions worldwide and it was decided, primarily by John and Benny Lee, that it made commercial sense to buy Panavision. While we were borrowing substantial amounts of money to do this, it was never intended that we would bankroll these sums for an elongated period of time. 'Black Monday', the writers' strike and the Serious Fraud Office investigation were events which, when added to the financing problems, would have been terminal for the Group.[8]

Despite this further change in ownership the studio continued to improve. In 1989 'T' stage (42 × 67 × 18 ft) came into operation, and the studio car park was upgraded for *Robin Hood – Prince of Thieves*. The generating substation was phased out, to become from February 1992 'P' stage (90 × 33 × 21 ft). Unfortunately, this stage could not be sound-proofed because of its specialist structure.

1991 productions at Shepperton included *Chaplin* (Richard Attenborough), *Blame it on the Bellboy* (Mark Herman), *Wuthering Heights* (Peter

Kosminski), *The Crying Game* (Neil Jordan), and nine television series productions.

1992 features included *Damage* (Louis Malle), *Turn of the Screw* (Rusty Lemorande), *The Muppet Christmas Carol* (Brian Henson), *Splitting Heirs* (Robert Young), and fourteen television series and film productions.

When Shepperton Studios was acquired by the Lee Group in 1984 it came under the control of people who knew its value and how to use it. Mills & Allen, the previous owner, had seen the studio only as an investment. Today the studio is owned by banks as collateral for loans taken out by Lee International. At some future date the banks will divest themselves of one of their assets – Shepperton Studios. To date, the banks have appreciated the value of this asset and the importance of the studio within the British and international film industry. The question remains: is there a future within the film industry for a studio such as Shepperton (or indeed Pinewood)?

Clearly Shepperton's future is in the hands of its present owners, but it is also in the hands of British politicians who have the power, if not the will, to create the fiscal environment in which films can be produced in Britain on a fair competitive basis, both with Europe and with the US. In 1948 the government of the day stepped in to support the British film industry. However, over the years that industry has been its own worst enemy in terms of business practices, restrictive practices, accounting procedures and, in far too many cases, simple greed. Most of the criticism fired at the industry has been deserved, but today's industry climate is somewhat healthier regarding the attitude of the professionals working in it. A welcome degree of responsibility has filtered through, both from producers and from unions, to create an increasing confidence in the ability of British films to continue being among the best in the world. Regrettably, British politicians remain sceptical, perhaps with good reason considering the government's past involvement in the industry.

Perhaps Norman Loudon's vision of a studio within a theme park or zoo was not so fanciful after all. For over sixty years the studio has been one of the great survivors of the British film industry. Throughout its stormy history it has always been an independent studio for independent producers – a maverick within a vertically integrated establishment.

Shepperton is the only major British film studio to have been supported by direct government intervention, albeit through its parent company. According to Sidney Gilliat: 'Shepperton was financed by government, was run by government and was almost destroyed by government!'[9]

Shepperton has survived incompetence, greed and, more recently, being used as a pawn by City whizz-kids, a meal-ticket for some within the industry and collateral for a disastrous expansionist escapade.

Supporters of the studio and of the studio system can take heart. From 1 January 1992 people have been encouraged to call the studio Shepperton Studios again, rather than Lee International Film Studios Shepperton. So, what's in a name? Durability, it would seem, and the ability to wake up from a dream that turned into a nightmare.

At the time of writing, British Lion is alive and well. When British Lion ceased to trade in 1977, it signified the end of an era, but in 1987 Peter

Snell, the Canadian who was Head of Production and Managing Director of British Lion Films from 1972 to 1974, purchased the company shell of British Lion Film Productions Limited and the British Lion trade-mark from Thorn-EMI Screen Entertainment (TESE). British Lion Television is the latest development in Snell's plan to continue ressurecting British Lion.

Perhaps it is appropriate that the story of Shepperton Studios is best summarised by the film industry's own trade paper. In 1976, *Screen International* commented:

> The premature burial of the British film industry and the 'inevitable' demise of the studios have gone hand in hand for years. There are those who think, with some justification, that Shepperton has been 'ripped off left, right and centre' over the decades.
>
> It has been, at different times, a lever, a strippable asset and a conscience, though more often, and folk in their righteous or unrighteous fury tend to forget this, a splendid film-making centre.[10]

Notes

1. Author's interview with Charles Gregson, 10 January 1992.
2. Ibid.
3. Author's interview with Nigel Hurdle, 31 March 1992.
4. *Eyepiece*, January/February 1988.
5. Extract from Offer Document dated 4 September 1987, for the proposed acquisition of Panavision Incorporated by Lee International plc.
6. Ibid.
7. Author's interview with Nigel Hurdle.
8. Ibid.
9. Author's interview with Sidney Gilliat, 27 February 1993.
10. *Screen International*, 17 January 1976.

8

IS THERE A FUTURE?

Shepperton Studios have survived the traumas of the last sixty years. But is there a future for a major film studio such as Shepperton?

In 1992 I posed this question to a cross-section of those working in the film industry, both in the UK and the US. There follow some of the answers I received.

The film studio as a place where feature films are made has long been an anachronism. After the Second World War there were some twenty-three studios in, or near, London, varying in size from Merton Park, Marylebone and Bushey, to Pinewood, Shepperton and Elstree (ABPC and MGM). At that time the demand only came from producers of first and second feature films and there was roughly a balance of demand and supply, the government having released all studio property from requisition.

The gradual expansion of television foreshadowed a change in the needs for studio space as we saw the spectre of fully-manned studios being unable to retain their complements of staff. This, together with a reduction in the number of films being produced, caused the closure of some of the smaller and medium-sized studios and others found a new role in property development.

Television also needed more studio space and Ealing, Lime Grove and National Studio were acquired by the BBC and ITV companies. It was not long before the bigger studios began to realise that they needed to cater for television requirements and Pinewood, Shepperton and Elstree built smaller stages to accommodate this kind of business.

For a time, the studios were able to accommodate our national output, aided by American finance and, subsequently, tax advantages. However, the last three years have seen a dramatic collapse in studio requirements. Even Pinewood has at long last been forced to go 'four-wall' and Elstree has largely been converted to a supermarket. Nor should we forget that many films are being made on location as technical developments allow directors more freedom to create a greater realism in their work, both for cinema and television films and series. What is left of the film industry in Britain can only be stimulated by financial considerations, but these are unlikely to be forthcoming from government policies at the present time. It must also be remembered that the rates of exchange do not favour the cost of sterling expenditure over the dollar at present and competition for production throughout the world remains intense.

163

So what of Shepperton and Pinewood for the future?

They must continue to be service centres for facilities, stage space and expertise. Past reputations must count for something and perhaps the widening of the role in television for the independent producer will create some additional demand. Let us at least encourage the use of the studios to maximise their value and hope that a cyclical resurgence of film-making will not be far away.

Kenneth Maidment

British studios can be a success, given adequate funding. There is a great future for Shepperton and Pinewood studios, given adequate cooperation from Her Majesty's government. Look at what happens in France and Germany. It is a pity that the Eady Fund was abandoned. It was a big help. Perhaps it can be brought back in some form.

James Hill

The history of Shepperton will be a most important contribution to the history of the cinema.

I found my working days at Shepperton most productive, professional and more than pleasant. The future of the major studios is doomed. By the year 2000 not one of the present working studios in the world today will be standing. We have lost the 'dinosaur' and now the 'studio'.

It is not an economic problem, or the result of escalated value of real estate. The studios were built by pioneer picture-makers who fought to bring their product to the screen and to keep improving. Always 'make it better'. They sought and built talent, writers, directors, actors, artisans, etc., and a world to entertain. Today those studios are retreads; the new technical inventions make them obsolete.

The entire complexion of the studio has changed. The studios were built by creators. Today practically the entire entertainment world is owned overseas. The management is populated by other than creators. Deals are the important issue. It is a 'Do it yourself' world.

We, who were fortunate enough to have lived in the world of Shepperton, MGM, Paramount and the likes, were very fortunate. The so-called money-oriented power structures of management do not care for building a future, nor are they equipped to do so. The major studios, the dream factory, will never be again.

George Sidney

I personally think there is always a place for a well-run studio giving independents a place to go should they need a space for the unusual. Where else would you find the ease of operation, as I did at Pinewood, when we created an underground coal mine, complete with horse stables and rail system, in my film for Disney, *Escape from the Dark*? Where else would you have the space to create all those hand-painted tapestries and re-created chambers of power as we did at Shepperton on *Anne of the Thousand Days* and *Mary, Queen of Scots*?

I have shot epics on natural locations all over the United Kingdom and a lot of them leave a lot to be desired! And I shall forever miss that small patch of water at Shepperton where, when I was planning walks for Henry VIII and trysts for Mary Stuart, dodging [Roman] Polanski making *Macbeth* and [Ken] Hughes making *Cromwell*, I would hear the echo from the past of Robeson canoeing up the river in *Sanders of the River.*

Charles Jarrott

I would sincerely hope that neither Shepperton nor Pinewood will go the way of other studios we have seen disappear during the last decade. The role of a studio is crucial to any film industry, not so much for the bricks and mortar, but as a base for all the craftsmen and their unique talents. It is hard to imagine that there would ever be a situation whereby all films are produced entirely on location, and it is a fallacy to think otherwise.

We have all seen the total cynical disregard of those who control our industry in relation to studios. EMI Elstree, which I once ran, is now a bomb site and I doubt whether a studio phoenix will ever rise again on the same site. During my term of office there I had the sad task of closing MGM Borehamwood which, again, was cynically emasculated and put out of business for a short-term gain which in the event never materialised. Indeed, the entire history of the film industry in Britain is a mixture of greed and total incompetence; the fabric of a once flourishing industry manipulated by property speculators and conglomerates in the most ruthless manner. The film industry is not a poor industry, taken as a whole – it is a very rich industry – but there has never been any concerted attempt, for many years, to put back what has been taken out. One would hope that, somehow, a halt will be called to the devastation, and that previous trends will one day be reversed. I emphasise the word 'hope', though in my heart I doubt whether those who currently control the purse strings will ever stifle their short-term greed.

Bryan Forbes

Shortly after being demobbed from the Royal Navy, I went under contract to London Films as an Assistant Director. As far as I am concerned, the next few years were the glory days of Shepperton. Always one production occupying 'A' and 'B' stages and another on 'C' and 'D', with usually some spectacle or water sport going on in the 'Silent Stage' 'H', after it had been brought over from Worton Hall and re-erected.

In the crowded restaurant a table was always reserved for Sir Alex Korda, who was forever due for lunch but never turned up, thus keeping the whole studio on its toes. Alex finally came down to direct *Home at Seven*, simply to remind Carol Reed and David Lean that it was possible to make a picture in three weeks.

This is not the place to go into the legion of Alex stories, except to emphasise that Shepperton was Korda and his brother, Vincent: Alex at 146 Piccadilly, with his direct line through to the studio, and Vincent in his awesome Art Department. A mix of all the refugee talent from UFA, via Paris, and a new generation of young bloods who were all, subsequently, to make names for themselves.

The decline in the fortunes of Shepperton can certainly be traced to the slump in the British film industry, but surely the main factor was the move out of sets and into the filming of interiors on location (made possible by improved stock and equipment). A studio today is only useful for process work, fantasy sets and for things that cannot conveniently be filmed, or found, on location.

Sadly, I do not believe there are enough Batmen, Supermen and Bonds to keep Shepperton flourishing.

Guy Hamilton

Shepperton Studios played a substantial and very important part in my life. Not only did I meet and fall in love with my wife there, but I found my way into the film industry in England after returning from Hollywood.

Super memories. On a summer's day, all the extras would sit outside the Old House on the grass taking the sun. Halcyon days. Lunch down at a pub by the river, or in the Old House bar. Lunchtime, or evening, a country club atmosphere would prevail. Actors, technicians and friends would come to Shepperton for lunch and you never had to work there to come into lunch. The gate men were always happy and friendly.

Tunes of Glory was one of the first stunt jobs I had there. Fred Haggerty and I were the Stunt Co-ordinators on that super film and we played very small parts in the film. After that, I did many stunts and played many parts in productions at Shepperton. The first show I directed there was a television show called *Up, Up She Goes*. Through the years, I have made many television episodes in that lovely studio.

Shepperton always had a new film coming in. The same with Pinewood. As a stunt man and director, I would work between the two studios. In the 50s and 60s the British film studios had it made. The American film-makers came to England for actors and the best crews in the world and our prices were right; everyone got value for money. But that was then; now is now. I believe Shepperton, Pinewood and Elstree will all disappear.

Tony Richardson was one of the first directors to walk away from the studios and the high costs. The same is happening here in America and has been for years. Studio costs all around the world seem to escalate every few months. Yes, you can still cut a deal with a studio, but not to the degree you can with an outside location. When you put a deal together now in the US, one of the paramount questions is 'Union, or non-union?'

I have just spent four years producing and directing *Zorro* in Spain. With the budget I had, I would not have been able to make this show in a studio. We did consider England when we had our original meeting on the production.

Unhappily, I cannot see a hope for the Sheppertons of the world. More television shows are shooting everything on location. Costs are too high. Shepperton has one big plus – its big stage 'H'. I understand that companies making commercials have an infatuation for that stage, but we all know they have more money than sense. One day, the penny will drop and they will cultivate sense and cut back on the money. Poor old Shepperton will have had it by then.

Ray Austin

I regret the passing of working in a studio. I am sure a lot of people today love making everything on location – it's more exciting. But for me, in my department (wardrobe), I loved being in a studio. The thing about going away for months at a time and doing the whole thing on location is something, now that I'm older, I don't want to do at all. It sounds old-fashioned, but I just love to get in a car and go to a studio.

Julie Harris

I have regretfully to say that I don't think there is a future for a studio such as Pinewood or Shepperton. I must also add that I know nothing about raising money for films. I'm very lucky – I've had the best of this business and I don't think anyone is going to have such a good time as I've had. That is because of the demise of the studio system. One looks around and sees people doing the odd one film, becoming a success and going to America, or becoming a failure and fading out completely.

The other problem is that there are no Kordas any more. Whatever one says about Korda, he was a wonderful, brash opportunist and a very good organiser. If someone seriously wanted to put a huge fortune into films, there's no one to talk to nowadays. There's no one who is a leading light in the British film industry. I think all these things go together with property prices and studio rentals. I don't think modern films can afford studios. The only films that can are commercials who have more money than we have to make films. It is a great pity. I have spent the last ten years in America where they do spend money and do have people who know how to run studios. The industry there is very successful because they don't just make single pictures, but a programme of pictures. If two or three are successful, they are in the clear.

For that reason, I believe we've seen the last of the studios in Britain, which is very sad. When I go to places like Shepperton – and I've had some wonderful times at Shepperton and I love the studio – I look at it and I'm almost in tears. I don't think Pinewood has degenerated quite so much, but it is like watching a very dear relative die. I hope I'm wrong.

Freddie Francis

I am constantly being asked my view on the future of studios as we know them. I believe there is a future, but not perhaps for the expected reasons.

The glory days of studio-based continuous production have been over for a very long time and never will they return. But studios, of all sizes, certainly have a role to play in present and future activities.

Some scripts require the kind of management only possible within the confines of a closed set in a security-controlled studio environment. 'Period' can be created and sustained without difficulty in a studio as the technique that goes into the reproduction of the past (and the future) is obtainable on site. Again, a story which calls for large numbers of people, including crowd, can, of course, be shot anywhere, but the facilities needed to dress the artists and do their hair, to store their costumes and to feed and pay them, are not generally available when working in disused school halls, redundant factories and empty warehouses.

Invariably, the most expensive item in a budget is time. A shoot that is technically difficult, for whatever reason, is likely to benefit from the multitude of services and facilities instantly available to users of studios like Shepperton. Offices, construction services, cutting rooms, catering, equipment supplies, special effects expertise, storage (timber, materials, props, set-pieces, equipment of all kinds), dubbing suites, even production accountants, insurance brokers and media lawyers are usually on the spot, immediately to hand, when a production is studio-based.

Absolutely *yes*, there will always be a place for a well-run studio – Shepperton, for example.

Sydney Samuelson CBE

The first film studios (glass-roofed) were built in California in the early silent days. As talkies came in, they were rebuilt and sound-proofed until every company had their own studios with their own trademark and logo. Occasionally some movies, mostly Westerns, were made on location in the deserts and mountains of California and Nevada, but for over ninety years the film business was synonymous with film *studios.*

To some extent that situation has changed as producers and directors, searching for 'realism', shot scenes in actual locations. Two reasons were given. First, the 'real thing' was much more impressive than studio-made sets. Second, working on location proved often to be less costly than using the huge and expensive studios where costs were often enormous – heat, light, telephone, offices, secretaries, executives and crews, highly paid and often not used enough to warrant the expense.

So, over the years, more and more films were made on actual locations – and very good some of them were – but, there were several drawbacks to working in the open air in all weathers, a major one of which was just that – the weather. A bad day of rain or black clouds could set a movie back by days and cost millions. In recent times, an example was the BBC television series, *A Year in Provence.* Allegedly set in the sunny South of France, the series encountered the dreaded mistral, high winds, continual rain and mud. The weather improved later and the results on the small screen looked good and sunny, eventually, but at horrendous cost.

Robert Redford told television viewers of the horrid weather sometimes encountered on his film *A River Runs Through It.* Ben Elton, making a film of one of his novels in Australia, recently talked about the incessant rain that ruined take after take in a part of the desert which had rarely seen rain in previous years. That great film *The Crying Game* ran into bad weather while shooting in Ireland. There are many other examples where the advantage of actual locations was outweighed by the extra cost of dealing with inclement weather and difficult terrain.

It seems that filming in the studios is safer and can often be much cheaper. As long as the production company is not saddled with outrageous overheads or feather-bedding of the crew, working in a well-run studio is often preferable and more convenient to coping with indifferent weather and uncomfortable terrain.

Although there is much to support this argument, we must remember that the huge moviegoing public really doesn't *care* if the scenes are authentic against 'real' background, or cleverly shot at Shepperton, Pinewood, Elstree or Twickenham; not only do they not care, but, most of the time, your average moviegoer wouldn't know a genuine location if he or she fell over it on the way to the ice-cream girl.

Peter Noble

If the history of most of our film studios were examined sufficiently closely, it would soon become only too clear that those which combined their own film-making activities with the operation of studio premises have run into trouble again and again through losses incurred from the films so made, rather than from shortfalls in studio space usage.

Elstree drew in its horns sharply after heavy losses on their films in the late 20s and early 30s and became little more than a 'quickie' factory up to the Second World War. Gaumont-British lost its money on the films it made to fill Shepherd's Bush in the 30s and had to close the studio down from 1936 until that same war. Ealing, after a good run, ran into the same sort of trouble for precisely the same reasons and first fell into the maw of Rank and John Davis and then were closed down altogether and sold. The same fate befell the postwar Gaumont-British when, after Box had filled the stages with loss-making films, his contract was terminated and the studios shut down and sold.

Altogether during my career I find I have worked at, or had connections with, no fewer than sixteen different British studios of which three now remain – Shepperton, Pinewood and Twickenham. The others include Shepherd's Bush, Stoll, Nettlefold, Ealing, Riverside, Teddington, Islington, Elstree, Denham, Isleworth, Bray and Welwyn Garden. Big or small, they have all bitten the dust. Beaconsfield now functions only as a film school whose graduates are either looking for work in Britain, or finding it in California.

Some of the closures may have arisen through obsolescence, unsuitability or lack of the right connections, but the principal cause overall was losses on film-making. The trouble with British film production is that the abolition of Quota and Eady Levy is death. Any studio will be in trouble without government help. All our major studios were built around the 1927 Quota Act. You can't have an industry unless you have protection against leakage of our top talent to the US.

Anyone who looks at the history of a studio such as Shepperton must accept the fact that no studio is a sacred edifice which must always remain inviolate. The National Film Finance Corporation, via Douglas Collins, tried to sell off a large part of the Shepperton lot in 1959. I opposed that, as I opposed any such attempt up to the end of my Chairmanship of Shepperton Studios. The fact remains that there should then have been three studios instead of four on any rational basis at that time. I thought the one to go should be Elstree and others privately agreed with me. I had thought then that John Davis of Rank felt that it should be Shepperton. In the end these discussions came to nothing. Shepperton is still there, but today it only has two others to compete with. The right one has gone at last.

Sidney Gilliat

Although I really didn't work at Shepperton very often (mostly I was based at Pinewood for sixteen to seventeen years, it seems), Shepperton was my

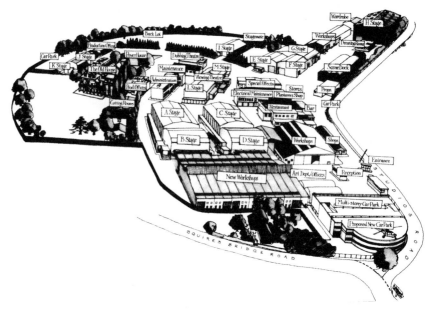

Plan of Shepperton Studios, 1994

favourite studio. I loved all the nonsense of the [Old] House and the big black and white tiled floor which we had to cross to get to the restaurant and bar. In my day it was a converted conservatory. I remember the story of the dotty lady who threw herself from the gallery into the hall and died, naturally enough. A lot of actors rather wished that they could follow her course, having been to 'rushes'. I *was* shattered to be present for some late post-synch on some film I did there when they were literally carting out the last files, filing cabinets and racks of empty coat-hangers as the place was turned into a 'four-wall' studio. I was bitterly sad and shortly after went off to live in France. Shepperton was quite the happiest studio for me. Its end marked, for me anyway, the end of British films. After that, it was merely a studio rental job.

Sir Dirk Bogarde

FILMOGRAPHY

The ownership and management changes over the years at Shepperton Studios have resulted in incomplete records of production. This filmography is as accurate as can be determined from records currently available (1993). Films listed relate to the year of production, but where it was not possible to establish this, the year of distribution is used. Details of any inaccuracies or omissions will be welcomed by the author (c/o the publishers) for consideration in any future updated edition of this book.

Key: * (a Worton Hall production)
     † (British Lion Production Assets [BLPA])

1932 Five shorts: *Aerobatics*; *Capture*; *Pursuit of Priscilla*; *Reward* and
        The Safe.
      Reunion (Ivar Campbell)
      Watch Beverley (Arthur Maude)

1933 *Colonel Blood* (W. P. Lipscomb)
      Doss House (John Baxter)
      Drake of England (part) (Arthur Woods)
      Eyes of Fate (Ivar Campbell)
      Golden Cage (Ivar Campbell)
      Moorland Tragedy (M. A. Wetherell)
      Paris Plane (John Paddy Carstairs)
      She Was Only a Village Maiden (Arthur Maude)
      Side Streets (Ivar Campbell)
      Song of the Plough (John Baxter)
      Taking Ways (John Baxter)
      Three Men in a Boat (part) (Graham Cutts)
      The Wandering Jew (part) (Maurice Elvey)
      The Wishbone (Arthur Maude)

1934 *By-Pass to Happiness* (Anthony Kimmins)
      Designing Women (Ivar Campbell)
      The Dictator (part) (Al Santell/Victor Saville)
      Falling in Love (part) (Monty Banks)
      How's Chances (Anthony Kimmins)
      The Iron Duke (part) (Victor Saville)
      Lady in Danger (part) (Tom Walls)

171

Lest We Forget (John Baxter)
Lily of Killarney (part) (Maurice Elvey)
Once in a New Moon (Anthony Kimmins)
Rolling Home (Ralph Ince)
Sabotage (Adrian Brunel)
Sanders of the River (part) (Zoltan Korda)
White Ensign (John L. F. Hunt)
Youthful Folly (Miles Mander)

1935 *Birds of a Feather* (John Baxter)
Emil and the Detectives (Milton Rosmer)
Father O'Flynn (Wilfred Noy/Walter Tennyson)
Maria Marten (*or The Murder in the Red Barn*) (George King)
Radio Pirates (Ivar Campbell)
Two Hearts in Harmony (William Beaudine)

1936 *The Captain's Table* (Percy Marmont)
The Crimes of Stephen Hawke (George King)
The Crimson Circle (Reginald Denham)
David Livingstone (James A. Fitzpatrick)
Grand Finale (Ivar Campbell)
Happy Days Are Here Again (Norman Lee)
Hearts of Humanity (John Baxter)
King of the Castle (Redd Davis)
Men of Yesterday (John Baxter)
Mill on the Floss (Tim Whelan)
Murder by Rope (George Pearson)
On Top of the World (Redd Davis)
Reasonable Doubt (George King)
The Robber Symphony (part) (Friedrich Feher)
Second Bureau (Victor Hanbury)
Secret of Stamboul (Andrew Marton)
Show Flat (Bernard Mainwaring)
Sporting Love (part) (J. Elder Wills)
Such is Life (Randall Faye)
Sweeney Todd (George King)
Wings Over Africa (Ladislao Vajda)
Wolf's Clothing (Andrew Marton)

1937 *Academy Decides* (John Baxter)
Auld Lang Syne (James A. Fitzpatrick)
The Bells of St Mary's (James A. Fitzpatrick)
Double Exposures (John Paddy Carstairs)
The Elder Brother (Frederick Hayward)
For Valour (Tom Walls)
House of Silence (R. K. Neilson Baxter)
It's Never Too Late to Mend (David MacDonald)
Last Adventurers (Roy Kellino)
Last Rose of Summer (James A. Fitzpatrick)
Merry Comes to Town (George King)

Mr Stringfellow Says No (Randall Faye)
Overcoat Sam (Wallace Orton)
Return of a Stranger (Victor Hanbury)
School for Husbands (Andrew Marton)
Screen Struck (Lawrence Huntington)
Song of the Road (John Baxter)
Talking Feet (John Baxter)
Thunder in the City (part) (Marion Gering)
Ticket of Leave Man (George King)
Under a Cloud (George King)
Wake Up Famous (Gene Gerrard)
Wanted (George King)
When the Poppies Bloom Again (David MacDonald)
Wife of General Ling (Ladislao Vajda)

1938 *Dream of Love* (James A. Fitzpatrick)
Georges Bizet, Composer of Carmen (James A. Fitzpatrick)
John Halifax, Gentleman (George King)
Kate Plus Ten (Reginald Denham)
Life of Chopin (James A. Fitzpatrick)
Old Bones of the River (part) (Marcel Varnel)
Old Iron (Tom Walls)
Second Best Bed (Tom Walls)
Sexton Blake and the Hooded Terror (George King)
Silver Top (George King)
Stepping Toes (John Baxter)

1939 *French Without Tears* (Anthony Asquith)
Riding High (David MacDonald)
Spy for a Day (Mario Zampi)

STUDIO CLOSED FOR WAR WORK

1946 *London Town* (Wesley Ruggles)
The Shop at Sly Corner (George King)
White Cradle Inn (Harold French)*

1947 *An Ideal Husband* (Alexander Korda)
Bonnie Prince Charlie (Anthony Kimmins)†
The Courtneys of Curzon Street (Herbert Wilcox)
A Man About the House (Leslie Arliss)
Mine Own Executioner (Anthony Kimmins)*

1948 *Anna Karenina* (Julian Duvivier)
Call of the Blood (John Clements/Ladislao Vajda)
The Fallen Idol (Carol Reed)
Night Beat (Harold Huth)*†
Spring in Park Lane (Herbert Wilcox)
The Winslow Boy (Anthony Asquith)†

1949 *Britannia Mews* (Jean Negulesco)
Elizabeth of Ladymead (Herbert Wilcox)

173

The Last Days of Dolwyn (Emlyn Williams)*†
Saints and Sinners (Leslie Arliss)*†
The Small Back Room (Michael Powell)*†
That Dangerous Age (Gregory Ratoff)
The Third Man (Carol Reed)†
You Can't Sleep Here(I Was a Male War Bride) (Howard Hawks)

1950 *The Angel With the Trumpet* (Anthony Bushell)†
The Black Rose (Henry Hathaway)
Circle of Danger (Jacques Tourneur)*
Cure for Love (Robert Donat)*
Curtain Up (Ralph Smart)
Flesh and Blood (Anthony Kimmins)
Gone to Earth (Michael Powell)†
The Happiest Days of Your Life (Frank Launder)*†
Into the Blue (Herbert Wilcox)*
The Late Edwina Black (Maurice Elvey)*
The Lost Hours (David MacDonald)*
The Mudlark (Jean Negulesco)
My Daughter Joy (Gregory Ratoff)†
Night and the City (Jules Dassin)
Seven Days to Noon (John Boulting)†
State Secret (Sidney Gilliat)*†
The Wonder Kid (Karl Hartl)†
The Wooden Horse (Jack Lee)†

1951 *The Elusive Pimpernel* (Michael Powell)†
Lady Godiva Rides Again (Frank Launder)†
The Lady With the Lamp (Herbert Wilcox)
Pandora and the Flying Dutchman (Albert Lewin)
The Tales of Hoffman (Michael Powell)†

1952 *The African Queen* (John Huston)
An Outcast of the Islands (Carol Reed)†
The Beggar's Opera (Peter Brook)
Circumstantial Evidence (Don Birt)
Cry, the Beloved Country (Zoltan Korda)†
Derby Day (Herbert Wilcox)
The Gift Horse (Compton Bennett)
The Holly and the Ivy (George More O'Ferrall)†
Home at Seven (Ralph Richardson)†
Mr Denning Drives North (Anthony Kimmins)†
The Sound Barrier (David Lean)†
Trent's Last Case (Herbert Wilcox)
Who Goes There! (Anthony Kimmins)†

1953 *Appointment in London* (Philip Leacock)
Beautiful Stranger (David Miller)
The Captain's Paradise (Anthony Kimmins)†
Folly to be Wise (Frank Launder)†
The Intruder (Guy Hamilton)

Laughing Anne (Herbert Wilcox)
The Man Between (Carol Reed)†
Moulin Rouge (John Huston)
Profile (Francis Searle)
The Red Beret (Terence Young)
The Ringer (Guy Hamilton)†
Single-Handed (Roy Boulting)
The Story of Gilbert and Sullivan (Sidney Gilliat)†
They Who Dare (Lewis Milestone)
Twice Upon a Time (Emeric Pressburger)†

1954 *An Inspector Calls* (Guy Hamilton)
Aunt Clara (Anthony Kimmins)
Bang, You're Dead (Lance Comfort)
Beat the Devil (John Huston)
The Belles of St Trinian's (Frank Launder)†
The Colditz Story (Guy Hamilton)
Devil Girl From Mars (David MacDonald)
Eight O'Clock Walk (Lance Comfort)
The Green Scarf (George More O'Ferrall)
The Heart of the Matter (George More O'Ferrall)†
Hobson's Choice (David Lean)†
It's a Great Day (John Warrington)
Josephine and Men (Roy Boulting)
Malaga (Richard Sale)
Raising a Riot (Wendy Toye)
The Teckman Mystery (Wendy Toye)

1955 *Carrington VC* (Anthony Asquith)
Cockleshell Heroes (José Ferrer)
The Constant Husband (Sidney Gilliat)
The Deep Blue Sea (Anatole Litvak)
The End of the Affair (Edward Dmytryk)
Gentlemen Marry Brunettes (Richard Sale)
Geordie (Frank Launder)
The Good Die Young (Lewis Gilbert)
I Am a Camera (Henry Cornelius)
A Kid for Two Farthings (Carol Reed)
The Man Who Loved Redheads (Harold French)†
Private's Progress (John Boulting)
Summer Madness (David Lean)
They Can't Hang Me (Val Guest)
Three Cases of Murder (Wendy Toye/David Eady/
    George More O'Ferrall)

1956 *The Admirable Crichton* (Lewis Gilbert)
The Baby and the Battleship (Jay Lewis)
Charley Moon (Guy Hamilton)
Dry Rot (Maurice Elvey)
The Extra Day (William Fairchild)

The Green Man (Robert Day)
The Hide Out (Peter Graham Scott)
A Hill in Korea (Julian Amyes)
The Iron Petticoat (Ralph Thomas)
Loser Takes All (Ken Annakin)
Manuela (Guy Hamilton)
The March Hare (George More O'Ferrall)
My Teenage Daughter (Herbert Wilcox)
The Passionate Stranger (Muriel Box)
Richard III (Laurence Olivier)
Sailor Beware (Gordon Parry)
The Secret Tent (Don Chaffey)
Three Men in a Boat (Ken Annakin)

1957 *Behind the Mask* (Brian Desmond Hurst)
The Birthday Present (Pat Jackson)
Blue Murder at St Trinian's (Frank Launder)
Bonjour Tristesse (Otto Preminger)
Fortune is a Woman (Sidney Gilliat)
Happy is the Bride (Roy Boulting)
A King in New York (Charles Chaplin)
The Long Haul (Ken Hughes)
A Novel Affair (Muriel Box)
Saint Joan (Otto Preminger)
Second Fiddle (Maurice Elvey)
Seven Waves Away (Richard Sale)
The Smallest Show on Earth (Basil Dearden)
The Story of Esther Costello (David Miller)
Town on Trial (John Guillermin)

1958 *Carlton-Browne of the FO* (Roy Boulting)
Danger Within (Don Chaffey)
The Horse's Mouth (Ronald Neame)
Jack the Ripper (Robert S. Baker)
Killers of Kilimanjaro (Richard Thorpe)
Law and Disorder (Charles Crichton)
Life is a Circus (Val Guest)
The Man Upstairs (Don Chaffey)
Orders to Kill (Anthony Asquith)
The Silent Enemy (William Fairchild)
Tread Softly Stranger (Gordon Parry)
The Truth About Women (Muriel Box)
The Whole Truth (John Guillermin)

1959 *The Angry Silence* (Guy Green)
Friends and Neighbours (Gordon Parry)
Idle on Parade (John Gilling)
I'm All Right, Jack (John Boulting)
Jet Storm (Cy Endfield)
Left, Right and Centre (Sidney Gilliat)

A Model for Murder (Terry Bishop)
The Mouse That Roared (Jack Arnold)
The Mummy (Terence Fisher)
Next to No Time (Henry Cornelius)
Our Man in Havana (Carol Reed)
Room at the Top (Jack Clayton)
Subway in the Sky (Muriel Box)
Suddenly Last Summer (Joseph L. Mankiewicz)
Tarzan's Greatest Adventure (John Guillermin)

1960 *City of the Dead* (John Moxey)
Cone of Silence (Charles Frend)
Dead Lucky (Montgomery Tully)
The Entertainer (Tony Richardson)
Expresso Bongo (Val Guest)
Faces in the Dark (David Eady)
The Flesh and the Fiends (John Gilling)
A French Mistress (Roy Boulting)
The Grass is Greener (Stanley Donen)
The Greengage Summer (Lewis Gilbert)
Greyfriars Bobby (Don Chaffey)
The Guns of Navarone (J. Lee Thompson)
The Hands of Orlac (Edmond T. Greville)
The Horsemasters (William Fairchild)
Mysterious Island (Cy Endfield)
Nearly a Nasty Accident (Don Chaffey)
The Night We Got the Bird (Darcy Conyers)
Offbeat (Cliff Owen)
Pure Hell at St Trinian's (Frank Launder)
The Queen's Guards (Michael Powell)
Suspect (Roy Boulting)
Spare the Rod (Leslie Norman)
Surprise Package (Stanley Donen)
Tarzan the Magnificent (Robert Day)
The Trunk (Donovan Winter)
Tunes of Glory (Ronald Neame)
The Unstoppable Man (Terry Bishop)
Weekend With Lulu (John Paddy Carstairs)
Yesterday's Enemy (Val Guest)

1961 *The Barber of Stamford Hill* (Casper Wrede)
The Day of the Triffids (Steve Sekely)
The Day the Earth Caught Fire (Val Guest)
Dentist on the Job (C. M. Pennington-Richards)
The Devil's Daffodil (Akos Rathony)
Foxhole in Cairo (John Moxey)
The Frightened City (John Lemont)
Girl on the Boat (Henry Kaplan)
The Golden Rabbit (David MacDonald)
Hair of the Dog (Terry Bishop)

177

HMS Defiant (Lewis Gilbert)
Information Received (Robert Lynn)
The Innocents (Jack Clayton)
It's Trad, Dad (Dick Lester)
A Kind of Loving (John Schlesinger)
The Kitchen (James Hill)
Nothing Barred (Darcy Conyers)
On the Fiddle (Cyril Frankel)
Only Two Can Play (Sidney Gilliat)
Over the Odds (Michael Forlong)
The Painted Smile (Lance Comfort)
The Prince and the Pauper (Don Chaffey)
The Road to Hong Kong (Melvin Frank)
Take Me Over (Robert Lynn)
Two and Two Make Six (Freddie Francis)
The Valiant (Roy Baker)
The War Lover (Philip Leacock)

1962 *The Amorous Prawn* (Anthony Kimmins)
Billy Liar (John Schlesinger)
The Break (Lance Comfort)
The Cool Mikado (Michael Winner)
Danger By My Side (Charles Saunders)
The Devil's Agent (John Paddy Carstairs)
The Dock Brief (James Hill)
Doomsday at Eleven (Theodore Zichy)
Heavens Above (John Boulting)
Hide and Seek (Cy Endfield)
I Could Go On Singing (Ronald Neame)
The King's Breakfast (Wendy Toye)
The L-Shaped Room (Bryan Forbes)
The Main Attraction (Daniel Petrie)
Mix Me a Person (Leslie Norman)
Mystery Submarine (C. M. Pennington-Richards)
Night of the Prowler (Francis Searle)
Night Without Pity (Theodore Zichy)
Sammy Going South (Alexander Mackendrick)
Serena (Peter Maxwell)
The Small World of Sammy Lee (Ken Hughes)
Station Six – Sahara (Seth Holt)
Stolen Hours (Daniel Petrie)
Two Guys Abroad (Don Sharp)
Two Left Feet (Roy Baker)
The Victors (Carl Foreman)

1963 *A Jolly Bad Fellow* (Don Chaffey)
Becket (Peter Glenville)
Catacombs (Gordon Hessler)
The Comedy Man (Alvin Rakoff)
Dr Strangelove (Stanley Kubrick)

The Eyes of Annie Jones (Reginald Le Borg)
First Men in the Moon (Nathan Juran)
The Horror of it All (Terence Fisher)
It's All Happening (Don Sharp)
The Long Ships (Jack Cardiff)
Lord Jim (Richard Brooks)
A Matter of Choice (Vernon Sewell)
Psyche 59 (Alexander Singer)
The Pumpkin Eater (Jack Clayton)
Ring of Spies (Robert Tronson)
Saturday Night Out (Robert Hartford-Davis)
The Servant (Joseph Losey)
Walk a Tightrope (Frank Nesbitt)
The Yellow Teddy Bears (Robert Hartford-Davis)

1964 *Allez France* (Robert Dhery)
The Amorous Adventures of Moll Flanders (Terence Young)
The Bedford Incident (James B. Harris)
The Black Torment (Robert Hartford-Davis)
Curse of Simba (Lindsay Shonteff)
Curse of the Fly (Don Sharp)
Darling (John Schlesinger)
Daylight Robbery (Michael Truman)
Do You Know This Voice? (Frank Nesbitt)
Dr Terror's House of Horrors (Freddie Francis)
The Earth Dies Screaming (Terence Fisher)
East of Sudan (Nathan Juran)
Every Day's a Holiday (James Hill)
Gonks Go Beat (Robert Hartford-Davis)
I've Gotta Horse (Kenneth Hume)
Joey Boy (Frank Launder)
Just for You (Douglas Hickox)
Khartoum (part) (Basil Dearden)
King and Country (Joseph Losey)
Night Train to Paris (Robert Douglas)
The Projected Man (Ian Curteis)
Rotten to the Core (John Boulting)
The Sicilians (Ernest Morris)
Space Flight IC-1 (Bernard Knowles)
The Tomb of Ligeia (Roger Corman)
Troubled Waters (Stanley Goulder)
Witchcraft (Don Sharp)
The Young Detectives (Gilbert Gunn)

1965 *Casino Royale* (John Huston/Ken Hughes/Val Guest/Robert Parrish/
       Joe McGrath/Richard Talmadge)
Cul de Sac (Roman Polanski)
Daleks Invade Earth (Gordon Flemyng)
Doctor Who and the Daleks (Gordon Flemyng)
Drop Dead, Darling (Ken Hughes)

Georgy Girl (Silvio Narizzano)
The Great St Trinian's Train Robbery (Frank Launder)
Life at the Top (Ted Kotcheff)
Modesty Blaise (Joseph Losey)
Monster of Terror (Daniel Heller)
The Murder Game (Sidney Salkow)
The Night Caller (John Gilling)
Othello (Stuart Burge)
Promise Her Anything (Arthur Hiller)
The Psychopath (Freddie Francis)
The Return of Mr Moto (Ernest Morris)
Sands of the Kalahari (Cy Endfield)
The Skull (Freddie Francis)
The Spy Who Came in From the Cold (Martin Ritt)
A Study in Terror (James Hill)

1966 *Berserk* (Jim O'Connolly)
Calamity the Cow (David Eastman)
The Family Way (Roy Boulting)
Fathom (Leslie Martinson)
Half a Sixpence (George Sidney)
A Man for All Seasons (Fred Zinnemann)
River Rivals (Harry Booth)
The Spy With a Cold Nose (Daniel Petrie)
Torture Garden (Freddie Francis)
The Trygon Factor (Cyril Frankel)

1967 *Danger Route* (Seth Holt)
Don't Raise the Bridge, Lower the River (Jerry Paris)
Duffy (Robert Parrish)
Girl on a Motorcycle (Jack Cardiff)
Great Catherine (Gordon Flemyng)
Hostile Witness (Ray Milland)
Mrs Brown, You've Got a Lovely Daughter (Saul Swimmer)
Oliver! (Carol Reed)
Salt & Pepper (Richard Donner)

1968 *The Adding Machine* (Jerome Epstein)
Battle of Britain (part) (Guy Hamilton)
The Best House in London (Philip Saville)
The Birthday Party (William Friedkin)
The Body Stealers (Gerry Levy)
The File of the Golden Goose (Sam Wanamaker)
The Looking Glass War (Frank R. Pierson)
Negatives (Peter Medak)
Otley (Dick Clement)
Play Dirty (André de Toth)
Project Z (Ronald Spencer)
The Reckoning (Jack Gold)
The Smashing Bird I Used to Know (Robert Hartford-Davis)

Till Death Us Do Part (Norman Cohen)
A Touch of Love (Waris Hussein)
Twisted Nerve (Roy Boulting)
2001 – A Space Odyssey (part) (Stanley Kubrick)

1969 *Anne of the Thousand Days* (Charles Jarrott)
Cromwell (Ken Hughes)
Every Home Should Have One (James Clark)
The Last Grenade (Gordon Flemyng)
Loot (Silvio Narizzano)
The Mind of Mr Soames (Alan Cooke)
The Oblong Box (Gordon Hessler)
The Promise (Michael Hayes)
Scream and Scream Again (Gordon Hessler)
A Severed Head (Dick Clement)
Take a Girl Like You (Jonathan Miller)
The Three Sisters (Laurence Olivier)
When Dinosaurs Ruled the Earth (Val Guest)

1970 *Dad's Army* (Norman Cohen)
A Day in the Death of Joe Egg (Peter Medak)
Fright (Peter Collinson)
The House That Dripped Blood (Peter John Duffell)
I, Monster (Stephen Weeks)
Macbeth (Roman Polanski)
Puppet on a Chain (Geoffrey Reeve)
Scrooge (Ronald Neame)
There's a Girl in My Soup (Roy Boulting)
Wuthering Heights (Robert Fuest)
Zee and Co (Brian G. Hutton)

1971 *Crucible of Terror* (Ted Hooker)
Fun and Games (Ray Austin)
The Magnificent 6 ½ (Peter Graham Scott)
Mary, Queen of Scots (Charles Jarrott)
Psychomania (Don Sharp)
Romeo and Juliet (Franco Zeffirelli)
She'll Follow You Anywhere (David Rea)
Something to Hide (Alastair Reid)
Tower of Evil (Jim O'Connolly)
Whoever Slew Auntie Roo (Curtis Harrington)
Young Winston (Richard Attenborough)

1972 *Alice's Adventures in Wonderland* (William Sterling)
And Now the Screaming Starts (Roy Ward Baker)
The Asphyx (Peter Newbrook)
Asylum (Roy Ward Baker)
Bequest to the Nation (James Cellan Jones)
The Boy Who Turned Yellow (Michael Powell)
Creeping Flesh (Freddie Francis)
The Day of the Jackal (Fred Zinnemann)

Follow Me (Carol Reed)
Hitler – The Last Ten Days (Ennio de Concini)
The Homecoming (Peter Hall)
It's a 2'6" Above the Ground World (Ralph Thomas)
The Last Chapter (David Tringham)
The Lovers (Herbert Wise)
Luther (Guy Green)
Tales From the Crypt (Freddie Francis)
The Wicker Man (Robin Hardy)
With These Hands (Don Chaffey)

1973 *The Beast Must Die* (Paul Annett)
Butley (Harold Pinter)
Craze (Freddie Francis)
The Internecine Project (Ken Hughes)
Soft Beds and Hard Battles (Roy Boulting)
Tales That Witness Madness (Freddie Francis)

1974 *Brannigan* (Douglas Hickox)
Conduct Unbecoming (Michael Anderson)
Great Expectations (Joseph Hardy)
The Land That Time Forgot (Kevin Connor)
Lisztomania (Ken Russell)
The Man Who Fell to Earth (Nicolas Roeg)
Mister Quilp (part) (Michael Tuchner)
Return of the Pink Panther (Blake Edwards)

1975 *The Adventure of Sherlock Holmes' Smarter Brother*
     (Gene Wilder)
The 'Copter Kids (Ronald Spencer)
The Omen (Richard Donner)
The Pink Panther Strikes Again (Blake Edwards)
Sinbad and the Eye of the Tiger (Sam Wanamaker)

1976 *Jabberwocky* (Terry Gilliam)
The Marriage of Figaro (Jean-Pierre Ponelle)
Queen Kong (Frank Agrama)

1977 *The Boys From Brazil* (Franklin Schaffner)
Dominique (Michael Anderson)
Force 10 From Navarone (Guy Hamilton)
The Four Feathers (Don Sharp)
The Medusa Touch (Jack Gold)
Prey (Norman J. Warren)
The Revenge of the Pink Panther (Blake Edwards)
The Strange Case of the End of Civilisation As We Know It (Joe
     McGrath)
Superman (part) (Richard Donner)

1978 *Alien* (Ridley Scott)
Dracula (John Badham)
The Martian Chronicles (Michael Anderson)

Murder By Decree (Bob Clark)
The Odd Job (Peter Medak)
Saturn 3 (Stanley Donen)
The Thief of Baghdad (Clive Donner)

1979 *All Quiet on the Western Front* (Delbert Mann)
Flash Gordon (Michael Hodges)
SOS Titanic (William Hale)

1980 *The Elephant Man* (David Lynch)
Eye of the Needle (Richard Marquand)
History of the World Part One (Mel Brooks)
Little Lord Fauntleroy (Jack Gold)
Priest of Love (Christopher Miles)
Ragtime (Milos Forman)
A Tale of Two Cities (Jim Goddard)

1981 *Brimstone and Treacle* (Richard Loncraine)
Five Days One Summer (Fred Zinnemann)
Gandhi (Richard Attenborough)
The Hunger (Tony Scott)
The Pirates of Penzance (Wilford Leach)

1982 *The Hound of the Baskervilles* (Douglas Hickox)
Jigsaw Man (Terence Young)
The Keep (Michael Mann)
Lords of Discipline (Franc Roddam)
The Missionary (Richard Loncraine)
Privates on Parade (Michael Blakemore)
The Sender (Roger Christian)
Sherlock Holmes' Sign of Four (Desmond Davis)

1983 *Bullshot* (Dick Clement)
The Company of Wolves (Neil Jordan)
The Far Pavilions (Peter Duffell)
The Zany Adventures of Robin Hood (Ray Allen)

1984 *The Bride* (Franc Roddam)
Doctor and the Devils (Freddie Francis)
1984 (Michael Redford)
A Passage to India (David Lean)
Reunion at Fairborough (Herbert Wise)
2010 (Peter Hyams)
Water (Dick Clement)

1985 *Absolute Beginners* (Julien Temple)
If Tomorrow Comes (Jerry London)
Link (Richard Franklin)
Out of Africa (Sydney Pollack)
Ping Pong (Pochih Leong)

1986 *Cry Freedom* (Richard Attenborough)
84, Charing Cross Road (David Jones)

Hearts of Fire (Richard Marquand)
The Princess Bride (Rob Reiner)
Shanghai Surprise (Jim Goddard)

1987 *Gorillas in the Mist* (Michael Apted)
The Lonely Passion of Judith Hearne (Jack Clayton)
Poor Little Rich Girl (Charles Jarrott)
White Mischief (Michael Radford)

1988 *Bert Rigby, You're a Fool* (Carl Reiner)
Endless Game (Bryan Forbes)
Eric the Viking (Terry Jones)
Henry V (Kenneth Branagh)
How to Get Ahead in Advertising (Bruce Robinson)
Mountains of the Moon (Bob Rafelson)
Strapless (David Hare)

1989 *About Face* (John Henderson)
Back Home (Piers Haggard)
Free Frenchmen (Jim Goddard)
Killing Dad (Michael Austin)
Nuns on the Run (Jonathan Lynn)
Shell Seekers (Waris Hussein)

1990 *Hamlet* (Franco Zeffirelli)
A Kiss Before Dying (James Dearden)
The Rainbow Thief (Alejandro Jodorowsky)
Robin Hood – Prince of Thieves (Kevin Reynolds)
Three Men and a Little Lady (Emile Ardonilo)

1991 *Blame it on the Bellboy* (Mark Herman)
Chaplin (Richard Attenborough)
The Crying Game (Neil Jordan)
Under Suspicion (Simon Moore)
Wuthering Heights (Peter Kosminski)

1992 *Damage* (Louis Malle)
The Muppet Christmas Carol (Brian Henson)
Splitting Heirs (Robert Young)
Turn of the Screw (Rusty Lemorande)

Television Series

1959 *The Third Man* (British Lion/National Telefilm Associates
[USA])

1961 *Danger Man* (second series) (ATV)
Man of the World (ITC)
Sentimental Agent (ITC)

1968 *The Ugliest Girl in Town* (ABC [USA])

1972 *Jumbleland* (Thames TV)

1981 *Winds of War* (Paramount Pictures [UK])

1982 *Gilbert and Sullivan* (Brent Walker)

1984 *Ellis Island* (Telepictures Films)

1988 *Spooks* (Corruna)

1989 *The Choice* (BBC TV)
     The Secret Life of Ian Fleming (Ian Productions)

1990 *Gwain and the Green Knight* (Thames TV)
     Manhattan Project (HBO)
     Red Dwarf IV (Grant Naylor/BBC)
     Smith & Jones (Talkback/BBC)
     To Be the Best (Gemmy Productions [UK])
     You Bet (series 4) (LWT)

1991 *Big Break* (BBC)
     Bye Bye Columbus (Greenpoint)
     Ex (Talkback/BBC)
     Murder Most Horrid (Talkback/BBC)
     Pressgang (Richmond Film & TV)
     Red Dwarf V (Grant Naylor/BBC)
     Thomas the Tank Engine and Friends (Britt Alcroft)
     You Bet (Series 5) (LWT)
     Young Indiana Jones (Lucas Films)

1992 *The Borrowers* (series 1) (WTTV)
     Calling the Shots (BBC TV)
     Covington Cross (Thames TV)
     Foreign Affairs (TNT)
     Inspector Morse (Zenith)
     Jeeves and Wooster (Hat Trick Productions)
     The Paradise Club (Zenith/BBC)
     The Philip Knight Story (Walker Film Company)
     Red Dwarf VI (Grant Naylor/BBC)
     Smith & Jones '92 (Talkback/BBC)
     You Bet (series 6) (LWT)
     You Me and It (Wall to Wall TV)

BIBLIOGRAPHY

The British Film Industry (London: Political and Economic Planning, 1952).

Dunham, Harold, *The Life and Times of G.B. (Bertie) Samuelson* (research document, unpublished).

Halliwell, Leslie, *Halliwell's Film Guide.*

Hirschorn, Clive, *The Columbia Story* (London: Pyramid Books, 1989).

Jones, David, *Film Fanatic's Guide* (Braunton: Merlin Books, 1988).

Kine Year Book (1933–1940 and 1970).

Korda, Michael, *Charmed Lives* (USA: Random House Inc., 1979).

Kulik, Karol, *Alexander Korda: The Man Who Could Work Miracles* (London: W. H. Allen, 1975).

Lane, Margaret, *Edgar Wallace – A Biography* (London: 1939).

Low, Rachael, *British Film Production in the 1930s* (London: Allen & Unwin, 1985).

Maskelyne, Jasper, *Magic – Top Secret* (London: Paul, 1949).

National Film Finance Corporation Annual Reports (1950–85).

Ramsey, Winston G. (ed.), *The Blitz Then and Now* (London: Battle of Britain Prints International).

Reit, Seymour, *Masquerade* (New York: Hawthorne, 1978).

Robinson, Martha, *Continuity Girl* (London: Robert Hale, 1937).

Shepperton Studios Limited Annual Reports (1960–71).

Stevenson, William, *A Man Called Intrepid* (London, 1976).

Tabori, Paul, *Alexander Korda – A Biography.*

Thomas, Tony and Solomon, Aubrey, *The Films of 20th Century-Fox* (USA: Citadel Press, 1979).

Trevelyan, John, *What the Censor Saw* (London: Michael Joseph, 1973).

Winchester, Clarence (ed.), *The World Film Encyclopedia*, London, (Amalgamated Press, 1933).

INDEX

187

188

190

191